In *The Leadership Principles of Jesus*, the authors ostensibly offer ideas, suggestions, techniques, and action steps for Christians in their church organizations and activities—but in fact this book is a worthwhile tool for any organization: business or social, profit or non-profit, sectarian or secular. This is a brilliant synthesis of tried and true organizational leadership principles as viewed through the prism of the Christian message.

James A. Autry, Author
Love and Profit, The Art of Caring Leadership and
Confessions of an Accidental Businessman

A great book about the greatest leader of all time. Great leadership principles never die. This book proves it.

Arthur R. Bauer, President
American Media Incorporated

There have been many excellent books addressing Judeo-Christian ethics as they may apply to running organizations and maintaining wholesome relationships with others. However, Batten and Howard have made a great contribution to all of us by addressing a very basic organizational need, namely how to lead and motivate people by using principles taught by Jesus. I particularly enjoy the thoroughness of their research. This is not a thirty minute emotional charge to excellence; but a very rational explanation of the basic teachings of Christ as they apply to leadership.

George Bragg, Chairman
Markwood Capital Alliance

It has become popular to write management books playing off the teachings of Jesus. However, until Joe Batten and his coll~ ~gues wrote *Leadership Principles of Jesus*, most writers have gott~ ng. As Joe correctly points out, Jesus was not a mana~ ~ LEADER. This book presents, with simple and dra~ the "upside down" leadership principles Jesus help church workers everywhere become ~ have become more Christ-like.

President, Pea. ~ellman
~ian Living

[Additional endorsements at end of book]

The LEADERSHIP PRINCIPLES *of* JESUS

MODERN PARABLES OF ACHIEVEMENT AND MOTIVATION

JOE BATTEN • GAIL BATTEN
WARREN HOWARD

COLLEGE PRESS
PUBLISHING COMPANY
Joplin, Missouri

Published by College Press Publishing Co., Joplin, MO
Printed and Bound in the United States of America
All Rights Reserved

    LB   – *The Living Bible,* © 1971.

    CEV   – *Contemporary English Version,* © 1991, 1995.

    PHILLIPS – *J. B. Phillips: The New Testament in Modern English,*
                  © 1958, 1960, 1972.

Cover Design by Mark A. Cole

Library of Congress Cataloging-in-Publication Data

Batten, Joe D.
    The leadership principles of Jesus: modern parables of achieve-
ment and motivation / Joe D. Batten, Gail Batten Cunningham,
Warren R. Howard.
      p.   cm.
    Includes bibliographical references.
    ISBN 0-89900-782-1 (pbk.)
    1. Christian leadership. 2. Jesus Christ—Leadership.
3. Leadership—Religious aspects—Christianity. I. Cunningham,
Gail Batten, 1951–1996. II. Howard, Warren R. (Warren
Remington), 1926– . III. Title.
BV652.1.B375 1997
253—dc21   97-11019
                                            CIP

Dedication

To Gail Batten, deceased in 1996.
Beloved daughter of Joe and Jean
She inspired everyone she touched.

✳✳✳✳

Please read her poem
Reply to Darkness,
in the appendix.

To David —

Joe Batten

To contact the authors:

Joe Batten Associates
4505 S.W. 26th Street
Des Moines, IA 50321
(800) 234-3176
(515) 285-8069
Fax: (515) 285-5672

Warren R. Howard
17452 Amaganset Way
Tustin, CA 92780
(714) 544-2976
Fax: (714) 542-6234

ACKNOWLEDGMENTS

Thanks especially to Paul Liston who made many valuable suggestions on wording and punctuation. Thanks also to our agent Don Brandenburgh. In addition to finding publishers, he helped us organize our ideas and arrange them in the most effective way.

Members of Christian Writer's Fellowship (authors, lecturers, and critiquers) have been indispensable. We love you and thank you.

We are indebted to the numerous authors listed in our references. Our professional colleagues and Christian friends have been an inspiration and have supplied the laboratory where we have learned from constant experimentation. We wholeheartedly thank our wives, Jean Batten and Jean Howard.

We thank our families for their patience. We especially thank our Father in Heaven for the guidance and encouragement of His Spirit and His Word. May our book glorify Jesus, equip many servant/leaders, and advance His Kingdom on Earth.

TABLE OF CONTENTS

FOREWORD

Christians are optimistic — especially when faced with adversity. Optimistic Christians are happy, expect challenges, live life.

Optimistic behavior threatens people in the secular world who fail to understand the Christian's source of strength, which often in turn threatens the Christian's position, socially or in the workplace.

Christians have faith and believe in possibilities. Christ tells us, "With God all things are possible."

"Grassroots Christians" must become as "tough-minded" as the earliest Christians. We can "Make disciples of all nations."

In addition to prayer, the most effective way to develop the courage and conviction of first century Christians, is to follow their lead, creating small groups of like-minded believers, dedicated to learning to use the Bible's proven methods in our workplaces, neighborhoods and families.

The Leadership Principles of Jesus shows us how to develop small groups of Christians who learn to demonstrate, through their lives, just how God's wishes for His people become reality.

The hard school of personal experience, leading organizations involved in activities as diverse as insurance marketing, church and other boards, Sunday School teaching, Jaycees, Boy Scout troop leadership, various chairmanships, and other real life responsibilities, frustrated me because I didn't understand the lessons, so effectively communicated in practical, *How to do it format* of *The Leadership*

Principles of Jesus. This book is an ideal guide for individual and small group study, and action.

Anything is possible — through Christ — when Christians are taught how to lead the way. By becoming living witnesses miracles happen.

Authors Batten, Batten and Howard are well known for their contributions and effect on many lives and businesses, through personal involvement and writings. The latest work of this active trio, *The Leadership Principles of Jesus*, could change the world.

This foreword has been prayerfully written by Jerry Carey, an active, seeking Christian, trying to make a difference, just as you are, through prayer, patience and behavior.

In the real world, it's not easy. This book will make it easier.

Jerry Carey
Group Vice President,
The Principal Financial Group

INTRODUCTION

This book will equip you to glorify Christ, develop quality relationships, and achieve dynamic results in every phase of your life.

In an age of exponential change, millions of people hunger for fundamental truths, principles, and values. They cry out for the emotional security and a sense of purpose needed to cope with change. More importantly, they need emotional and spiritual ammunition for ever-increasing growth and improvement. However, these needs often go unmet, because in many churches and other organizations the leadership holds dogmatically to traditions that frustrate members and nullify God's Word. Like the Pharisees and teachers of the Law, we find it very hard to examine and change what needs changing.

Scientists and scholars often miss *the Big Picture* by their *tunnel vision*. But even scientists and scholars experience little progress without a difficult struggle against ignorance and the hard work of continual experimentation. God gives us brains, materials, forces and tools. Whether we understand it or not, these gifts present overwhelming evidence of God's love, design, power, and presence. Many don't believe, because the evidence, to them, *seems too amazing to be true*. In reality, the evidence actually proves *too amazing to be false!* God designs, creates, and sustains all nature and all true science. When we see the *Big Picture* we understand reality from God's viewpoint!

> How many are your works, O LORD! In wisdom you made them all;
> the earth is full of your creatures . . . When you send your Spirit,
> they are created, and you renew the face of the earth
>
> (Ps 104:24,30).

Part One (chapters one through seven) covers the dynamics of living
your life in Christ by focusing on possibilities, strengths, goals, priorities, and hard work. Organizations all over the world achieve
tremendous results with these dynamic principles. Church small
groups find them highly effective.

We challenge you to memorize these seven principles starting
with *Possibilities.*

Dynamics of Achievement

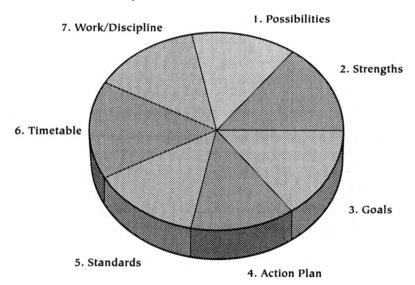

Part Two (chapters eight through sixteen) covers the dynamics of
inspiration and motivation that completes *The Leadership Principles of
Jesus.* The true motivator is Christ Himself.

We challenge you as you read these chapters to let His Spirit fill
your hearts and minds. Let Christ motivate you to live for Him and to
be highly productive in His Church and His world.

Dynamics of Motivation

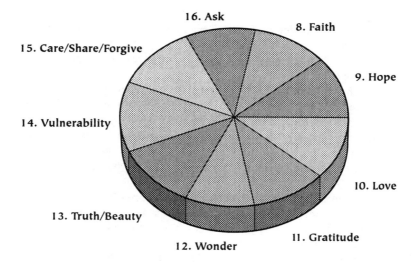

Here is an expanded list of the themes of each chapter:[1]

PART ONE: The dynamics of knowing and accomplishing God's will.

1. Possibilities: Let yourself perceive all the possibilities you can envision.
2. Strengths and Gifts: Know what you can and will expect from yourself and how to develop and use your spiritual gifts and strengths.
3. Goals: Determine specific achievable components of your vision.
4. Action Plan: Decide the "what, where, when, who, how, and why" of the vision Christ has for you.
5. Standards: Determine how your goals will be realized with excellence.
6. Timetable: Schedule your priorities and develop your "life calendar."
7. Work and Discipline: Apply your gifts and skills to your ministry effectively.

PART TWO: Spiritual dynamics for letting God motivate you.

8. Faith: Believe in yourself, others, and Christ.

   9. Hope: Believe in and learn from your experiences. Expect the best.
  10. Love: Tap into the power that makes it all happen according to God's will.
  11. Gratitude: Develop the highest form of mental and spiritual health.
  12. Wonder: Let life *in*. Seek, quest, admire, enjoy. Appreciate God's Creation.
  13. Truth and Beauty: Savor the joy of each passing "now."
  14. Vulnerability: Dissolve your emotional defenses. Let Christ strengthen you.
  15. Caring, Sharing, Forgiving: Guarantee growth, change, and fulfillment.
  16. Asking: Complete the other principles in the two circles.

In our years of working, leading, and consulting, this book's dynamic approach has been very effective. This challenge applies just as much to everyday, grassroots Christianity as it does to success and relationships in secular organizations. Nothing has such an impact as vibrant, Christ-centered living. These dynamic principles show *how* Jesus lived and *what* He taught His Disciples to teach the whole world. *The greatest leader who ever lived,* His example and principles work as effectively today as they did 2,000 years ago. They apply to *all people.* He reveals the vital connection between the *Big Picture* and the small picture, *God's viewpoint* and the world's viewpoint.

When Joe first published his book *Tough-minded Management*, it produced two outstanding responses: "These principles come right out of the teachings of Christ." "They will work in church relationships just as well as they do in secular organizations."

Now that book has sold more than 2 million copies.

Grassroots Christianity grows spontaneously all over the world through the following:

  ◆ The spread of Christ's Message, inspired by His Holy Spirit.
  ◆ The overwhelming wonder of the Creation. It uses no words or speech, but its "voice" goes out to every person in the world. (See Ps 19:1-4.)

If we reduce our personal world to the mere material, to the secular only, we miss the *Big Picture* and *God's existence.* So Paul said, "What may be known about God is plain to them," plainly perceived in the things that exist. We have no excuse if we fail to know God and show gratitude for what He gives to us (Rom 1:18-21).

The Leadership Principles of Jesus[2]

One leader in a large international company told us with a bitter, pained look, "Give me one good reason why we don't have a lot of enthusiasm and motivation in this division. I've personally attended all kinds of seminars on motivation, communication, human relations, and you name it. I've made sure we're doing all the right things here. But these lazy clunks just don't react.

"*Enthusiasm,*" he said in a measured, abrasive manner, "is all I'm asking for."

Do you see what was happening? As Emerson said, "What you are speaks so loudly, I can't hear what you are saying." And this man was calling for something he simply didn't exemplify. So his leadership was not real; it was not authentic. In short, it was phony. Like all of us, he first had to put *himself* on the hook! Jesus put it this way: "If your eyes are good, your whole body will be full of light. But if your eyes are bad, your whole body will be full of darkness. If then the light within you is darkness, how great is that darkness!" (Matt 6:22-23).

The essence of all modern, valid principles of achievement and motivation were spelled out in the *Sermon on the Mount* by Christ, the toughest-minded and most effective Example and Teacher of all time.

LEADERSHIP BY RESULTS? Isn't it better and more simply said by Christ in the statement, "By their fruit you will recognize them" (Matt 7:16)? This implies that the principles, priorities, and practices for the workers in any organization should relate recognition and compensation for each individual worker to his or her *actual performance* — not to color, race, creed, old school ties, physical appearance, and other related trivia.

INVOLVEMENT, COMMITMENT, AND CONVICTION? The *Beatitudes* permit nothing less than tough-minded inner conviction. They require compassion, hard work, discipline, love, and confrontation to even partially fulfill their stretching expectations. You simply cannot make a continuous and vigorous effort to develop these into the *fruit of the Spirit* without involved and committed relationships with the people around you.

Read the beatitudes to see how apparent weaknesses become our greatest strengths. In secular society these beautiful attitudes may look like weaknesses, but to Jesus they are strengths, therefore:

Blessed are the poor in spirit, for theirs is the kingdom of heaven.
Blessed are those who mourn, for they will be comforted...
Blessed are those who hunger and thirst for righteousness, for they
will be filled.
Blessed are the merciful, for they will be shown mercy . . .
Blessed are you when people insult you, persecute you and falsely
say all manner of evil against you because of me. Rejoice and be
glad, because great is your reward in heaven, for in the same way
they persecuted the prophets . . . (Matt 5:3-12).

CONFRONTATION AND INTERFACE? These transactions fill the
New Testament. The following potent Scripture teaches us confrontation, interface, and accountability:

Whosoever therefore shall break one of these least commandments, and shall teach men so, he shall be called the least in the
kingdom of heaven: but whosoever shall do and teach *them*, the
same shall be called great in the kingdom of heaven. For I say unto
you, That except your righteousness shall exceed *the righteousness*
of the scribes and Pharisees, ye shall in no case enter the kingdom
of heaven (Matt 5:19-20, KJV).

That's telling it like it is!

EFFECTIVE COMMUNICATION? We know that one of the principal
problems in every organization is communication. Too much paperwork, too much irrelevant conversation, memoranda, correspon-
dence, hinting, "diplomacy," and oblique innuendoes. Many pundits
tell us sagely to "reduce the complex to the simple." Christ said it
this way:

Whatsoever you have to say let your "yes" be a plain "yes" and
your "no" be a plain "no" — anything more than this has a taint of
evil (Matt 5:37, Phillips).

PERFORMANCE STANDARDS? How about this?

Be ye therefore perfect, even as your Father which is in heaven is
perfect (Matt 5:48, KJV).

PROFITABILITY? Christ puts it plainly:

Even so every good tree bringeth forth good fruit, but a corrupt tree bringeth forth evil fruit (Matt 7:17, KJV).

TRUST AND INTEGRITY? Trust and integrity create a foundation of granite. Jesus stated it this way:

Therefore whosoever heareth these sayings of mine, and doeth them, I will liken him unto a wise man, which built his house upon a rock: And the rain descended, and the floods came, and the winds blew, and beat upon that house; and it fell not: for it was founded upon a rock (Matt 7:24-25, KJV).

The company, school, family, church, government, or any other organization that does not structure everything it believes and does on trust and integrity may generate profit or demonstrate profitability for awhile, but ultimately crumbles. It builds on sand.

And every one that heareth these sayings of mine, and doeth them not, shall be likened unto a foolish man, which built his house upon the sand. And the rain descended and the floods came, and the winds blew, and beat upon that house; and it fell: and great was the fall of it (Matt 7:26-27, KJV).

Effective, experienced people know these statements simply as facts of life. The wise person focuses on the *Big Picture*. The foolish person focuses on the small picture.

POSITIVE LISTENING, OPEN-MINDEDNESS AND SENSITIVITY? Everyone accepts these as essentials for organized, productive, and profitable people. Note how clearly the tough-minded Light of the World presents the distilled and beautiful essence — and the answer — to these needs.

Don't criticise people, and you will not be criticised. For you will be judged by the way you criticise others, and the measure you give will be the measure you receive.

Why do you look at the speck of sawdust in your brother's eye and fail to notice the plank in your own? How can you say to your brother, "Let me get the speck out of your eye," when there is a plank in your own? You hypocrite! Take the plank out of your own eye first, and then you can see clearly enough to remove your brother's speck of dust (Matt 7:1-5, Phillips).

BUILD ON STRENGTHS? Don't dwell on weaknesses! Every successful person knows that personal oblivion comes from dwelling on
weaknesses of self, people and things. To be positive and successful
seek out, identify, relate to, and *apply* strengths. Christ speaks
squarely to our frequent dilemma in choosing between these two
options when he says the following:

> Love your enemies, bless them that curse you, do good to them
> that hate you, and pray for them which despitefully use you, and
> persecute you (Matt 5:44, KJV).

Many readers may disagree with this, but don't knock it until
you've *tried it*, and *tried it*! Try to see everything from God's viewpoint, the *Big Picture*.

LEADERSHIP BY EXAMPLE? Matthew said it even better.

> For he taught them as *one* having authority, and not as the scribes
> (Matt 7:29, KJV).

Jesus is one with God, and therefore when He speaks, He speaks
with Authority and Power. He focuses our eyes on eternity!
The greatest statement on the essence of leadership was and is,
"Follow me."

JOB ENRICHMENT OR HIGH EXPECTATIONS? Do you have the guts
to expect the best — not the worst — from your fellow creature and
from life itself?
And here again, Christ says it so much better than we can.

> Ask, and it shall be given you; seek, and ye shall find; knock, and
> it shall be opened unto you: for every one that asketh receiveth;
> and he that seeketh findeth; and to him that knocketh it shall be
> opened (Matt 7:7-8, KJV).

As Christians, we don't have to adopt the victimist mentality, always
down-in-the-mouth, solemn, and expecting the worst in health, performance, compensation, love or morals. Christ commands us to *trust
in* God's love and to *expect* and go *after* excellence that lasts forever.
What secular leader can match or top this?
Without doubt, the most beautiful and potent teaching available
to us daily from Christ concerns the need of a troubled world for "a
living way to go," for inspiration and moral guidelines. Everyone,
regardless of their religious background, whether executive, teacher,

minister, artisan, farmer, or homemaker, the following sublime precept cuts to the heart of the human condition, and gives us all we need:

> Treat other people exactly as you would like to be treated by them — this is the meaning of the Law and the Prophets (Matt 7:12, Phillips).

But wait! There's one most important word from Christ! You say you believe in these things, but, after all, you're only *one* person? And what can *one* person do?

> You are the world's light — it is impossible to hide a town built on the top or a hill. Men do not light a lamp and put it under a bucket. They put it on a lamp-stand and it gives light for everybody in the house. Let your light shine like that in the sight of men. Let them see the good things you do and praise your Father in Heaven (Matt 5:14-16, Phillips).

How's that for the *power of example?*"

Will you *do* it?

Before you read the first chapter of this book, take time to read through the Sermon on the Mount in Matthew, chapters five through seven. Commit yourself to understanding what Jesus taught His disciples 2,000 years ago. Believe the power and practicality of His words for everyday life. *By immersing yourself into the Word of Life and prayer, the Spirit of Christ will motivate you to achieve in your life all that God wants you to achieve!*

Will *you* do it?

REFERENCES

1. Joe Batten, *Tough-Minded Leadership* (New York: AMACOM, 1989), adapted from 176.

2. Joe Batten, *Expectations and Possibilities* (Santa Monica: Hay House, 1990), adapted from 199-204.

DYNAMICS OF ACHIEVEMENT

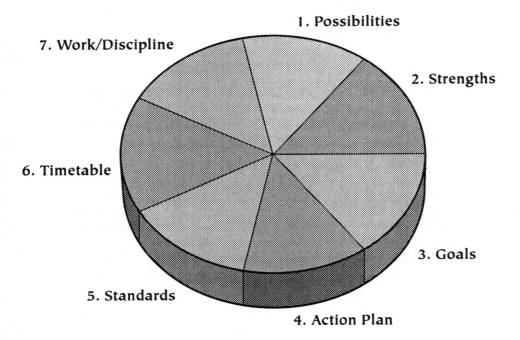

1. Possibilities

7. Work/Discipline

2. Strengths

6. Timetable

3. Goals

5. Standards

4. Action Plan

Part One: The Dynamics of Achievement

◆ *Achieve dynamic results in your church work.* If secular organizations use the dynamic principles of Christ wisely and shrewdly, grassroots Christians can certainly show churches how to use His principles and priorities even more effectively.

◆ *God's message to us is the life of Christ.* Our strengths, spiritual gifts, and values take on great power because He helps us grow in them. Through Christ we can see how the small picture fits into God's *Big Picture!*

Greater Than You Think!

Jesus shows us the perfect way to develop healthy relationships. He trained the disciples by forming them into a small group that lived intimately with Him for three years. He demonstrated and explained to them what Heaven is all about and also what is important for living in human society.

Our prayer for you is this: As you read through this book, may the Spirit of Christ open your heart and help you discover what really pleases God (Rom 12:1-2). God created us to love each other and to do good works. He wants us to be productive, not unproductive in our walk with Him. When Jesus chided the disciples for their lack of faith, He was not focusing on weaknesses. He was stressing that God would do through them *far more than they could imagine.* (See Eph 2:10; Titus 2:14; 3:8,14; Phil 2:12-13; Matt 17:20; Eph 3:20.)

In ministry to others, we emphasize Christ's threefold priority (see John 15:5-8, 12-17 and 26-27):

1. Base everything that we think and do upon our love for Him and His words.
2. Love each other and relate to one another in healthy, intimate small groups.
3. Reach the people in our circle of influence with the love and wisdom of Christ.

All Truth Is God's Truth

Moral law came though Moses, but kindness, love, and truth came through Christ. If we hold to Christ's teaching we will know the truth, and the truth will make us free. Mary chose to sit at Jesus' feet and learn from Him while Martha was "worried and upset by all the preparations that had to be made." Jesus said, "Only one thing is needed. Mary has chosen what is better and it will not be taken away from her." (See John 1:17; 8:31-32; Luke 10:38-42.)

Jesus told Pilate, "Everyone on the side of truth listens to me" (John 18:37b). God spoke from Heaven to tell Peter, James and John, "This is my Son. . . . Listen to Him" (Matt 17:5).

It's no wonder that what works in modern relationships (in America, Japan, or anywhere else) are the same principles that Jesus taught, especially in His *Sermon on the Mount.* They work in church relationships. And they work in business and *all other* relationships.

All Science Is God's Science

Jesus was with God in the Creation of all things. Everything was created by, for, and through Him. Nothing was made that was not made by, for, and through Him. No truth of science has ever been discovered that wasn't given to us by God, because God makes all true science possible. God created this world as a "training school" for us. He designed it for the purpose of revealing to us what we need to know about Heaven. Jesus told Nicodemus, "If you don't believe when I tell you earthly things, how will you believe if I tell you heavenly things?" (see John 3:12). When scientists say, "We no longer need the God-hypothesis" they deceive themselves and anyone else who believes their claim. Scientific discoveries don't surprise God and Christ because all technology *comes* from God. And God has an even greater technology, the truth about Heavenly things. (See John 1:1-3, 10; Col 1:15-20; Heb 1:1-3, 10.)

Getting Us To See God's Vision

Jesus often appealed to His disciples, "If you have faith as small as a mustard seed, . . . [n]othing will be impossible for you" (Matt 17:20). "With God all things are possible" (Matt 19:26). It's important for us to read the very words of Christ, not only what others write about His words. Little faith, low productivity, and poor quality in our relationships come from never making the commitment and risk necessary to follow Jesus. We need to balance intellectual learning with daily living in "Christ's school of experience."

Obey Christ, even if it is risky, and the truth will become more clear. Jesus said, "If anyone chooses to do God's will, he will find out whether my teaching comes from God or whether I speak on my own" (John 7:17). When the angel Gabriel appeared to Zacharias and told him that his wife Elizabeth would have a son named John, Zacharias said, "How can I be sure of this? I am an old man and my wife is well along in years" (Luke 1:18). He doubted. But when

Gabriel appeared to Mary with the news that she would be the mother of Jesus, she said, "How will this be, since I am a virgin?" (Luke 1:34). Mary believed Gabriel but wanted to know more about such a great honor. Great things are possible with us if we choose to believe and do God's will.

The Unlimited Power of Christ

We please God when we are productive. Jesus said, "This is to my Father's glory, that you bear much fruit, showing yourselves to be my disciples" (John 15:7-8). Peter said, "For this very reason, make every effort to add to your faith goodness; and to goodness, knowledge; and to knowledge, self-control; and to self-control, perseverance; and to perseverance, godliness; and to godliness, brotherly kindness; and to brotherly kindness, love. For if you possess these qualities in increasing measure, they will keep you from being ineffective and unproductive in your knowledge of our Lord Jesus Christ" (2 Peter 1:5-8).

"The only thing that counts is faith expressing itself through love" (Gal 5:6). Faith and love are the most powerful forces in the world. We pray that this book will help you glorify Christ in all of your relationships by recognizing and using the truths that God has revealed through Christ, truths that many in the world may be using more effectively than God's own people. (See Luke 16:8.)

Our first seven chapters describe systematically how to build our lives on God's spiritual gifts and strengths, maximize our possibilities, reach achievable goals, accomplish God's will successfully, and glorify Christ.

Chapter one deals with creating an inspiring vision from your dreams and possibilities.

Chapter two stresses discovery and use of spiritual gifts and strengths.

Chapter three covers the value of setting and reaching goals.

Chapter four focuses on your Action Plan for productivity in God's Kingdom.

Chapter five discusses standards for serving Christ with excellence.

Chapter six tells us how to keep priorities in perspective.

Chapter seven covers Work and Discipline: using the first six dynamic principles.

CHAPTER ONE
POSSIBILITIES

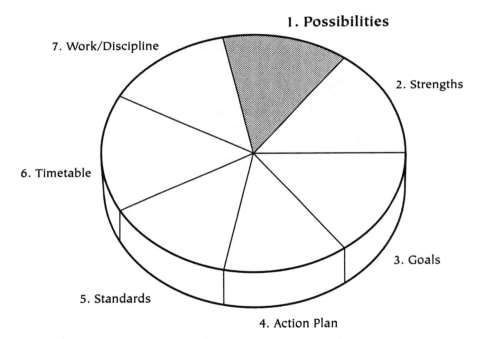

Reflect on the vital place that *your possibilities* have as the above circle applies to *your life*!

1

CLIMB EVERY MOUNTAIN —

DEVELOP YOUR BEST POSSIBILITIES

Man with God's help and personal dedication is capable of anything he can dream.
Conrad Hilton

I tell you the truth, if you have faith as small as a mustard seed, you can say
to this mountain, "Move from here to there" and it will move.
Nothing will be impossible for you.
Jesus (in Matt 17:20; emphasis added)

Key Points

Excellent organizations discover and exploit their best possibilities. To become effective and productive workers in Christ's Kingdom we must seek out whatever He makes possible. This chapter provides readers with insights and principles for putting dynamic life into their daily ministries, into their vision for Christ's Kingdom. God's Word tells many stories about people who realized their possibilities by trusting in Christ. Individuals can help churches turn possibilities into realities, especially with small groups.

✷✷✷✷

Climate is important, whether we are part of a church or a secular organization. Jesus often spoke about loving each other, and being united with each other as He is united with God. He faced criticism from the leaders of His nation because they exemplified a

27

climate of fear, self-righteousness, and partiality. From the start to the end of the Bible God reveals Himself as One who is fair, reasonable, and impartial.

It's no surprise that human organizations stress the importance of a climate that will inspire productivity and excellence. What is surprising is that in this secular groups are often more resourceful and successful than churches are. Jesus teaches us that we will know the truth and the truth will set us free. But that won't happen if we are not free to discover what the truth is. God has designed tremendous capability into the physical world, and scientists have been free to discover many of God's physical blessings. Shouldn't we be more innovative in God's Church? The leaders of God's own people had chained themselves and the people by human traditions. When the Prophets tried to call His nation back to His principles, the leaders and people persecuted them and rejected God's words. When Jesus tried to set people free, they condemned and crucified Him. Jesus prayed that all believers would be united as He and God are united, yet believers remain divided.

In this chapter we develop the idea that Christians, indeed all people, can discover better possibilities for serving Christ by looking at the success of other organizations that constantly evaluate their possibilities, combine them with people's strengths, and stretch toward higher, more valuable goals.

Your Dream and Your Vision

How do we move toward a transcendent vision? A person can't begin and sustain a steady ascent toward dreams without the fuel of faith, hope, love, and gratitude based on a growing awareness of his or her strengths.

Knowing your spiritual strengths stimulates and encourages dreams. Ask yourself these seven questions:

1. What would you ideally most like to *be*?
2. What would you ideally most like to *do*? *Being* should precede *doing*.
3. What kind of experiences help you feel more *complete*?
4. What kind of relationships are most helpful in making you feel encouraged, multiplied, compounded, and built-up?
5. In what kind of situations do you most want to share yourself?

6. In what circumstances can you most vulnerably let others *in* and you *out*?

7. What kind of happenings best help you feel a sense of exceeding yourself?

The tough stuff of possible dreams must be fashioned and crafted out of reality. And reality starts with asking, listening, and hearing. What you imagine is what will transpire. What you believe is what you will achieve.

Joe Batten[1]

Joe's Work in Japan

I'll always remember what happened in Sendai, Japan, on a recent trip. Some 375 executives of a huge automaker were gathered for a seminar on Tough-Minded Leadership. For seven hours I presented principles and techniques for making sure the company was truly value-led.

At the end of the day, every single person lined up, with reams of notes, shook my hand and said, "Mr. Batten, tomorrow I will *start to do* these things." Some even said, "*tonight* I will start to do these things."

The CEO of the company then invited me into his private dining room and said, "Forgive me for not shaking hands. My palms are wet because I'm feeling so emotional about what I have learned today. All these principles are practical and we can start using the following immediately:

◆ Confront all our possibilities and develop the best ones.
◆ Build on strengths.
◆ Use crystal clear vision to develop specific and excellent goals."

In a letter received since that seminar, the CEO listed the following results that are already apparent:

◆ Heightened morale
◆ Accelerated personal growth
◆ Focused effort
◆ All previous quality standards exceeded
◆ General increase in a variety of performance indicators

The CEO also indicated that this is only the beginning and the entire workforce is committed to *continuous improvement*. They have targeted going *beyond* reengineering.

What We Think and Say Is What We Become

"Men grow when inspired by a high purpose, when contemplating horizons," said Alex Carrel. "The sacrifice of oneself is not very difficult for one burning with the passion for a great adventure."

So where do we find our great adventure in the church? Where do we start? What are we saying to one another about the world in which we live and the future that lies ahead? Let's quit saying, "The church is out of it. Everything is bound to go wrong. There is something basically bad about all human beings. All human history is evil, irrational, without purpose." When we begin to talk this way, and when we begin to think this way, we begin to *become* this way. Don't react with gloomy, cynical, and despairing expectations or almost always those expectations will be borne out.

We call people of all ages and kinds regardless of vocation, to appraise the past and present dispassionately; let us respond objectively to the challenge of criticism and set targets for ourselves. Let's undertake the stretching dream for greater understanding of the role that Christ calls us to fulfill? Our ministry matters to God, and we can glorify Christ by perceiving and following the vision He has for us.

It Takes Work to Dream

We need to dream bigger dreams, not the easy things. Somehow, in our modern organizations an outlook appears to be all too prevalent which will not, cannot, restore the ability to dream that so many people have lost. Why? In part, because hard work—physical and mental—has become relatively unknown in America.

Perhaps the main problem is simply that "fatty" brain cells making thoughts jumbled and uncoordinated are no substitute for "real" gray matter. Wouldn't it be better to have mental muscles than mental misery? Then it would be easy to look for strengths instead of weaknesses, to dream instead of complain.

We can't dream if we don't develop our spiritual dimension. We can't trust ourselves if we overemphasize, or dwell on, our own weaknesses. If we could learn to use the potential that God has designed into our bodies and brains, who knows the upper limits of *His possibilities*? He has given us a brain with *one trillion* brain cells. We currently use only a minute fraction of them.

You Find What You Dream and Envision

Would it be safe, then, to say this? "The church is great wherein people have a genuine zest for living each day and for every moment trying to replace put-downs with great dreams." Perhaps the very notion of having vision instead of merely criticizing frightens many because judging others has become the basis for their existence. Again they have become imprisoned by their weaknesses. They are liberated and empowered by their strengths.

Jesus tells us to use our ears and eyes wisely. According to Luke, one of the thieves that died with Christ had the vision to believe in Him and ask to be remembered when Jesus came into His kingdom. This man, as bad off as he was, had his capacity to dream revived by Jesus' powerful presence. In spite of his dilemma he was able to believe in the *Big Picture!* (cf. Luke 23:40-43).

Luke also tells of the woman who poured expensive perfume on Jesus and kissed His feet. She was forgiven much because she loved much. Jesus' host, Simon the Pharisee, didn't perceive how great Jesus was, and he didn't love like the woman. Simon, with all his wealth and power, wasn't able to understand the marvelous vision God gave to the woman. (See Luke 7:36-50.)

The story of Joseph is one of the greatest in the Bible of a person who realized wonderful dreams from God. His brothers hated him; they sold him into slavery; his master's wife falsely charged him with rape; and the king's servant whom Joseph befriended in prison forgot his promise. Joseph triumphed over a series of great troubles, and with God's help became the ruler of all Egypt. God enabled Joseph to save the Jewish nation from a seven-year famine.[2]

The Shrewd and Dishonest Manager

"The master commended the dishonest manager because he had acted shrewdly. For the people of this world are more shrewd in dealing with their own kind than are the people of the light. I tell you, use worldly wealth to gain friends for yourselves, so that when it is gone, you will be welcomed into eternal dwellings.

Whoever can be trusted with very little can also be trusted with much, and whoever is dishonest with very little will also be dishonest with much. So if you have not been trustworthy in handling worldly wealth, who will trust you with true riches? And if you have not been trustworthy with someone else's property, who will give you property of your own?

No servant can serve two masters. Either he will hate the one and love the other, or he will be devoted to the one and despise the other. You cannot serve both God and Money."

The Pharisees, who loved money, heard all this and were sneering at Jesus. He said to them, "You are the ones who justify yourselves in the eyes of men, but God knows your hearts. What is highly valued among men is detestable in God's sight" (Luke 16:8-15).

From God's Point of View, We Can Learn from Others

From God's point of view all secular organizations are temporary. If temporary human organizations can do things wisely to perceive and grasp opportunities and possibilities, then God's people should be able to do this even more wisely and effectively. Unfortunately this is not always true. That's why Jesus gave us the parable of the shrewd manager in Luke 16.

Secular organizations must use possibilities wisely and effectively if they are to survive and be successful. If they are not wise they will lose their customers and their most talented people. Highly successful companies innovate constantly using entrepreneurial teams. Top leaders develop the vision and mission of the organization with input from all the employees. Then they decentralize, delegate, and *empower* their most capable people. They select these teams of highly motivated, talented people from all key departments and from all levels of the company. The best companies often include suppliers and customers on teams of their own employees. Some even change from calling their people employees and use terms like team members, associates or partners. The leaders build a climate that is totally positive, sensitive to the customer's needs and wants, and stresses cooperation, not competition. They discover the best and most vital needs and opportunities with positive listening and extensive experimentation. Discovering the possibilities that serve the customer best also optimizes the strengths and gifts of the team's members (our chapter two).

Team Taurus: People on the Ford Taurus team examined and took apart the 12 top competitive cars in that class to determine what was the best. The team came up with 400 features of excellence. When the first Taurus came off the production line it had 360 of the 400 features. A wide variety of people were on the team from design, production, assembly, marketing, and service. In addition to examining competitive cars the team early on visited assembly plants, manufacturing facilities, suppliers, and insurance companies. They asked everyone, "What do you want to see in this car?"

On the Ford assembly line alone they came up with 1,000 ideas. These ideas (none were asked for on previous cars) led to:

◆ Many significant innovations.

◆ Lower design and production times and costs by a large percentage.

◆ Excellent implementation, which was badly neglected on previous cars.

◆ Increased involvement, and this produced commitment and conviction. The Taurus became everyone's baby.

Social scientists know that we change more for emotional reasons than for intellectual ones. Ford made sure that every person from assembly line worker to car owner was emotionally involved with this total quality car. Later, when customers discovered bugs in cylinders of cars made in a certain plant, Ford contacted all the owners, set up appointments, installed new motors, and provided a loaner car, all free.

What resulted from Ford's dedication to excellence?

Four years after their introduction, the Ford Taurus and its Mercury equivalent, the Sable, were selling faster than ever. In 1988 Ford earned a stunning 25 percent on equity. And despite several new model introductions by General Motors in early 1989, Ford continued to build its market share in the midsize category.[3]

IBM: In the '50s Univac had the most advanced computer in the world. It worked great for accounting and other business uses, but Univac devoted its efforts primarily to the computer's scientific use. IBM also had developed a computer for scientific work, but Watson saw the possibilities for the payroll and accounting market. Since his computer was not right for payroll and accounting, he worked closely with customers, hired capable computer scientists, and experimented extensively with better designs. In four years IBM took the lead in the computer market even though its own design was inferior to Univac's for another ten years. Univac had the best machine but never became a factor in computers.

In 1950 Univac's marketing research people predicted that only 1,000 computers would be sold by the year 2000. Because they weren't sensitive to customers' needs and wants, they allowed IBM to become the market leader. By 1984 more than 1 million computers were sold. By 2000 many hundreds of millions of a wide variety of computers will be in use. IBM succeeded by focusing on the possibilities.[4]

Matsushita: The Japanese giant electronic firms, Toshiba and Hitachi, believed that Japanese farmers were too poor to afford a TV. They saw and sold only to the luxury market. Matsushita was a small company at the time, but they manufactured a TV and sold it door-to-door to the farmers. Matsushita discovered that the farmers didn't know that they were too poor to own TVs. The farmers were actually very excited with this new invention. With a TV they could see the world.

By being ready for unexpected possibilities Matsushita (brand name Panasonic) became a world leader with its products. Konosuke Matsushita, founder of the company, referred to Joe's *Tough-Minded Management* as his "secular bible."[5]

Taco Bell: In 1983 Taco Bell was getting "sicker" compared with other fast food restaurant chains. Their CEO decided to take a "voyage of discovery" to save the company. Their greatest insights were:

◆ We decided to listen to our customers.
◆ We had been making the fast food business too complex.
◆ We were far behind our major competitors in every way.

Taco Bell created a vision:

◆ They looked at all the possibilities.
◆ They asked customers, "What do you want?" The answers were simple: good food, served hot and fast, a clean environment, and affordable cost.
◆ They unleashed their possibilities by thinking in totally new ways, innovatively.
◆ They decentralized by eliminating district managers, creating market managers, and giving restaurant managers more power.
◆ They ignored their traditional-thinking people who "knew" what customers wanted without asking them, and whose dogmatic attitude only caused slower service at higher cost. They attacked head on the phenomenon described by John Steinbeck: "It is the nature of man as he grows older to protest change, particularly change for the better."

What resulted from this new vision? Taco Bell reached a growth rate in profit of 31% while the industry struggled. They redefined their vision: *To be number one in share of stomach.* When they heard comments like, "Your goal is far fetched," or, "There are too many changes," *they knew they were on the right track.* Now they're delivering food to wherever people are, to vending machines, supermarkets, schools, retail outlets, street corners, etc. Taco Bell recognized what customers really wanted and needed.[6]

What Jesus Said about Possibilities

Jesus and His disciples faced great obstacles, but they also faced greater opportunities and possibilities. Jesus kept asking His followers to have more faith, because God could do anything they asked. God can do things people find impossible. Jesus did many marvelous miracles that His disciples had never seen done before. He healed every conceivable sickness and raised people from the dead. He used the forces of nature as the One who had created them. He walked on water, multiplied food for thousands, stopped a storm, and turned water into wine. When they crucified Him He rose from the dead.

What important possibilities does Jesus want people to recognize? After feeding the 5,000 He told the people, "Do not work for food that spoils, but for food that endures to eternal life, which the Son of Man will give you. . . ."

Then they asked Him, "What must we do to do the works God requires?"

Jesus answered, "The work of God is this: to believe in the one he has sent" (John 6:27-29).

He explained His priorities to His followers: Become fully mature through faith in Him. Be filled with inexpressible joy. He wanted all people to know that He came to save the whole world and to give every person the opportunity for eternal life. He said, "I am the way, and the truth and the life. I came that they might have life more abundantly." He meant for us to have *total quality life* with each other and eternally with God. With Jesus every person in the world can realize astounding possibilities. Do we understand Jesus' possibilities, or are we distracted by human traditions, conceits, and worries?

Why Churches Need to Consider Possibilities

It may not be obvious to some church leaders and some church members, but many churches today need to listen to the parable of the shrewd manager. Jesus united His followers in a few general principles:

◆ Believe on the One whom God sent.
◆ Treat others as you would like to be treated.
◆ Love God, and love your neighbor as you love yourself.
◆ Don't criticize others; criticize yourselves.

He condemned human traditions that ignored God's purpose, despised the "sinners" God loved, led to self-righteous pride, and nullified God's Word. Jesus brought freedom for all those who would continue in His Word. (See John 8:31-32.)

But we church members don't always think for ourselves or feel free to follow Jesus. We sometimes treat innovation, discovery, and change as bad words. Jesus came as a Doctor to heal the sick, as a Savior to reach and save sinners, but His church often has great difficulty in following His example and obeying His wishes. We can be divided by technical theories, dogmatic opinions, and traditional habits. We find it difficult to encourage people to think for themselves, even though John said, "You do not need anyone to teach you" (1 John 2:27). And Jesus praised God, "because you have hidden these things from the wise and learned, and revealed them to little children" (Matt 11:25).

Two people described by Paul in Romans 14 had widely different views of God's will, but Paul said that Christ accepts both of them. The strong one must not look down on the weak one, and the weak one must not judge the strong one. Paul prayed for this kind of unity when he said, "May the God who gives endurance and encouragement give you a spirit of unity among yourselves as you follow Christ Jesus, so that with one heart and mouth you may glorify the God and Father of our Lord Jesus Christ. Accept one another, then, just as Christ accepted you, in order to bring praise to God" (Rom 15:5-7).

God provides great possibilities if we will love Him, love each other, and truly listen to the voice and needs of our neighbors around us in the world. We can learn from the secular organizations whose people may be wiser in their concern about their future than we are about our future.

How Can Grassroots Christians Help Churches See Possibilities?

Grassroots Christians can help churches and the whole world understand the best of what we have learned from working in the marketplace. The shrewd manager in Jesus' parable was commended by his master because he prepared wisely for his future. Jesus also approved his foresight and practical actions, not his dishonesty. Jesus used this man's shrewdness to show the children of light, the people of God, that we also should be very careful and wise concerning our own future. We should learn how to make friends for ourselves in heavenly places, in other words, make a friend of God.

"God's customers" are all those Christ wants us to bring into His Kingdom. "God's customers" should be our customers. We should be listening to them in the way that successful secular organizations listen to the voices of their customers. Christ is the Savior of the whole world, all people that God has created. God is not willing that a single person be lost. He wants all to come to repentance. (See 2 Peter 3:9.) Every knee will eventually bow and every tongue confess that God is great. Do we in the church understand and appreciate how much God wants to save the spoiled, not spoil the saved? Isn't this what Paul meant when he said, "I make myself a slave to everyone, to win as many as possible" (1 Cor 9:19-23)?

The experts leading God's people asked, "Why does your teacher eat with tax collectors and 'sinners'?" On hearing this Jesus said, "It is not the healthy who need a doctor, but the sick. But go and learn what this means, 'I desire mercy, not sacrifice.' For I have not come to call the righteous, but sinners" (Matt 9:11-13).

Nothing is more joyful than discovering Christ and the true meaning of eternal life. Christ gives His church the possibility of spreading the manifold wisdom of God to the whole world. God loves every person in the world. He made every one. Jesus wants us to leave the 99 to find every single lost one.

If Jesus could use the shrewd manager to illustrate our need for wisdom, we today need to appreciate what God gives to wise people in the world: wisdom that comes from practical secular experience. Jesus often found the religious experts and leaders to be blind, arrogant, and prejudiced. He commended and associated more with outcasts and "sinners" than He did experts, leaders, and teachers of the law. The people in authority often hated the very ones that Jesus loved and accepted. These "sinners" were more willing to repent, and even had greater faith than the leaders of Israel. Look at the following people Jesus commended or befriended:

- The Roman Centurion with the dying servant (Matt 8:5-13).
- The man born blind that the Pharisees cast out because he was "steeped in sin" (John 9).
- Zacchaeus the chief tax collector and "real sinner" (Luke 19:1-10).
- The Samaritan woman at the well (John 4:4-42).
- The woman caught in adultery (how did the man get away?) (John 8:1-11).
- The "sinner" woman who anointed Jesus' feet in the home of Simon the Pharisee (Luke 7:36-50).

◆ The Syrophoenician woman with great faith, willing to take "the crumbs" (Mark 7:24-30).
◆ Paul, who called himself the greatest of sinners (1 Tim 1:15).
◆ The Twelve Disciples, none of whom were religious professionals.
◆ Mary Magdalene, out of whom Jesus cast seven demons (Luke 8:2).

Small Groups Bring Out God's Possibilities

The use of small groups has proven to be one of the most effective ways to develop and build healthy long-term relationships. The quality and effectiveness of our relationships develop best in small, intimate groups where possibilities can be shared and worked on.

How do we get small groups up and operating? In many companies and churches small groups have become the basic building blocks for constantly bringing new people into a living relationship with Christ as well as with each other. Churches all over the world using small "cell-groups" have grown explosively into large communities. They organize their church life around small groups to better accomplish God's priorities.

Common Questions about Small Groups

1. **What is a small group?**

Six to twelve people. Groups meet weekly for the purpose of improving every dimension of relationships, service, spirit, vision, etc. They enable individuals, groups, and churches to play a more vital role in God's kingdom, to provide the type of community that will bring in, welcome, and encourage new believers.

2. **Who are members?**

Anyone who wants to be part of God's growing family. All people committed to growing spiritually and working with God and each other to bring God's possibilities to reality. He reveals tremendous possibilities when we see ourselves as fellow workers with Him to reach the world with His message of life.

3. **What is unique about small groups?**
    ◆ They emphasize current and potential strengths and spiritual gifts.
    ◆ They identify your weaknesses and strengths to determine:
    —What additional strengths are needed
    —What is needed to further develop existing strengths

—That forgiveness is made real with intimate and loving support.

◆ Spiritual gifts and strengths enable individuals to develop the best relationships in the group, in the family, on the job, or with social contacts.

4. **What results do small groups produce?**
    ◆ Greater empowerment and renewal of people to be truly proactive.
    ◆ Greater enhancement of individual responsibility and growth in spiritual maturity.
    ◆ Greater service to others in the group.
    ◆ Reduction in destructive thinking; replacement of fear with love and confidence.
    ◆ Improved team spirit; new appreciation for the intimate "family" climate.
    ◆ Constant focus on and guidance from the group's vision and mission.
    ◆ Constant discovery of new possibilities fed by their dreams.

5. **What other things do small groups accomplish?**
    ◆ Discoveries are integrated with the group's basic philosophy and God's will.
    ◆ There is a high degree of interpersonal discussion, interaction and intimacy.
    ◆ Leadership develops spontaneously and effectively.
    ◆ Facilitators and members learn to be tough-minded and tenderhearted.
    ◆ Just discovering possibilities for new and better relationships is inspiring.

Sample Agenda from an Exciting Small Group

This approach for unleashing the potentials and capabilities of the *grassroots Christian* creates virtually unlimited possibilities. It is based totally on positives, strengths, and spiritual gifts. In small groups meaningful *involvement* maximizes the possibility of devout *commitment* carried out with enthusiastic *conviction. Grassroots faith* brings about effective renewal for both individuals and groups. With Paul we can say, "I can do everything through him who gives me strength" (Phil 4:13).

The following example shows how most groups interact during a typical small group meeting:

A small group met for a potluck dinner at 5 PM one Sunday

evening. The meal was finished by 6 PM, and the discussion went like this:

1. **Icebreaker (20 minutes):** The eleven present in the group each described a dream or possibility that they could work for in the church. Each person in the group was asked to use not more than two minutes. Only two or three people in this group had any previous experience discussing dreams or possibilities. It was exciting to see people's face light up with the thrill of this new experience. Some sharing of needs took place also.

2. **Relating Life to the Bible (10 minutes):** The leader then had different people read the following verses:

- ◆ 1 Timothy 1:12-16 where Paul wrote that he was the worst of sinners.
- ◆ Acts 10:25 where Peter told Cornelius not to worship him, because he was only a man himself.
- ◆ Acts 14:13-15 where Paul told the crowd that wanted to worship Barnabas and him not to do it: "We too are only men, human like you."
- ◆ James 5:17 where James referred to Elijah, the great Old Testament prophet, as "a man just like us."
- ◆ Exodus 4:10-17 where Moses said, "I can't speak. Send someone else." God had commanded him to go back and bring His people out of Egypt.

3. **Group Discussion (30 minutes):** The whole group then discussed the idea that God can select, train and use anyone He wants. God will use each of us to do what He calls us to do. We can be just like the people mentioned in the Bible. God made them what they were, and *they were all humans just like us!* The members of this small group realized that God wants to use each of us to become like Christ and to spread His good news. All involved had a heightened understanding that grassroots Christians follow *the Christ-road of highly effective ministry*. Our example inspires others and spreads like yeast through the whole loaf of bread.

4. **Individual Prayers (20 minutes):** The group leader then had all of us in the circle pray for our own dream and for the dream of the person on our left. Praise, thanks for His gifts, and specific needs of individuals were included. The leader started the prayer, and each person to the right went in turn always praying for themselves and the person that had just prayed (on the left).

5. **The Group's Vision (10 minutes):** Finally the leader described the vision of what this group of people could achieve with God's help over the next five years:

- Bring friends, relatives, neighbors, etc. to know Christ and to experience fellowship.
- Help the church to multiply the present number of groups.
- To develop mature and intimate friendships with each other and experience in this group relationship the same kind of love for one another that Jesus and His disciples experienced.
- To be a truly loving support group.

Suggested Implementation Sequence for Starting Small Groups in a Church or Other Organization

1. For small groups to succeed, leadership support at the top level of the organization is crucial. Senior pastors and elders must make a commitment to encourage and be part of creative idea development and implementation. The leaders should attend some of the many available seminars and conferences on successfully organizing and implementing the cell-group system.
2. Make a decision to implement small groups.
3. Appoint a guidance committee, a small group task force.
4. Train guidance committee members in the small group process. (See the recommended reading at the end of this chapter. We used a 13-week "hands on" course for all trainees.)
5. After group leaders are trained they personally invite six to eight members for each of their groups to be sure that all involved want to be in their specific group.
6. Each group should plan to multiply into two groups when its attendance is over 12. It's vital not to have too many in a group.
7. From the group's start each leader trains an "intern" to lead the next "daughter" group. This is one of the keys to reaching people and bringing them into God's family.
8. Various types of small groups can be started based on people's needs:
   - Basic fellowship groups which bring friends and relatives into the group.
   - Support groups for those with special needs such as marriage enrichment, divorce recovery, parenting, substance abuse recovery, etc.
   - Life application Bible study groups for all ages.
   - Task force groups with specific short or long term assignments.
   - Leadership training groups. It is vital for leaders in training to read the available literature on small groups. See the *Recommended Reading* at the end of this chapter.

◆ Leadership team of elders and pastors. This team can best lead the whole congregation by example and as an intimate small group. Read Acts 6:1-7 to see how Jesus' leaders functioned.

Conclusion

Some secular organizations use the dynamic principles of Christ with amazing results. Christians can certainly learn the same principles effectively. You can show your church how to serve Jesus more productively and effectively. *Christ will lead you to achieve dynamic results in your life.*

Read on and learn to identify your spiritual gifts and strengths in chapter two. Delight yourself in the Lord, and His Spirit will use your gifts, strengths, and dreams to make the desires of your heart come true (see Ps 37:4).

RECOMMENDED READING/VIEWING

The following books give valuable knowledge on how small groups work in a variety of situations:

1. On what secular organizations are doing—

Joe Batten, *Tough-Minded Leadership,* (AMACOM) and *Building a Total Quality Culture,* (Crisp Publications).

Michael Hammer & James Champy, *Reengineering the Corporation,* (HarperBusiness).

Robert H. Waterman, Jr., *Adhocracy: The Power to Change,* (Norton) and *The Renewal Factor,* (Bantam Books).

Peter Drucker, *Innovation and Entrepreneurship,* (Harper & Row).

Tom Peters, *The Pursuit of Wow!,* (Vintage); *The Tom Peters Seminar,* (Vintage); *Liberation Management,* (Alfred A. Knopf); *Thriving on Chaos,* (Alfred A. Knopf).

_____, *A Search for Excellence,* with Robert H. Waterman, Jr., (Warner Books); and *A Passion for Excellence,* with Nancy Austin, (Warner Books).

Charles Garfield, *Second to None,* (Avon Books); and *Peak Performers,* (William Morrow).

Wolfe J. Rinke, *The 6 Success Strategies for Winning at Life, Love & Business,* (Health Communications).

2. On small groups and the cell-group church—

Linus Morris, *The High Impact Church*, (Houston: Touch Publications, 1993).

Ralph Neighbor, *Where Do We Go from Here?*, (Houston: Touch Publications, 1990). *The Cell-Church Magazine*, (Houston: Touch Outreach Ministries, Quarterly), 1-800-735-5865.

Serendipity New Testament for Groups, New International Version; Steve Sheely, *Ice-Breakers and Heart-Warmers*, (Littleton, CO: Serendipity House, 1990), 1-800-525-9563.

Mike Slaughter, *Beyond Playing Church*, (Anderson, IN: Bristol House, LTD, 1994).

Bill Donahue, *Leading Life-Changing Small Groups*, (Zondervan/Willow Creek Resources). Very valuable for training and coaching leaders.

Rick Warren, *The Purpose Driven Church*, (Zondervan).

Dale Galloway, *20/20 Vision: How to Create a Successful Church*, (Scott Publishing).

Carl George, *Nine Facets of the Effective Small-Group Leader* video library series, (Center for Development of Leadership for Ministry). These nine videos are vital for training staff and volunteer leaders. Phone 1-909-396-6843, Fax 1-909-396-6845.

_____, *Prepare Your Church for the Future*, (Revell).

_____, *The Coming Church Revolution*, (Revell), with Warren Bird.

Paul Meier, Gene A. Getz, Richard A. Meier and Allen R. Doran, *Filling the Holes in Our Souls*, (Moody Press). Very good on caring in small groups.

REFERENCES

1. Joe Batten, *Tough-Minded Leadership*, adapted from 177.

2. Genesis, chapters 37-50; also read David Seamands, *Living with Your Dreams*, (Wheaton: Victor Books, 1990).

3. Robert H. Waterman, Jr., *Adhocracy: The Power to Change*, (New York: Norton, 1992), 83-86.

4. Peter Drucker, *Innovation and Entrepreneurship*, (New York: Harper & Row, 1985), 43-44.

5. Ibid., 44. Joe Batten, *Building a Total Quality Culture*, (Menlo Park, CA: Crisp Publications, 1992), 23.

6. Michael Hammer & James Champy, *Reengineering the Corporation*, (New York: HarperBusiness, 1993), 171-181.

CHAPTER TWO
STRENGTHS

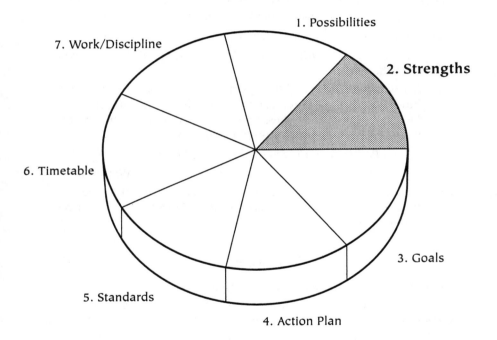

1. Possibilities

7. Work/Discipline

2. Strengths

6. Timetable

3. Goals

5. Standards

4. Action Plan

**We challenge you to absorb into your mind each step
in the above circle, starting with *Strengths*!**

2

DEVELOPING YOUR SPIRITUAL GIFTS AND STRENGTHS

*I pray that out of his glorious riches he may **strengthen** you with power through his Spirit in your inner being, so that Christ may dwell in your hearts through faith. I remind you to fan into flame the gift of God. . . . For God did not give us a spirit of timidity, but **a spirit of power, of love and of self-discipline**.*
The Apostle Paul (in Ephesians 3:16-17 and 1 Timothy 1:6-7; emphasis added)

Jesus Christ changes people (if they are willing to pay the price of being changed) so that they quite naturally and normally live as "sons and daughters of God."
J.B. Phillips, *Your God Is Too Small*

Key Points

Excellent secular organizations help their members maximize their strengths, talents, and capabilities. Jesus taught His disciples to use their strengths and talents to advance God's Kingdom on earth as it was in heaven. He wants us to develop values of eternal quality. Grassroots Christians can use strength-building methods as individuals and in small groups to strengthen themselves and their congregations spiritually. It's exciting to be *strengthened with power and to receive a spirit of power, love, and self-discipline through His Spirit!*

****

We discover and develop our strengths best in a climate that encourages dreams and possibilities. The habit of looking constantly for possiblilites and opportunities inspires us. We volunteer for new projects and experiments, and we discover talents and abilities that we never thought we had. Synergism and creativity work together, and we grow to fill a more useful role in God's family. One more thing: this growth in our abilities happens faster and better when we work with others in a small group than when we act as "Lone Rangers."

◆ We identify strengths, talents, and capabilities.
◆ We develop these effectively and discover more latent talents.
◆ Our weaknesses surface, especially as we try to work with others in the group.
◆ We learn to convert our weaknesses into strengths.
◆ We compensate for weaknesses by focusing on complementary strengths.
◆ The strengths of others actually make the team more effective.

Increased Self-Knowledge Means Spiritual Growth

The power of the maxim "know yourself" is as old as civilized thought. You only "know yourself" by knowing your spiritual strengths. Until we recognize and build strengths into the standards and values of school, government, church, small group, synagogue, home, and workplace, we will continue to stay plateaued in our quest toward the highest of human possibilities that God has designed us for.

Weakness can't help us, because a weakness is only an absence, a fault, a zero, a vacuum, a nothing. Once we realize that the only tools and building material we possess are our present and potential strengths, we can begin to focus intently on:

What *is* instead of what *isn't.*

What *can* instead of what *can't.*

What *will* instead of what *won't.*

What *does* instead of what *doesn't.*

What *has* instead of what *hasn't.*

Begin an all-out search for greater awareness, development, and use of all your strengths and potential strengths. Make this your new spiritual frontier. Strengthen yourself for tomorrow by beginning in your spirit today.

Joe Batten[1]

God Can Help Us Learn from Our Experience in Secular Organizations

After a Tough-Minded Leadership Seminar: Jim looked tightly controlled and deadpan. He was one of the forty who attended, and I had no idea whether Jim considered this seminar useful or enjoyable. At the end of the day, as the others filed out, he shuffled up to me. In a halting voice he stuttered, "Joe, you told us that you used to stutter and that you learned how to overcome it. All day long I've been thinking, 'Can he help me?'

"You mentioned several times 'All of us have much more potential than we realize. We can overcome weaknesses and replace them with strengths.' *Can you help me* with my stuttering?" He trembled with strain and 'pain' as he spoke.

We arranged to meet at regular intervals in Pittsburgh for mentoring sessions. The overall quest was for him to *become all that he could be,* to focus constantly on possibilities and *strengths.* I stuttered for 30 years, so I knew from my early experience that stuttering, in the absence of any congenital problem, could be caused by mental, emotional, and spiritual strictures. As Jim began to cultivate his emerging strengths he also learned that "vulnerablilty is invincible." He included in his prayers,

"Not my will, Oh Lord, but Thine be done."

"Be still and know that I am God."

In time his strictures released, smoothed out, and ultimately his stuttering was gone. He succeeded in building up his strengths and consigning his negative, defensive, and fearful thoughts to the past. Jim became a Vice President of Human Resources for a major, Fortune 500 company, and is now a popular and dynamic public speaker.

A Growing Video Products Firm: People in the functional groups in the company quarreled over every little thing. Problems cost them millions. The VP of operations got deeply involved and even hired a consultant. Nothing worked, so he drew together a temporary team of twelve and begged them to just meet weekly and talk about the problems. He would be available if they needed him.

Within a few weeks things began to look better. The team surprised him by not even asking him for advice. Later they asked him to attend a meeting to give expert input on a technical point. At the meeting, he found a sharp looking agenda on his seat. They placed him sixth on the agenda. The meeting moved at a crisp pace. Several outside people appeared before he did. A person from UPS discussed and solved a difficult handling problem.

The VP had his chance to give the requested input. As the meeting closed he had only one minor concern. The youngest team member, a girl, had her head down taking notes. "They're giving the dirty work to the junior woman; it figures," he thought to himself. The meeting ended, and the girl looked up from her notes and said, "That will do it for this week. I pass on my role as chairman. Whose turn is it next?"

This example shows the unexpected and dramatic effect of involving workers. It illustrates the "compelling, natural human thirst to be engaged." A person can't be *committed and have conviction unless that person is deeply involved!* It shows how unknown strengths are discovered and developed in the process of just doing what has to be done.[2]

What Happens in the Learning Organization?

People are led instead of being driven, inspired by praise rather than criticism.

No one likes to work for a *know-it-all*. They like to work for a *learner* who leads by example. Learning requires experimenting, and experimenting means trying anything that looks promising. *Try, try, and try again* when you want to find new solutions to old problems, discover problems you didn't know you had, and find innovative ways to do things far better than you ever did them before.

Delegate if you want to learn. The lower down in the organization we encourage experiments, the more we involve people, the more we tap hands-on knowledge, and the more we can achieve valuable improvements promptly. We uncover previously *hidden and vital strengths* in the front-line workers. How do we encourage such continuous improvement? How do we become expert in helping all the people in the company to *maximize their talents and strengths*? What will inspire them to work together as a team and not be blind to their potential? How can we reinvent the way we do things effectively and continuously?

- ◆ We have to allow mistakes and even encourage them. When we discover something new and valuable we usually take many steps in the process. We can't look at them as failures but as steps in the learning curve. *If a thing is worth doing, it is worth doing wrong the first time.* If we must be perfect the first time, we will be afraid to try anything very important.
- ◆ This means that experimentation becomes the road to better

quality, lower cost, higher productivity, and turned-on workers. The old myth, *"If it's not broke don't fix it!"* will be replaced
by constant progress rather than gradual undetected deterio-
ration.

◆ It's not unusual for people to have grandiose dreams of success. Soichiro Honda said, "To me success can only be
achieved through repeated failure and introspection. In fact,
success represents the 1 percent of your work which results
only from the 99 percent that is called failure."[3]

What Jesus Said about Talents and Strengths

Jesus taught in stories that were easy to remember, not like the
lawyers who described most things in technical abstract language. In
one of His most famous parables (the talents) He used the investment of time, effort, and money as symbols of how God wants each
of us to invest our lives totally in the Kingdom of Heaven. It's not
food and clothing that we should consider most important. It's life
itself, and above all eternal life. He said, "Seek first his kingdom and
his righteousness, and all these things will be given to you as well"
(cf. John 6:27 and Matt 6:33).

Look at how Jesus responded when Paul was frustrated over a
disability that he called "a thorn in my flesh"? Paul pleaded three
times to have it removed, but the Lord said to him, "My kindness is
all you need. My power is made strongest when you are weak.(CEV)"
So Paul commented, "I will boast all the more gladly about my weaknesses, so that Christ's power may rest on me. That is why, for
Christ's sake, I delight in weaknesses, in insults, in hardships, in persecutions, in difficulties. For when I am weak, then I am strong"
(2 Cor 12:9-10).

Paul also wrote to Timothy, "But for that very reason I was
shown mercy so that in me, the worst of sinners, Christ Jesus might
display his unlimited patience as an example for those who would
believe on him and receive eternal life" (1 Tim 1:16).

God uses things that look and feel like unnecessary pain, sickness, and trials. He gives us strengths that we could develop in no
other way. He makes us strong in circumstances where we often look
weak. The poor in spirit will surely inherit the kingdom of heaven,
and the (courageous) meek will inherit the earth! This is how to
understand the amazing *Beatitudes* that Jesus taught us in His *Sermon
on the Mount*. (See Matt 5:1-12.)

Techniques of Strength-building

Some people have taken this phrase *"build on strengths — don't focus on weaknesses"* to mean that we should ignore weaknesses, overlook them — permissiveness. It is important for the reader to understand this is *not* what we mean. When you set out to show somebody else how his or her performance can be improved (whether it be your child, your spouse, your boss, or even yourself) it is important to be aware of weaknesses, but then leave them in God's hands — *forget them*. You will gain nothing except to compress, paralyze, or squeeze that person into insignificance by focusing on a weakness. The true part of wisdom is to concentrate on strengths, gifts and accomplishments and to nurture, build, give direction and "how-to" with regard to particular strengths. This is being proactive.

You are the sum of your strengths. If we believe that a person's greatest need is a need for significance, it follows that our own feelings of significance grow in direct relationship to a growing awareness of our strengths as leaders, parents, and total people. The converse is also true. When we search for, dwell on, and reiterate a person's weakness, we stultify that person's possibilities, reduce feelings of significance, inhibit growth on and off the job, and seriously hamper performance. This is *counter*productive! It doesn't glorify God.

When we overemphasize the weaknesses of people we shackle them with a miserable self-image. On the other hand, when we strive diligently and truthfully to help them understand, and *use* their strengths we *set them free*.

Clear-eyed, objective, and consistent affirmation of strengths is one of the great pleasures for committed, expectant people. They discover this adds zest and gusto to all their relationships — with their families and with those with whom they work. We can't overemphasize this because of the very common error that people make focusing on weaknesses.

If you want to reap the rewards that God promises to those who serve Him, you must make a fundamental decision: to expand people, not compress them; to build on their strengths, not focus on their weaknesses. It isn't always easy. It requires weaving together a group (or a family) of basically self-led people, all doing what God has enabled them to do best so as to achieve singleness of purpose and unity of direction.

If you decide to strive for excellence and seek exceptional performance, then you must back your decision with demonstration, not just conversation, and begin building on strengths — starting with yourself. You also need to *help others* realize that the one best way to grow as individuals is to build others up constantly.

This takes a lot of study, prayer, and self-discipline. Be careful to include your own strengths along with those of the people you teach. Don't just sit back and oversee what goes on. Use your own talent to accomplish specific tasks. Involve yourself directly and deeply in the achievement of transcendent spiritual dreams and objectives.

It's Important To Make People Feel Strong

Serial Printer Division of Dataproducts: Kouzes and Posner tell the story of a general manager who turned five years of company losses into a $3.6 million profit — the first year his division had ever made a profit. He had many talented people, but they didn't get along, and they had no vision of what the possibilities were. He did it by "strengthening everyone's abilities to contribute to the success of the organization." He stressed "the importance of *team* effort" instead of divisiveness, and he constantly encouraged everyone to do their best.

Every two weeks he met with a small number of about 25 people. He repeated this until he had met with all 310 people. Then he started the cycle over again. Everyone talked. They could influence decisions on both the big and the small details, from where the company stood to the poor "lighting over the benches." He gave them "the sense that they were part of a team." He built their confidence, and made them feel "in command of what was going on." In dramatic semiannual meetings, he lined the walls with photographs of all of them. He presented achievement awards to those who had made the greatest contributions. This man knew that he had to strengthen others before they could help him pull the division and the company out of their downhill slide.

A leader empowers others by strengthening them. The leader does this by working side by side with them and by knowing and understanding each worker. Executives that are loners get fired most often. They are "people who prefer to work independently of others, who are highly critical of their staffs," and control all projects and problem solutions. These fired executives have poor people skills and think "team discussion and participation is a waste of time."[4]

Identifying Strengths

Many times we have seen truly productive and beautiful things happen with individuals and with client organizations when they begin to understand and practice systematic methods of strength building. The following method works great:

1. Seat group of 15 or less people in a circle.
2. Have each of them write down 10 strengths they identify in themselves. Then have them each share their list with the group.
3. Ask each person to look at the other members of the group one at a time and mentally identify one significant strength in each person. This practice opens up the mind to the importance and value of strengths. The participants learn to define strengths and express themselves in ways they have never thought of before. Many of the people involved learn for the first time in their lives to think of themselves as *walking bundles of strengths*.
4. Starting at any point in the circle, choose the first subject. Ask the person on his or her left to name one significant strength about that person. Then proceed on around the circle until everyone has shared a strength-oriented perception of that person.
5. Move on to the second subject, then the third, and so on until everyone has had a turn. Provide the guidance needed to keep the remarks totally positive and strength based. Permit *no* negatives of any kind, especially no sarcasm or negative humor.

Every single person in a group of 15 hears 14 strength-based comments about himself or herself from 14 different personalities in 14 different ways. Many people of even mature years hear, for the first time, the kind of affirmation and reassurance most of us hunger and thirst for.

This is usually the first time people have ever been asked to identify, perceive, and articulate strengths — and *only* strengths — in anyone else. Now they do so 14 times, and their minds literally start to reroute brain circuits. A vital process of spiritual renewal takes place. This has led to amazing spiritual and career growth in those introduced to this method.

In a seminar we held in Milwaukee with company presidents we worked one whole day on this strength-identifying exercise. At the end of the day they felt that they *knew one another better than they did their own team members* with whom they had worked many years. In another seminar two people who worked together in the same company developed a totally new relationship with each other. Neither had realized before this exercise the amazing strengths that each other had been capable of.

We have also used the above method in church small group

meetings with remarkable success. Typical comments have been,

1. This is the most positive and uplifting support I've received in all my life.
2. In one meeting I've learned more wonderful things about the people in our group than I have in many years of attending church with them.
3. We ought to let all the other groups know how gifts and strengths help us serve God, and how vital it is to tell each other these things.
4. I'm really motivated to love others and to appreciate how much God loves me.

Important Benefits

- ◆ High levels of confidence and self-esteem; liberating knowledge of self.
- ◆ New insights into the wants, needs, and possibilities of team members, family members, and most important of all, self.
- ◆ Improved capacity to spring back resiliently from disappointment and setbacks.
- ◆ Much greater capacity for longer work days and other manifestations of stamina. When the body is basically healthy, most fatigue is caused by an orientation to weakness.
- ◆ The ability to recognize and use strengths in all areas of life, as well as in your career.

Whenever we dwell on our own weaknesses, we tend to look for and relate to weaknesses of everything and everyone around us.

Booker T. Washington said:

There are two ways of exerting one's strengths:

- ◆ One is pushing down
- ◆ The other is pulling up

One of the Biggest Challenges

Weaknesses expose our character *flaws*, the areas we need to look at honestly and attempt to change. One of the biggest challenges facing many people today is that they are afraid to face themselves honestly and seek out ways to grow and make changes. Growth often produces pain but like the old adage says, "no pain no gain."

We can be our own greatest enemy in the growth and change process. So what can you and I do? Begin *now* to make healthy choices in your life. Don't make decisions based on whether or not others like you or approve of your ways. We alone can make changes in our lives and we need to start now, not yesterday or tomorrow. We can climb that mountain, but it all begins with you and me and the choices we make.

A Word on Spiritual Gifts and Fruit of the Spirit

The many strengths that we have talked about so far can be organized under either the heading of *Spiritual Gifts* or *Fruit of the Spirit* as described by Paul. We will go into more detail on the Fruit of the Spirit in *Part Two: The Dynamics of Motivation*.

One church that we are involved with in making the transition from a traditional, program-based design to a cell-church dynamic used the principles and materials available from *Heart to Heart Ministries*. Don and Katie Fortune base their system of Motivational Spiritual Gifts on Paul's statement:

We have different gifts [strengths, faculties, talents, qualities], according to the grace given us. If a man's gift is prophesying, let him use it in proportion to his faith. If it is serving, let him serve; if it is teaching, let him teach; if it is encouraging, let him encourage; if it is contributing to the needs of others, let him give generously; if it is leadership, let him govern diligently; if it is showing mercy, let him do it cheerfully.[5]

The seven gifts are,
1. Perceiver or Prophet
2. Server
3. Teacher
4. Encourager or Exhorter
5. Giver
6. Administrator or Leader
7. Compassionate Person

The pastor of this church spoke on four successive Sundays describing the above gifts. Then all members voluntarily filled out questionnaires to help individuals identify their gifts. This was a key step in choosing people to be trained for leading small groups. With this information they started a 13-week training course to prepare group leaders, interns and hosts. Next, ten small groups were started with five more groups planned.

Conclusion

In the first chapter we focused on how Christians can learn from secular organizations to discover and maximize possibilities. In this second chapter we learned that excellent companies train people to build strengths and capabilities. Churches need to learn all they can to be productive as servants of God. *This is why Jesus told the story of the shrewd manager!* Christ has a worldwide, all-time vision for us. He commissions us to make maximum use of our strengths and talents. He wants every person to repent and come into His Kingdom, He's not willing that any should perish. And, as Paul felt constrained to emphasize, we should follow him as he followed Jesus: "We proclaim him, admonishing and teaching everyone with all wisdom, so that we may present everyone perfect in Christ. To this end I labor, struggling with all his energy, which so powerfully works in me" (Col 1:28-29). Remember the word "good" comes from the word "God."

RECOMMENDED READING

Leith Anderson, *Winning the Values War in a Changing Culture*, (Bethany House Publishers).

R. Ruth Barton, *Becoming a Woman of Strength*, (Harold Shaw Publishers).

J.D. Batten, *Tough-Minded Leadership*, (AMACOM).

Stephen Covey, *Seven Habits of Highly Effective People* (Simon & Schuster).

Dr. Larry Crabb, *Inside Out*, (NavPress).

Don & Katie Fortune, *Discover Your God-Given Gifts*, (Chosen).

Emmet Fox, *The Sermon on the Mount*, (Grosset & Dunlap).

E. Stanley Jones, *The Christ of the Mount*, (Abingdon).

Robert H. Schuller, *The Be (Happy) Attitudes*, (Bantam Books).

REFERENCES

1. Joe Batten, *Tough-Minded Leadership*, adapted from 177.

2. Tom Peters, *Thriving on Chaos*, (New York: Harper & Row, 1987), 346-347.

3. Ibid., 315.

4. James M. Kouzes and Barry Z. Posner, *The Leadership Challenge*, (San Francisco: Jossey-Bass Publishers, 1987), 166-168.

5. Romans 12:6-8; also see Galatians 5:22-23; Colossians 3:12-17 and 1 Corinthians 13:1-13. Also refer to Don & Katie Fortune, *Discover Your God-Given Gifts*, (Grand Rapids: Chosen, 1987).

CHAPTER THREE
GOALS

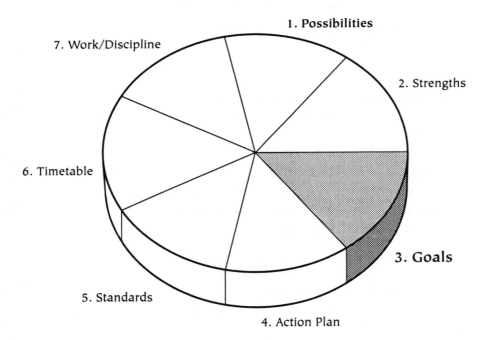

Reread the Sermon on the Mount in Matthew 5-7 and reflect on the goals Jesus taught the Twelve Disciples

3

WHERE DO YOU GET
YOUR GOALS?

*Do not store up for yourselves treasures on earth, where moth and rust destroy, and
where thieves break in and steal. But store up for yourselves treasures in heaven.
. . . For where your treasure is, there your heart will be also. . . . seek first his kingdom and his righteousness. . . .*
Jesus (in Matt 6:19-21, 33)

*Forgetting what is behind and straining toward what is ahead, I press on toward the
goal ... All of us who are mature should take such a view of things.*
Paul (in Phil 3:13b-15a)

In Search of Excellence, *Bob Waterman and I defined and measured excellence in
terms of long-term financial health. Truth is, we could hardly have cared less. But
we knew we needed to go through the drill to be taken seriously by the 5,000 con-
formists we hoped would buy the book. Nothing wrong with financial measures. . . .
But . . . I've got a new one-dimensional measure of excellence: Would you want
your son or daughter to work there? . . . Ethical? Profitable? Growing? Yes. Yes. Yes.
Also . . . spirited, spunky. And curious.
And a place where they're routinely told, "Do something great!"*
Tom Peters[1]

Key Points

In the first two chapters we covered possibilities and strengths.
In this chapter we will learn how highly successful organizations
integrate their goals with their people's goals and values. Many of

these companies use the principles that Jesus taught and modeled. God expects us to use the good things we learn on our jobs to help leaders and team members become better servants of Christ.

****

Goals in Secular Organizations

The most excellent organizations put people first in their goals and in their actions. This hasn't always been so. Many leaders still use *command and control* methods, but this management philosophy often assumes that people's goals oppose the goals and aims of the company. Isn't this a self-fulfilling prophecy? If we treat people as inherently lazy, won't they get the message and act out our assumptions? Do we believe that they won't take responsibility and that they will usually let us down? If we assume these things at the start, then that's probably how we'll judge them, no matter how things actually turn out. It's natural to blame people for what goes wrong when we already suspect them.

What happens when we believe that people want to work, handle responsibilities well, and learn everything they can? Here's what happens in organizations that put people first and treat people with honor and dignity, especially the customer:

Knowing and meeting customer needs is the most important goal: This story is typical of the most excellent companies: At America West the employees have the freedom to do anything that it takes to make customers happy. By mistake a man got aboard a flight about to leave for San Jose. When the destination *"San Jose"* was announced, he grabbed his things and tried to get off. It was too late to get him on the correct flight to *San Francisco*. He was *very upset*.

The flight attendant, also known as CSR (Customer Service Representative,) had only 5 or 10 minutes before her flight left. She took him to the counter, looked up his reservations on the computer, and made the decision to take him to San Jose. Once they got there she knew she could get him to San Francisco on ground transportation. She changed his reservation and sent a computer note to the supervisor in San Jose to have ground transportation ready. The traveler was really concerned because his uncle was to pick him up in San Francisco, so she put a note for his uncle into the computer. The customer became calm.

The America West CSR got him to San Jose, made sure his ground transportation was OK, and that his uncle had been notified.

She felt responsible because another America West CSR had origi-nally brought him to the wrong plane. Also, he didn't fly very much, and she wanted this to be a good experience for him.

But that's not the end. She checked on his return flight, which came three days later, on her day off. She went to the airport, met him, took him to his connecting flight, and gave him a tin of choco-late chip cookies. All this, because she loved her job and wanted to serve the needs of her customers.[2]

Christians and churches can learn a lot from this example, because it teaches us like Jesus' parables do (this CSR was a *"Good Samaritan"*). Christ expects us to recognize when *living parables* occur in the world around us.

Internalized goals: People work best and enjoy what they do when their goals match the company's goals. They want to be loved and respected, and they will be "fired up" if we show them that we really care about their own internal goals. Good companies work hard to create a climate where people reach their goals while working toward the company's goals. "You must show each of these people how, through superb performance and an eye to customer satisfac-tion, they can get what they want. In other words, 'You have to over-lay their goals onto the company's goals.'"[3]

Shared values: The America West stewardess impressed her supervisor when she showed up on her day off with the tin of cook-ies for the man who missed his flight to San Francisco. She felt responsible for the man. She wanted him to have a good impression of her and her company. She said, "I am doing it because I feel part of it, because I want the company to do well... to be a success." She respects America West and shares the same values and goals. She does her best voluntarily, because she believes in the company and makes the organization's goals and mission her own. What an example for Christians![4]

Keep things simple: Of necessity the technology may be complex (computers and highly engineered equipment), but the human orga-nization should be flexible and responsive to the needs of people. Handle things at the lowest level in the organization. Here teams work fast, effectively, and with quality results. Break down the barri-ers between people, and put the people with the necessary skills on each team. Consider how intimate small groups in either church or business can create a great climate!

Keep things small: Large scale no longer yields the benefits it used to. Versatility, flexibility, and fast change all make an organization able to meeι market demands. The old bureaucracy with command and control, and with many people isolated in specialized functional departments, is costly, slow to respond to needs, and does not innovate well enough. The Japanese have become world leaders in almost every field by *thinking small*. To them *small is beautiful*. It uses less resources in a world of finite resources, gives more mobility, and aligns with most people's desires and needs. Japan, a small country, took the lead and the markets in miniaturization. Because of their passion for reductionism they pioneered in the miniaturization of tape recorders, radios, VCR's, disk audio players, and video players.[5]

Charles Garfield writes, "*Business — especially American business* — was lulled into a deep sleep, unconsciously going through the mechanical motions of churning out products for a mass market secure in isolation, 'rich and confident in a world that was poor and pessimistic,' oblivious to the human and environmental consequences of its actions ... Technology began breaking up mass markets into smaller units and eliminating competitive barriers of geography and company size ... Democracy began to emerge as a social force in unexpected places around the world."[6]

Leaders are coaches: To fully unleash the talents of people we must free them from unnecessary rules, and give them the necessary tools. Leaders must keep the philosophy and vision alive by being available, on the team, and not isolated away in an executive suite. In the most excellent companies, the leaders serve rather than being served. They invert the traditional hierarchal pyramid. Didn't Jesus tell His disciples to "be servant leaders"? Invert the pyramid! We truly lead when we serve.

Balance profit with other important concerns: No longer do the best companies make monetary profit the only or even their major goal. In fact, we often optimize profit when we consider it a result of organizational excellence and service rather than the primary purpose for existence.

- ◆ *Environment* is becoming an important concern, especially if we learn from the way many *people's republics* destroyed it.
- ◆ *Concern for human welfare and improvement* motivates most customers and employees. The excellent companies always put people first as their most important goal.
- ◆ *Well being of all stake-holders* transcends the welfare of investors alone, although the investors are important.

Employees don't rally around profit as the chief value and the most productive motivator.

◆ *Treat all the people involved as partners:* Team members will be inspired if they see the company's goals and values lived out. For example, the employees of Levi Strauss developed its Aspiration Statement which included the following:

> We all want a company that our people are proud of and committed to, where all employees have an opportunity to contribute, learn, grow, and advance based on merit, not politics or background. Above all we want satisfaction from accomplishments and friendships, balanced personal and professional lives, and to have fun in our endeavors.[7]

◆ *To be a learning corporation* is the major goal that enables organizations to survive in the fast changing world around us. In America the service sector now employs 75% of the work force. Customer sensitivity, knowledge, and computer skills all depend on continuous learning.

◆ *Cooperative relationships (task forces and teams)* make goal-oriented planning successful. Teamwork and cooperation hold the systems together. Companies and churches that organize around *small, flexible groups* grow the fastest.[8]

How Did Jesus Focus on Goals?

1. He *organized* His close disciples to be a flexible, mobile, small group.
2. He *focused* on what people needed the most, including the eternal dimension.
3. He *stressed* learning in community on the job more than on academic knowledge.
4. He *emphasized* the importance of serving rather than being served and giving rather than receiving.
5. His major goals were principle- and people-oriented, not traditional and rule-oriented:
   ◆ Recognize the unlimited possibilities of God and believe that He will help you.
   ◆ Stress the need for individuals to love each other, their neighbors, and even their enemies.
   ◆ Help individuals to serve and give to others.
   ◆ Spread God's message and kingdom gradually over the whole world.

◆ Start building for Him by stressing entry-level attitudes, the Beatitudes.

◆ Make perfection the ultimate goal, produced in our lives as *the fruit of the Spirit*.

6. This life should be considered a training place for eternal life:

◆ It's not the end in itself but the means of making us in His image.

◆ We're not to despise and isolate ourselves from those who God wants to reach.

◆ Relationships, not wealth, develop character. Jesus saw potential in unlikely people.

7. Our joy can be complete even in trial and hardship.
8. God's leaders are to be servants and not like those that lord it over others.

Goals Are Vital

Meaningful, stimulating goals must be preceded and nourished by a dream. This gives goals a *being* flavor rather than a self-defeating focus on activities or *doing*. Having a dream also means that goals will be focused on aspirations beyond your immediate knowledge and skill level, thus providing stretch. Consider these areas for goal setting:

Economic, social, political, spiritual

Physical, mental, emotional

Personal, relational, occupational, ministerial

Your overall dream should provide a continuous need to improve and grow. Goals based on your dream should be attainable in order to satisfy a clearly stated vision. My dream has evolved from years of challenge, joy, difficulties, failures, and triumphs. It is stated so that it cannot ever be *fully* reached: "I will make the lives of others richer by the richness of my own."

Joe Batten[9]

Jesus Set the Greatest Goals of All

Look at the beatitudes in Christ's *Sermon on the Mount* to understand the goals that He blesses. They represent *entry-level attitudes* of new believers, childlike *attitudes of the heart*. Jesus said, "I tell you the truth, unless you change and become like little children, you will never enter the kingdom of heaven. Therefore, whoever humbles himself like this child is the greatest in the kingdom of heaven" (Matt 18:3-4). Later, He said, "Let the little children come to me, and do not hinder them, for the kingdom of heaven belongs to such as these" (Matt 19:14).

In the most famous prayer of all time, Jesus told His disciples to ask, "Father . . . your kingdom come, your will be done on earth as it is in heaven" (Matt 6:9-10). This prayer affirms the overall goal of God. Jesus identifies this major goal with the first beatitude, "Blessed are the poor in spirit, for theirs is the kingdom of heaven" (Matt 5:13). Notice how His goal statements go together: Children know they need help spiritually. They are *poor in spirit*. They hunger and thirst for *righteousness*. They are *meek* and *pure in heart*. Therefore the kingdom of Heaven belongs to them. They will inherit the kingdom and be satisfied; and they will also inherit the earth.

In the fourth beatitude Christ said, "Blessed are those who hunger and thirst for righteousness, for they will be filled." He is making us righteous and spiritually mature. When we believe, we start out with His righteousness freely attributed to us, as it was with Abraham. But then His Spirit leads us in the growth process enabling us to produce the fruit of the Spirit. Through our hungering and thirsting for righteousness, we will learn to do God's will. We will see His kingdom come. We have the kingdom of heaven within us. Heaven and earth belong to God and His Christ. We become God's children and co-heirs of all things with Christ: "Will He not give us all things?" (cf. Rom 8:17,32; Matt 6:33).

Jesus told the devil, "Man does not live on bread alone, but on every word that comes from the mouth of God" (Matt 4:4). Christ was stating God's goal, based on Moses' words in Deuteronomy 8:3, that those who hunger and thirst for righteousness will be satisfied, not only by physical food, but by knowing God's Word. In the middle of His Great Sermon, Jesus explained that we use our eyes to read, see, and understand things from God's point of view:

> For where your treasure is, there your heart will be also. The eye is the lamp of the body. If your eyes are good, your whole body will be full of light. But if your eyes are bad, your whole body will be full of darkness (Matt 6:21-23a).

Do you see how these teachings of Jesus are connected? Do you understand how they make up God's perfect plan and vision for each of us? Isn't it plain common sense to see the teachings of Christ as goal statements by which we work together with God and by the Living Presence of His Spirit? We build for eternity, and it's vital that we build "our house on rock not sand" (cf. Matt 7:24-27).

We don't have to see His teachings as "impossible demands" like the traditions the religious leaders based on the Law. According to Paul, "a man is not justified by observing the law, but by faith in Jesus Christ. So we, too, have put our faith in Christ Jesus that we may be justified by faith in Christ and not by observing the law" (Gal 2:16). We have the major goals that Jesus taught His disciples. Let us keep feeding on God's Word and see how the lives of the disciples recorded in the New Testament were worked out in agreement with these primary goals of Christ. His goals are not burdensome. We are to "encourage one another" and "spur one another on toward love and good deeds."

This is what Paul meant when he said, "Forgetting what is behind and straining toward what is ahead, I press on toward the goal to win the prize for which God has called me heavenward in Christ Jesus" (Phil 3:13b-14). This is not being motivated by fear, guilt or worldly ambition; it's "faith expressing itself through love" (Gal 5:6b).

Jesus came as the exact image of God, to make God known to us. From the Creation of all things God's plan for Jesus was for Him to be the Savior of the whole world:

> Let us fix our eyes on Jesus, the author and perfecter of our faith, who for the joy set before him endured the cross, scorning its shame, and sat down at the right hand of the throne of God. Consider him who endured such opposition from sinful men, so that you will not grow weary and lose heart (Heb 12:2-3).

Jesus told the twelve disciples on the night before His death on the cross, "I am going there [to my Father's house] to prepare a place for you. And if I go and prepare a place for you, I will come back and take you to be with me that you also may be where I am" (John 14:2b-3).

Read again chapter 15 of John's biography of Christ to see the goals that Jesus gives us for guiding our lives. God created us for good works, and we can glorify Christ by having life-goals that make us productive in His Kingdom. (See John 15 and 2 Peter 1:8.)

Paul and His Goals

Before he was called Paul, Saul obeyed his conscience meticulously. He had unique and important training under the Law of Moses. No one excelled him as a Pharisee of Pharisees, a perfecter of legalistic righteousness. He persecuted Christians, determined to destroy all Jews who joined the new Way.

But he had one major problem: his goals were wrong even though his conscience was clean. Christ appeared to Saul in blinding light as he approached Damascus. Falling to the ground Saul asked, "Who are you, Lord?"

"I am Jesus, whom you are persecuting," the Lord replied. "Now get up and stand on your feet. I have appeared to you to appoint you as a servant and as a witness of what you have seen of me and what I will show you" (Acts 26:14-18).

Paul later tells Timothy, "Even though I was once a blasphemer and a persecutor and a violent man, I was shown mercy because I acted in ignorance and unbelief. The grace of our Lord was poured out on me abundantly, along with the faith and love that are in Christ Jesus. . . . Christ Jesus came into the world to save sinners — of whom I am the worst. But for that very reason I was shown mercy so that in me, the worst of sinners, Christ Jesus might display his unlimited patience as an example for those who would believe on him and receive eternal life" (1 Tim 1:13-16).

Paul treated as mere rubbish everything that he had achieved as a Pharisee and as a scholar of the Law. In one of the most famous goal statements ever written, Paul said,

> I consider everything a loss compared to the surpassing greatness of knowing Christ Jesus my Lord. . . . [O]ne thing I do: Forgetting what is behind and straining toward what is ahead, I press on toward the goal to win the prize for which God has called me heavenward in Christ Jesus (Phil 3:8, 13b-14).

Following the life of Paul through the book of Acts, chapters 9-28 and through his thirteen letters is fascinating reading. Paul illustrates what happens when we let God set our goals, and when we allow those goals to be the basis of our life. Christ chose Paul as His primary messenger and ambassador to the world because of his teachable heart, his integrity and his intensity.

How can we learn from Paul's hard work and goal-oriented life? Through him Christ reveals His Good News to the people of the world. Today we have many vital truths unique to Paul's thirteen letters in addition to the other letters of the New Testament (cf. 1 Cor 4:8-13; 15:10; 2 Cor 6:3-10; Col 1:23; John 16:12).

What Can Grassroots Christians Do?

We can persuade church leaders to see how small teams in companies are secular models for small groups in the church. Jesus constantly used parables — stories of worldly situations to illustrate heavenly truths. He kept asking his opponents, "Have you never read?" (Matt 12:3,5; 19:4; 21:16,42; 22:31). They were overlooking the examples from their own history that also illustrated the lives and actions that pleased God. "Those who don't learn from history are *destined to repeat it*."[10]

We can adopt the goal of helping the church become a body of small groups that cultivate love and intimacy. We are not Lone Rangers in God's eyes, and we need to provide a spiritual climate like Jesus did for His disciples. God will bring those He wants into our fellowship if we will prepare to receive them as His children and not as strangers. We need to unite on principles and not divide over human traditions and opinions (read Romans 14).

We need to experiment with new ways to reach out to those who don't yet know Christ. Jesus and Paul certainly used methods not approved by the "teachers of the law." We can become more involved in learning how to love "sinners" like Jesus did rather than catering to the desires of comfortable people "inside the ark." Christ wants us to help Him "save the spoiled, not spoil the saved."

We can remember what we read and realize that *God hated* the *solemn assemblies*, carefully executed *fasts and sacrifices* of His people because they had overlooked the *spiritual ruin* of His nation. Don't we in His church have the same problems today? (Read Isa 29:13; chapter 58; and Amos chapters 5 & 6.)

When we who work in secular jobs see organizations treating people better than many traditional churches do, we need to think of the problem that Jesus had with the leaders of His own nation. Churches today certainly don't want to copy their ruthless, unbelieving treatment of Him and those He associated with. We can read in Acts of how Jesus' disciples were persecuted for their loyalty to Him and to His message. Legalistic self-righteousness, bigotry, and verbal abuse do take place in some churches. Cults and sects victimize people in the name of "dogmatic anointed leaders" who do all the thinking, make all the decisions, and bind hard burdens on their followers. Some of the books listed at the end of this chapter cover these abuses that give Christ a bad name.

A Small Group Discussion of Goals

We started a number of small group meetings with the ice-breaker, "What goals would you most like to reach for Christ in the next year?" After all had described their top priority goal, the group discussed them. Then we studied one or more of Jesus' parables to show how He illustrated the goals He wants us to work toward.

Every time we have done this with a new small group, almost every person present said, "I never thought about goals in this way. *It's very exciting.*"

Within small groups church members experience more freedom to talk about their lives and compare their experiences with the simple teachings of Christ. These groups certainly increase the quality of our relationships and help us to love each other as Jesus commanded.

There are dangers, however. Some people try to monopolize the group. Negative people tend to draw the group into unhealthy and unproductive areas. But a well trained leader can guide and facilitate the group to overcome these obstacles. No other type of organization builds relationships more effectively. Small groups enable people to experience intimate fellowship and apply the Bible practically to everyday life.

In secular society excellent organizations renew themselves using small teams with adequate guidelines, proper training, and dedicated employees. In all kinds of organizations, leaders adopt the small team and group method to solve problems, stimulate new thinking and create a family-like, people-sensitive climate. The best organizations in society put people first, especially their customers, suppliers, and employees.

Christ wants to reach all people that don't know Him. People are His "customers." We can use the stories we have told you and those experienced in your own life as *parables of God's Kingdom*. This is exactly what Jesus did. Most of His parables use secular people to illustrate important principles. When He used religious people in His Parables they didn't fare too well. They tended to be self-righteous and ruthless with others. We've used the parable of the shrewd/unrighteous manager as the theme of our book. Examine the following table of parables to see how they fit our theme:

Parable	Reference	Today's Parallel to Consider
Barren fig tree	Luke 13:6-9	Not meeting goals and standards.
Good Samaritan	Luke 10:30-37	A despised person meets God's goals.
Great Banquet	Luke 14:16-24	The guests had the wrong goals.
Growing Seed	Mark 4:26-32	God's goal of continuous improvement.
Hidden Treasures	Matthew 13:44-46	Great enthusiasm for great goals.
Lost Son/His Brother	Luke 15:11-32	Father's love; brother's jealousy.
Persistent Widow	Luke 18:1-8	A person intent on reaching her goal.
Pharisee/Tax Collector	Luke 18:9-14	A "sinner" had the best attitude.
Rich Fool	Luke 12:16-21	It's not wise to hoard possessions.
Rich Man/Lazarus	Luke 16:19-31	Poor man reached the higher goal.
Servants Waiting	Luke 12:35-40	Importance of working towards goals.
Sheep and Goats	Matthew 25:31-46	Judged by serving relationships.
Shrewd Manager	Luke 16:1-12	Commended for planning ahead.
Sinful Woman	Luke 7:41-47	The "sinner" had better goals.
Sower	Matthew 13:1-23	Good and bad hearts compared.
Talents/Ten Minas	Matthew 25:14-30	Good and bad investors compared.
Ten Virgins	Matthew 25:1-13	Good and bad planning compared.
Two Sons	Matthew 21:28-32	"Sinners" were more receptive.
Unmerciful Servant	Matthew 18:21-35	We should respond to right model.
Vine and Branches	John 15:1-17	Be productive in meeting goals.
Weeds in the Field	Matthew 13:24-43	Judged by goals and standards.
Wicked Tenants	Matthew 21:33-44	Destroyed for not meeting expectations.
Wise/Foolish Builders	Matthew 7:24-27	Build with strengths to meet goals.
Workers in Vineyard	Matthew 20:1-16	Right attitudes key to rewards.
Yeast	Luke 13:20-21	Christ is helping us reach His goals.

RECOMMENDED READING

Stephen Arterburn & Jack Felton, *Toxic Faith*, (Oliver Nelson).

George Barna, *User Friendly Churches*, (Regal Books).

_____, *Evangelism That Works*, (Regal Books).

Joe Batten, *Building a Tough-Minded Climate for Results*, (AMACOM).

_____, *Beyond Management by Objectives*, (AMACOM).

Kenneth Blanchard and Spencer Johnson, M.D., *The One Minute Manager*, (Berkley Books).

Bob Briner, *The Management Methods of Jesus*, (Thomas Nelson).

Dwight L. Carlson, M.D., *Why Do Christians Shoot Their Wounded?*, (InterVarsity Press).

Russell Chandler, *Racing Toward 2001*, (HarperCollins).

Ronald M. Enroth, *Churches that Abuse*, (Zondervan).

_____, *Recovering from Churches that Abuse*, (Zondervan).

Charles Garfield, *Second to None*, (Avon Books).

William D. Hendricks, *Exit Interviews*, (Moody).

Lynne and Bill Hybels, *Rediscovering Church*, (Zondervan).

Laurie Beth Jones, *Jesus CEO*, (Hyperion).

David R. Miller, *Breaking Free: Rescuing Families from the Clutches of Legalism*, (Baker).

Merrill J. Oster, *Vision-Driven Leadership*, (Here's Life Publishers).

Tom Peters, *Liberation Management*, (Alfred A. Knopf).

Mike Regele, *The Death of the Church*, (Zondervan).

Wolfe J. Rinke, *The 6 Success Strategies for Winning at Life, Love & Business*, (Health Communications).

Rick Warren, *The Purpose Driven Church*, (Zondervan).

REFERENCES

1. Tom Peters, *The Tom Peters Seminar*, (New York: Vintage Books, 1994), 219.

2. Charles Garfield, *Second to None*, (New York: Avon Books, 1992), 91-93.

3. Merrill J. Oster, *Vision-Driven Leadership*, (San Bernardino: Here's Life, 1991), 82.

4. Garfield, *Second to None*, 95-96.

5. Peters, *Thriving on Chaos*, 15-25.

6. Garfield, *Second to None*, 47.

7. Ibid., 52.

8. Ibid., 71.

9. Adapted from Joe Batten, *Tough-Minded Leadership*, 178-179.

10. A paraphrase of George Santayana's famous statement.

CHAPTER FOUR
ACTION PLAN

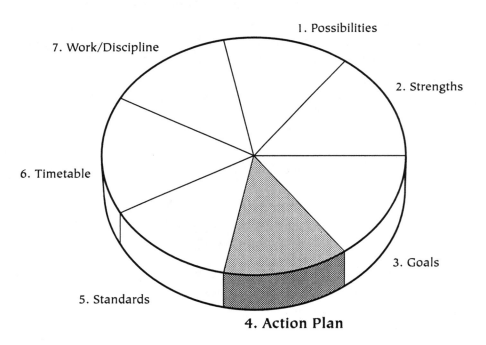

1. Possibilities

2. Strengths

3. Goals

4. Action Plan

5. Standards

6. Timetable

7. Work/Discipline

4

MEET THOSE WHO
KEEP ON GROWING

I am the vine; you are the branches. If a man remains in me and I in him, he will bear much fruit; apart from me you can do nothing. If anyone does not remain in me, he is like a branch that is thrown away and withers; such branches are picked up, thrown into the fire and burned. If you remain in me and my words remain in you, ask whatever you wish, and it will be given you. This is to my Father's glory, that you bear much fruit, showing yourselves to be my disciples.
Jesus (in John 15:5-8)

Key Points

How do excellent organizations maximize success by continuous experimentation and action orientation? Why did Jesus say, "I have no place to lay my head"? For the simple reason that He was living out God's action plan. He was busy with His Father's business. He is our model. His Spirit actively leads us and transforms us into spiritually mature followers. Churches need desperately to learn how to convert spectator Christians into action-oriented disciples. We challenge organizations of all kinds to learn from those that successfully use the amazing teachings of Jesus. We need to learn any way we can how to better serve our Lord.

✳✳✳✳

What Are Secular Organizations Doing?

To survive in a fast-changing world, organizations must make changes:

- ◆ They must come up with products that satisfy customers. In fact, they should delight their customers with the enhanced quality and capabilities of their products and services. If leaders don't keep ahead, domestic or foreign competition will out-perform them.
- ◆ Also, they must continually improve the quality of staple products, tailoring them more and more to the increased specialization required by customers. Specialized "niche" markets continue to replace the old high volume commodity type markets.
- ◆ Unfortunately for many companies that have been successful and grown large since the 1930s, only those who have adapted to rapid and radical change remain healthy. Many have evolved into ponderous, slow-moving bureaucracies with too many layers in the hierarchy, unrealistic and unwieldy strategic plans, secrecy and one-way communications, stifling negativism, commitment to the status quo, and tunnel vision.

Action-oriented Companies

3-M (Minnesota Mining and Manufacturing) has hundreds of small group venture teams. Anyone in the company who invents a product has a chance to manage it as if it were his or her own business. 3M doesn't kill new product ideas, and it doesn't shoot down those who pioneer new products and new ways of doing things. 3M accepts virtually any idea. Because of 3M's product diversity and worker persistence "a failed plastic cup for brassieres . . . became *the* standard U.S. worker safety mask." The worker had been told to stop work on the project, but he continued to do most of the development work at home.

3M fired another worker because he spent too much time trying to find a way of using "reject sandpaper minerals." He came to work anyway, and later became the vice-president of the Roofing Granules Division. "Product champions," even when they work underground . . . usually have a "coach" in the executive ranks who succeeded earlier as a "product champion."

3M considers innovation to be a *numbers* game where action takes priority over study:

- ◆ "Make a little, sell a little, make a little bit more."

◆ "Lots of small tests in a short interval... Develop in a series of small excursions..."
◆ "There is no limit on raw ideas."[1]

The Value of Action

Many people say, "I want to be . . ." or "I want to do . . . ." Nothing much usually results. *Wanting* alone doesn't really accomplish very much. We must make a *decision* and work at it. When we decide to act we move from good intent to an action plan that yields results.

In action planning we move from a dream-inspired goal to specific actions and experiments to reach our goals. We remain true to our mission and we work actively to turn our vision into a reality. Planning motivates and inspires the team working toward the vision. In fact, the vision may grow and change dramatically as the team experiments, cooperates, and tests its findings. We discover far greater truths by actively pursuing a dynamic, inspiring vision. The end results expand to be much more valuable than anything that could be planned for ahead of time.

The major benefits of this process of action-oriented planning are innovative thinking, inspired dedication, increased clarity of purpose, and superior rewards when the goals are reached.

HP (Hewlett-Packard) rewards action. It practices wide open communication with no secrets. HP wants capable, innovative people in all jobs. Their leadership generates commitment and excitement at every level in the organization. People have the freedom to work toward company objectives "in ways they determine best for their own areas of responsibility."

Some HP divisions have an "open lab stock" policy. They encourage engineers to bring equipment home with them for their own personal use. The learning they get from using the equipment reinforces the company's dedication to innovation, whether they use the equipment for company projects or not. As told in one of their "Bill and Dave stories," Bill Hewlett visited a plant on a weekend and found the lab stock area locked. He got a bolt cutter from the maintenance department, cut off the padlock, and left a note: "Don't ever lock this door again. Thanks, Bill."

Dave Packard tells the story of "a maverick's persistence": Chuck House was advised to discontinue work on a display screen monitor. Instead, he took samples on vacation with him and received a very positive response from customers he contacted while vacationing. When he got back to work he got the monitor rushed into production. It turned out that HP made and sold over 17,000 of these display monitors with revenues of $35 million. House later became the Director of Corporate R&D for HP. He explained, "I wasn't trying to be defiant. . . . I really just wanted a success for HP." To add a little humor, several years later Dave Packard "presented Chuck with a medal for 'extraordinary contempt and defiance beyond the normal call of engineering duty.'" Over the years, House has developed "pockets of innovation" throughout Hewlett-Packard, taking demoralized, unproductive groups and turning them into crackerjack innovators. He created the proper climate for innovation.

Right from the beginning HP decided not to be a "me-too" company. They didn't intend to copy the products of other companies but "to develop products that represent true advancement." They practice hands-on innovation as the action-plan most likely to bring long-term success.[2]

EDS (Electronic Data Systems) considers all its workers partners. It's a company of 72,000 people organized into teams of 10, making over $7 billion in revenue. All are "leaders" and "owners." Founder Ross Perot expected everyone to be on the team but also, he expected everyone to think for themselves. Soon after he sold EDS to General Motors (he was on the GM board) he told a GM manager to do something that needed to be done. The man told him that it wasn't in his job description. Perot responded, "I'll give you a job description: Use your head." The man responded with, "Can you imagine what chaos we'd have around here if everybody did that?"

Perot didn't look like a "team-player" because he wanted fast action on simple things. He hated the slow, "yes-man" climate which he had successfully avoided in EDS.[3] When asked to describe the essence of his leadership style, Perot said, "I love the members of my team."

Bell and Howell: Tom Peters and Bob Waterman tell of Peter Peterson's action orientation as president of Bell and Howell. Being new in the company he didn't know "what cannot be done." One day in the lab he looked through a zoom lens. "It was great." He hadn't considered it a consumer product. It was too expensive, and it "was something you used for football games." Peterson asked how much it would cost to make him one camera with a zoom lens. "They said, 'Just one? . . . We would probably spend around $500 on it.'" He told them, "[L]et's just do this." At a party of friends, he asked everyone to participate in a "sophisticated piece of marketing research." Each person that looked through the lens exclaimed, "My, this is marvelous: I've never seen anything like this in my life." Peterson concluded that the market would accept a lot more than we expect. We have to try out more new ideas rather than overanalyzing them.

He also said,

> Is there any way that we can experiment with this idea at low cost? The experiment is the most powerful tool for getting innovation into action. . . . [I]f we can get the concept of the experiment built into our thinking . . . more good ideas will be translated into action... [W]hy not sell a $150 movie camera [this was 1956] by direct mail? . . . Then we asked the key question: "What would it cost us to try out the idea?" The cost was only about $10,000. The point is that we could have spent $100,000 worth of time over-intellectualizing this problem. . . . Nine out of ten experts will tell you this idea just will not work. Yet it did and is now a basis of an important and profitable new business for us. It is possible for us all to get a little pompous about the power of an intellectual, rational approach to an idea that is often extremely complex.[4]

David Ogilvy (Ogilvy & Mather) says that good advertising depends on constant testing. How to start a job? Run an experiment. You can get feedback in a few hours. 95% of all products never get further than test markets. If companies don't test, they run up great costs and a bad name. Those who test with users and ads do well. Test what you promise. Test the media. Test the headlines. Test illustrations, cost level and commercials. Keep testing everything and you will keep improving.[5]

Bell Atlantic took fifteen to thirty days to hook up a carrier access service for customers with high speed video and data communications. New competitors had fiber-optic cables and could hook customers up in ¼ the time with better quality and lower cost. Bell Atlantic's analysis showed that a hookup required *only ten to fifteen actual hours of work*, but *the process took fifteen to thirty days because thirteen different handoffs* occurred among different work groups.

They decided to set up two reengineering work teams, one to come up with ideas, and the other to put them into operation in the real world. Customers wanted the hookup cycle time to be as short as one day. The teams designed a process that pulled all the functions together in one location under one supervisor. Previously the functions were geographically spread, managed separately, and in different departments. It took the design team one month to finish. Then the second team in a matter of several months had the cycle down to days instead of weeks. In a little more than one year they guaranteed three-day installation times, the best interval offered in the industry. Their labor costs in only one area dropped from $88 million to $6 million.

The design team is now working on the goal of zero cycle time. One person will take a customer's call and make electronically all the connections required to set up the service while the customer is on the line. This kind of action blows your mind.[6]

VeriFone dominates the U.S. market for credit card authorizations (60% of the market). It depends on computer networking more than any other company in the world. A large German banking group asked for a proposal and VeriFone went to work on it 24 hours a day. When the project team in California finished its day, it passed the project on to the team in Taipei. When the Taipei team finished its day's work, it passed the job on to the London project team. The London team then passed it back to California. VeriFone got the order, shocked the bankers, and shamed the competition. VeriFone allows no paper mail. All employees carry notebook computers and communicate with each other on a worldwide sophisticated electronic network. The company makes all information available to every employee.[7]

Optimizing the Plan

What key factors enable these organizations to take fast action, plan wisely, and thrive in a climate of constant change? How do they keep their plans flexible enough to follow their mission, realize their vision, and not disintegrate in anarchy?

◆ They actively listen to and cooperate with their customers. They know that more than 60% of all innovation comes from the marketplace. Constant experimentation makes for products that better fit the needs of customers. It results in constant improvement. Companies that don't communicate actively with customers don't really listen and can't respond with "cutting-edge" quality. Those who indulge in expensive R&D without active feedback from the marketplace waste lots of time and money on highly sophisticated but unneeded new products.

◆ They empower workers by passing authority down the line to the teams of workers at the lowest level in the organization. They give what Bob Waterman calls "solution space," enough room on the job to operate autonomously, creatively, and with inspired commitment. Like good parents that teach their children to operate within general guidelines, these companies delegate and decentralize power and responsibility. To get action, they take the risk of giving too much freedom and too much authority to their teams. In order to make important discoveries and find valuable innovations, they encourage failures. Remember, *the few experiments that are successful* result from *hundreds more that failed but supplied essential feedback.* Healthy peer pressure and accountability to each other produce better results than restrictive control "from above."[8]

◆ These excellent organizations have drastically reduced functional departments and management layers. In fact, some companies have virtually eliminated the hierarchy and do everything with small project teams. EDS, founded by Ross Perot, is the largest project company in the systems information business. It has all of its people on small teams. One top executive explained that the partners (employees) all work for each other. No "Boss" is needed. *Getting the job done* takes priority over who reports to whom. A leader in each group coaches the group and keeps communications wide open. The company builds *a climate of trust and action-oriented commitment* that produces highly effective individual and team performance. According to Tom Peters, "Word of mouth still can — and does — work as the chief organizing device... EDS owes a huge debt to its founder — the ideas of unmistakable accountability to teammates and customers, of getting the job done regardless of the official resources at your beck and call, are Ross Perot to the core."[9]

◆ They have reduced strategic long range planning to general guidelines only and relied on fast *continuous experimentation*. Big, expensive, and highly technical strategic plans can't accurately predict the unknown. They have a very low success rate and a very high cost. Less than one out of 20 is ever profitable. However, with small, bite-sized chunks a very large project can be successfully developed. The immediate feedback from "many small experiments plays an important role that is lacking in massive projects planned out ahead of time in an ivory tower climate."[10]

◆ The best kind of *action planning* comes from the combination of good customer feedback, team members with adequate authority, flexible project teams, and continuous low cost experiments. Workers not only become peak achievers, but they bring fast innovation, higher profitability, higher personal income, and the reward of great satisfaction to all involved.

More on Action Planning

◆ Waterman calls the best planning *informed opportunism*. Get all available facts (even unpleasant facts are friendly) and be ready for unexpected opportunities. The best opportunities can't be planned for, but planning does provide the information necessary for good communications. Those who know the most about their business and markets exploit unexpected opportunities the best. They trust their intuition because they have a wealth of valuable information stored in their unconscious.[11]

◆ Peter Drucker says that the most valuable successes come from the following:
1) Unexpected opportunities for innovation that no one could have predicted.
2) Unexpected changes in the market environment that go undetected by most companies.
3) Taking over market niches where bigger companies did the original research and innovation but were too bureaucratic and slow to maintain profitability.
4) Working closely with customers because this by far produces the most profitable and innovative breakthroughs.[12]

◆ Don't get bogged down in paralysis of analysis. On the other hand, don't fail to get all the necessary and available facts. It's not unusual for the innovator to lose "the fruits of his innovation" and only create an opportunity for somebody else. Big bureaucracies often have "tunnel vision." Scientific and technical innovators rarely do the necessary and obvious analyses. They "are reluctant to make these analyses precisely because they think they already *know*." This is why so many "great knowledge-based innovations have had a layman rather than a scientist or a technologist for their father."[13]

◆ Keep objectives simple and easily modified to take advantage of a fast changing marketplace. General principles in the *mission statement* should guide the project teams. It should be fluid enough to allow for creativity and innovation. It's important to continuously visualize the picture of the company's future state as described in the *vision statement*. The vision should allow for continuous modification from the feedback and synergism that results when the project team follows a dynamic and opportunistic *action plan*. Then achievements will greatly surpass those aimed for in a "sophisticated long range strategic plan."

◆ Allow for fast scrapping of the action plan if the feedback indicates this. Keep communications wide open and customers totally involved. Have them carry out experiments at all phases of the project. Companies can waste a lot of money unless the targeted customers show serious interest in the product being developed.

1) One division of a large bureaucratic company worked years developing a polyolefin filament that the customer (actually another division of the same firm) never did purchase. Also, the existing competitors kept lowering their prices to prevent the success of this new source of product.

2) A smaller company developed an inked ribbon for a large manufacturer of computer printers. All quality standards were met, but this customer already purchased ribbon from several long established sources of supply. They never did accept the inexperienced supplier as a source no matter how well the product was developed.

What Did Jesus Model and Teach?

He knew that His disciples would need a long learning curve. Just as God designed into the universe all that science has discovered, so there are many wonderful things we can discover in God's word. He designed His word to train His people for eternity, and the Bible enables us to prepare for eternity. Human beings will not discover anything that God doesn't already know. But we can learn by seeing how Jesus' teaching agrees with the truths discovered by human organizations.

1. Jesus challenged the status quo because the actions of the leaders did not match God's standards. The commercialization of the temple courts offended Him. He tipped over the tables of the money changers and drove out the livestock with a whip made of cord. (See John 2:14-17 and Matt 21:12-13.)

2. He challenged the "traditions of the elders" because of their outright hypocrisy and snobbery. He put people first because the Sabbath was made for people and not people made for the Sabbath. He associated with tax collectors, prostitutes, and other outcasts, because His Father had sent Him to "call the sinners rather than the righteous." He healed sick and crippled sinners and forgave their sins, because He was sent to the sick, who needed a doctor. The "healthy people" didn't need one. (See Matt 9:10-13; 12:1-7; 15:1-14.)

3. Early in His ministry He visited the synagogue in His hometown of Nazareth and read from the prophet Isaiah. At first they mar-

veled at His gracious words. He told them, "Today this scripture is fulfilled in your hearing." He warned them, "A prophet is honored except
in his hometown." He pointed out that Elijah had been sent to help a
Gentile widow only, even though they were many widows in Israel. He
also told them that only Naaman, the Syrian, was healed of leprosy
though there were many lepers in Israel. This infuriated those in the
synagogue because He implied that they were snobs. What did they
do? They tried to throw Him off a cliff. (See Luke 4:16-30.)

4. Jesus took risks in order to actively serve the people God
wanted Him to serve. He was action-oriented. His words and actions
offended the leaders and caused Him and His followers to be persecuted. He said that He did not come to bring peace, but rather division, because people in the same household would love their own
agenda more than they loved God. He risked His life and His welfare
daily, and He asked His followers to be willing to lose their physical
lives in order to find their real lives. (See Matt 10:34-42; 16:24-26.)

5. Jesus denied Himself to demonstrate God's love for "sinners."
To those who showed an interest in following Him He said, "I have
no place to lay my head." To a rich man he said, "Sell your posses-
sions and give the proceeds to the poor. Then come and follow
me." He expected commitment in those going with Him. To one of
them who wanted to wait for his father's funeral, He said, "Let the
dead bury the dead. You come and follow me." To another who
wanted to first take time to go home and say "Good-bye," He said,
"No one who puts his hand to the plow and looks back is fit for service in the kingdom of God." He asked His followers to take action
and appreciate the value and importance of the kingdom they were
entering. He expected them to make sacrifices because He would
give His own life for the sins of the world. In His death He actively
demonstrated God's overwhelming love for all people. (See Luke
9:57-62; 18:22.)

6. He focused on the transcendent value of every person in the
eyes of God. He wanted everyone to see and appreciate the Big
Picture, God's eternal point of view. He taught plainly that any
person who chose to do God's will would know where He got His
authority, whether it was from God or merely from Himself (John
7:16-18). He asked people to enter in at the narrow gate and to build
on the rock foundation — His message (Matt 7:13-14, 24-27). He
expected them to love Him and one another. He expected them to
believe and practice all that He taught them. He asked them to
demonstrate their love for God, and for their neighbors (Matt 22:34-
40). Jesus gave them no viable alternative. He asked them, "What

good will it be for a man if he gains the whole world, yet forfeits his soul?" (Matt 16:26).

Jesus expects us to follow Him actively. He told His followers "Heaven and earth will pass away, but my words will never pass away" (Matt 24:35). His parables use common earthly experiences to illustrate the transcendent value of the invisible heavenly realm. Jesus came to give us hope for the future and to teach us that this earth is not our real home. Our actions and our plans as individuals and as church families are vital to Christ. He opens our hearts to His priorities when we spend the time to read them, think about them, and sincerely seek God's guidance in prayer. We pray that God will use our modern parables as well as the ones that Jesus taught two thousand years ago. Our Father reveals things to little children, and we hope that grownups will also come to see for themselves the clarity of God's action plan. (See Rom 12:1-2.)

Action Was the Chief Characteristic of Paul's Life

1. He asked his readers to follow him as he followed Christ (1 Cor 11:1).

2. He reminded the disciples in Thessalonica that his relationship with them was like a father and mother with their children (1 Thess 2:7-11).

3. Of his thirteen letters, nine of them were written directly to the church members. He didn't depend on a highly educated hierarchy for explaining his words to the people.

4. In Luke's book of Acts, from the ninth chapter on, we have the dynamic story of Paul's very active life. Both Paul's and Luke's writings are filled with the most intense activity. We read of no spectator Christianity. We see tough-minded, focused energy.

5. Paul told the Christians in Colosse about the strength that Christ mightily inspired within him. He feared the deceit of false teachers, and he asked Christians not to be led astray by human wisdom and commands. (Read Col 1:27-2:23.)

6. His action-oriented statements include the following:
   - I worked harder than all the rest, but it was not I but Christ working in me. (See 2 Cor 11:23 and 1 Cor 15:10.)
   - Fight the good fight of the faith (1 Tim 1:18; 2 Tim 4:7).
   - Be strong, endure hardship, compete to win the victor's crown (2 Tim 2:1-7).
   - Imitate me (1 Cor 4:8-17).
   - Open wide your hearts (2 Cor 6:3-13).

◆ God's power is made perfect in weakness (2 Cor 11:21-33; 12:1-10).

7. He advises us not to judge those outside the church, but to discipline ourselves and "clean our own house." It's God's place to judge those outside the church, not ours (1 Cor 5:9-13).

Paul was an activist, not an ivory tower theologian. It's true that he was without equal in his zeal for the Law of Moses and in the intensity of his legalistic righteousness. But he also claimed to be "a blasphemer and a persecutor. . . . the worst of sinners" (1 Tim 1:12-16). Christ chose him as an example of His great patience. Paul gave up everything he had previously worked so hard to attain. Why did Paul change from his Jewish activism to be the most *action-oriented* of all the Apostles?

Here's how Paul became the Apostle to the Gentiles throughout the world:

When Jesus appeared to him and called him into His service on the way to Damascus, He told Paul how much suffering he would have to endure as His chosen messenger. Paul himself listed in several places the hardships and trials he endured for Christ and for the people Jesus wanted him to reach. Do you want a great example of an action-oriented life that gave to the world some of the most wonderful revelations of God's will? Read about the life of Paul in Acts, chapters 9-28. Read his letters starting with Romans and ending with Philemon. Paul never lamented what happened to him as he traveled over his world serving the people and obeying his Lord. Even in great adversity Christ constantly showered him with love. Persecutions, pain, and hardship may be seen as weaknesses in the modern world. Paul saw them as the necessary training for maturity, for developing us into the image of Jesus:

> I consider that our present sufferings are not worth comparing with the glory that will be revealed in us (Rom 8:18; 2 Cor 4:17).

> What is more, I consider everything a loss compared to the surpassing greatness of knowing Christ Jesus my Lord, for whose sake I have lost all things... I want to know Christ and the power of his resurrection and the fellowship of sharing in his sufferings, becoming like him in his death, and so, somehow, to attain to the resurrection from the dead (Phil 3:8-10; also read 1 Cor 4:8-18; 2 Cor 4:7-18; 11:16-33).

What Can We Do to Replace Obsolete Traditions?

We can learn from reality that parables still teach God's truths effectively. Modern stories illustrate the teachings of Jesus just as His own parables illustrated the principles He taught His audience. Can we see the parallel between Jesus' use of material things and the parables that we today can draw from our experiences in secular organizations?

1. We need to keep God's goals at top priority and not let human traditions and habits prevent us from working out God's vision. He wants people to be put first. He wants us to be "all things to all people" where it is practical and possible, so that we don't overlook the "easily forgotten" people that He wants us to reach out to. Can we recognize that the priorities of Jesus are simple to understand but require wisdom and courage to put into practice? He has three primary and overriding priorities:

- ◆ Love God and listen to His Word. His Spirit will guide, teach, and encourage us.
- ◆ Love one another, not only as we love ourselves, but also as Christ loves us.
- ◆ Love the people of the world and be sensitive to God's desire that all of them be reached with His good news.

2. We need to study how to avoid the mistakes of the leaders that put Jesus to death. We need to listen to what Paul taught about the false apostles and divisive people who wanted to be teachers of the law but didn't know what they were doing (cf. 1 Tim 1:3-11; Titus 3:9-11; Rom 16:17-19).

3. Jesus' priorities require action and application more than intellectual study and analysis (read this again and again):

- ◆ He focused on action-oriented parables because they illustrated best what God wanted to happen.
- ◆ Theology often focuses on intellectual debating among the learned and overlooks the needs of the poor, sick, alien, and uneducated. Do Christian leaders make a basic mistake when we believe that the major problems in the church are intellectual problems? Actually, the major problems in Christendom are caused by "heart failure" and a "blindness" to the example of Jesus and His words, the very words that the Holy Spirit has inspired. Jesus' priorities are easy to understand, but very difficult to apply, especially for leaders. The behavior of the leaders of Jesus' nation plainly showed this. God kept saying throughout history, "You

aren't listening! You are not obeying Me in your hearts!" Jesus targeted these corrupt leaders with many of His parables.

◆ We should accept each other as He accepts us, as He did tax collectors, prostitutes, and other outcasts (including Samaritans and Gentiles who were considered dogs by the religious leaders).

◆ We need to appreciate how much God allows us to learn by our mistakes. Jesus told stories from everyday experience to expose the snobbery practiced by the religious people of His day. These *snobs* hated Him because *He used secular stories to expose their hypocrisy*. Hopefully, we can be humble and wise enough to learn from the good things going on around us in the secular world. Doesn't Jesus expect this? Isn't it common sense? *We don't have to compromise God's will* any more than Jesus did when He used secular illustrations for spiritual principles.

What Can Christians Do?

If we have experience in excellent secular organizations, we can apply what we learn in church relationships:

◆ Exalt Christ because He has actually made success in the scientific and industrial world possible. Nothing good has been done without Him — *nothing*! We need to be just as prepared for action as modern organizations are in carrying out their priorities.

◆ Expect and ask church leaders to be as wise in their relationships as excellent secular leaders are in theirs. Action succeeds in God's kingdom just as much as it does in secular organizations. Whatever we do, let's do it in the name of the Lord. And whatever we do, let's work at it will all our heart, as working for the Lord, not as for men (Col 3:17,23).

◆ God's Spirit is living in us and guiding us to active, living relationships with the people around us. We need to let our lights shine brightly if we expect to follow Jesus' example and love others as He loves us. (Cf. 1 Cor 2:9-16; Matt 5:13-16.)

Ad Hoc task forces and *small "growth" groups* can do the following:

◆ *Bring maturity to all Christians involved.* Open up communications and friendships — let people discover God's will by their own study, discussion, and experience. Eliminate dogmatism and legalistic mind-control that grieves the Spirit. Small groups allow us to share personal experiences and learn from them together. We all have problems. It's a great help for us to have the love and assistance of Christians who have become our intimate friends.

◆ *Make us action-oriented.* We can learn to trust each other and love each other. Dedicate part of each meeting to sharing the problems we deal with personally. Encouragement helps us through hard times, and we learn to share our resources with one another. We have received freely and we need to give freely. Without small groups Christians can't be as helpful and intimate. If we haven't learned what Jesus taught about loving one another as He has loved us, what does that tell God about our love for Him? How can we truly please Him, if we don't spent time with each other, listen to each other, help one another, and show the world an exciting example of God's kingdom in action?

◆ *Help us glorify Christ in our church life.* We may already be doing this in family relationships and in our secular jobs. We need to have the freedom to follow Christ, to use effectively the good things we experience in the marketplace, and not be snobs or bigots. Jesus certainly gave us a great model to follow in the way He dealt with "outsiders." The dogmatic, snobbish leaders of His own people badly misunderstood God's plan and methods. They envied Jesus' popularity with the crowds, and they hated Him.

◆ *Help us contact people in our circles of influence (personal networks), and bring others to know Jesus.* When Jesus revealed the Father's plan to preach good news to the Gentiles, many reacted violently. His own people were very angry with Jesus for accepting "sinners." They had a severe case of "self-righteous pride" and "tunnel vision." We need to learn from this. We need an action-plan to live by in order to bring glory to God, Christ, and the Spirit. That means being willing to associate with people we may not like, because God loves these people just as much as He loves us.

Bible Classes that Inspire: We have covered small groups in some detail in previous chapters, but how about Bible Classes? We have experienced great relationships and exciting breakthroughs using small group techniques in larger Bible Classes. We have used an "icebreaker" to get the people in the class talking about their own life experiences. We wanted to develop a climate where the teachings of

Jesus could be seen as very practical for everyday problems and opportunities.

◆ For one icebreaker we asked the class, "Tell us from your own personal life about a person who really showed love to you, someone who makes you think of Jesus because of his or her tender, unselfish love."

◆ We also requested of the group: "Tell the group of your favorite action parable." Then we discussed some action-oriented parables: *The Parable of the Wise and Foolish Builders*, Matthew 7:24-27; *The Soil and Seed that Produced*, Matthew 13:1-23; *The Sons who Did and Didn't*, Matthew 21:28-32; and *The Sheep and the Goats*, Matthew 25:31-46.

◆ We converted what used to be a ten to twenty minute icebreaker into a class-long exercise combined with open discussion. In a class of twenty-five to thirty-five people we experienced an entirely new level of excitement, participation, and interest. Often people who have attended Bible Classes for forty or fifty years have never been asked to share their personal experiences or opinions. They often have the feeling that only those educated in theology should ever say anything. And that happens. The most educated people sometimes monopolize the discussions. Leaders in bureaucratic organizations employ mostly one-way communication, from the top down, but not from the bottom up. It's an exciting experience when we treat people with dignity and give them the opportunity to tell others what they have learned over years of personal experience.

◆ Another value comes from designing small groups and Bible Classes to get maximum participation from every member: When we get passionate *involvement* we get more *commitment* and a much higher level of *conviction*. Action breeds faith and faith breeds action, the type of action and faith Jesus continually asked for.

For Small Groups: Use the same ideas that we listed above for icebreakers. In each weekly small group meeting spend some time talking about how each person can actively help and support each other during the week. Encourage all to visit in each other's home, know each other's needs, and quietly do something to help each other in practical, friendly ways.

Conclusions

In the secular world the best organizations succeed through constant change and innovation. They free up people! They encourage people to take action and discover truths that have been previously unknown or unappreciated.

We Christians can actively seek to know God better and please Him more. But we've got to ask, seek, and knock. We've got to learn from others who practice successful leadership principles. Jesus used experiences like these in His parables. He offended many of *the most religious experts* who heard His words. They couldn't stand His accusations that they "nullified the word of God" with their traditions and merely human opinions. They weren't willing to admit their shortcomings, and actively seek new and vital truths. What about you and me? Are we ready? Will we do it? Let's not repeat history!

The Bible tells us, "For the word of God is living and active. Sharper than any double-edged sword, it penetrates even to dividing soul and spirit, joints and marrow; it judges the thoughts and attitudes of the heart. Nothing in all creation is hidden from God's sight. Everything is uncovered and laid bare before the eyes of him to whom we must give account" (Heb 4:12-13). We are confident. Christians will continue to seek out God's will. Christ will lead us into new paths that are true and vital.

RECOMMENDED READING

Leith Anderson, *Dying for Change*, (Bethany House).

Doron P. Levin, *Irreconcilable Differences*, (Signet).

David Packard, *The HP Way*, (HarperCollins).

Tom Peters, *Liberation Management*, (Alfred A. Knopf).

Frank Tillapaugh, *Unleashing the Church*, (Regal Books).

REFERENCES

1. Thomas Peters and Robert Waterman, Jr., *In Search of Excellence*, (New York: Warner Books, 1982), 127, 225-231.

2. David Packard, *The HP Way*, (New York: HarperCollins, 1995), 93, 107-108. Ibid., Peters and Waterman, *In Search*, 243-246. Garfield, *Second to None*, 135-136.

3. Tom Peters, *Liberation Management*, (New York: Alfred A. Knopf, 1992), 20, 24. Robert Waterman, Jr., *The Renewal Factor*, (New York: Bantam Books, 1987), 219.

4. Peters and Waterman, *In Search*, 138-139, 144.

5. Ibid., 137-138.

6. Hammer and Champy, *Reengineering*, 193-199.

7. Peters, *The Tom Peters Seminar*, 179-180.

8. Robert Shook, *Honda: The American Success Story*, (New York: Prentice Hall Press, 1988), 14.

9. Peters, *Liberation Management*, 24-30.

10. Drucker, *Innovation*, 34, 130, 135-136.

11. Waterman, *Renewal*, 256-276.

12. Drucker, *Innovation*, 30-36.

13. Ibid., 116.

CHAPTER FIVE
STANDARDS

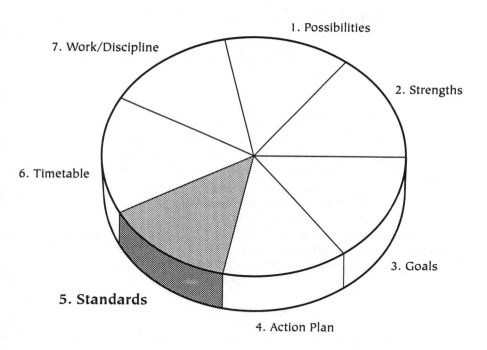

1. Possibilities

7. Work/Discipline

2. Strengths

6. Timetable

3. Goals

5. Standards

4. Action Plan

5

REACHING FOR YOUR VISION
BY MEETING YOUR GOALS
WITH EXCELLENCE

Be perfect, therefore, as your heavenly Father is perfect.
Jesus (in Matt 5:48)

[W]hatever is true, whatever is noble, whatever is right,
whatever is pure, whatever is lovely, whatever is admirable —
if anything is excellent or praiseworthy — think about such things.

We proclaim him . . . teaching everyone with all wisdom,
so that we may present everyone perfect in Christ.
Paul (in Phil 4:8 and Col 1:28-29)

So a revolution is brewing... the basics got lost in a blur of well-meaning gibberish
that took us further and further from excellent performance in any sphere. We got so
tied up in our techniques, devices and programs that we forgot about people. . . .
Tom Peters and Nancy Austin[1]

Key Points

The steps described in chapters one through four should be accomplished with excellence. In this chapter we stress the importance of standards, the conditions that will exist with jobs being done well, a mission being accomplished, and a vision realized. The best organizations use excellent values, vision, and principles to perfection. Jesus teaches us excellent standards and priorities for vision, use of talents, goal seeking, and discovering the most important truths. Churches need to have even more excellent standards than secular organizations. Christians who have experienced excellence in their jobs can bring excellence into their church relationships. Intimate small groups provide the ideal climate for developing a standard of excellence.

$$* * * *$$

The Importance of Excellence

How do organizations develop and maintain standards of excellence? Much depends on the excellency of leaders' attitudes and how they develop people. Excellent leaders do not spend their time protecting traditions, maintaining the bureaucracy, or using mind-control to force their views onto people. Great leaders develop excellent standards when both leaders and their people challenge the status quo, discover truths experimentally, and develop strengths for continuous improvement.

In this chapter we focus especially on how organizations develop *excellence* by the following:

- ◆ Working closely with and listening intensely to their customers
- ◆ Speeding up and maximizing innovation
- ◆ Teaching people to develop and use their strengths
- ◆ Learning from tough-minded, tender-hearted leaders.[2]

Customer Attention

Milliken & Company: Chief executive Roger Milliken has put his company at the top of the U.S. textile industry. According to quality guru Phil Crosby, Milliken's program is one of the two best in America, along with IBM's. Even John Jackson, IBM's retired vice president for quality, called it the best in the nation. A senior DuPont marketing executive said, "I've never seen the likes of this." He was a guest at one of Milliken's top management retreats.

Milliken cooperated closely in a year-long program with Levi Strauss to improve quality and serve this customer with excellence. Because Milliken's quality was so flawless, Levi eliminated incoming inspection of Milliken products. Milliken shipped directly to Levi's factory, eliminating the need for warehousing. The two companies got so good at coordinating shipments with machine schedules that when the trucks arrived at the plant, Levi attached their instruction tags as the trucks were unloaded. They delivered the material to the exact machine to be "cut and sewn."

Because of advanced communications linkups this close coordination could be done with great savings in cost and delivery time. Not only do they eliminate inspection, inventory, and warehousing, but "Levi's achieves previously unheard of flexibility." This enables them to compete effectively in the world of fast fashion changes.[3]

Excellence in Making Innovation Faster and More Effective

Peter Drucker has pointed out that the "home run mentality" simply does not succeed as effectively and economically as the "start-small and end-up-big" method of innovation. High cost R&D efforts may occasionally pay off, but they usually cost millions and take so long to complete that fast-moving competitors dominate the market.

Raychem: This company uses "Raychem in Response" for its motto, and it meets its customers needs. This means listening to them constantly. One of their engineers heard of an underwater leak at a North Sea offshore oil platform. Raychem had its researchers travel from California to the England location immediately. Within five days they had developed a truly new product, built and debugged it, and got it working for the customer. This product developed with speed and excellence became a $10 million business. On hearing this story a person from another more bureaucratic company said that in his company you'd be lucky to get your travel orders in five days.

Peters and Austin have got it right:

Touch. Feel. Do. Try. Fix . . . The scientific method rests foursquare on empiricism, which is to say, the experimenting mentality, not the home run — on paper — mentality. Get *hard* data. Get it quickly. That's the key. Get the market data, of course, but market data from *trying it* with a user as soon as possible. Get technical data, of course, but from *building* a prototype and *handling* it as the real world does, not keeping it bottled up forever in the pristine, sterile, temperature-controlled, dust-free lab or test kitchen.[4]

Data General: Tom West created the MV/8000 Eagle Computer with a small maverick group of engineers. He "signed up" only volunteers for the work. Each person had to want to do the job with excellence and give it his "heart and soul." The organization and the arrangements were simple, no charts, graphs or organizational tables.

Because of the climate of mutual trust, the team members were able to do their jobs without making each task so small that it was dull. They did their own special jobs, but all of them took an interest in the whole computer. This intense commitment and interest enabled them to finish the job on time. They designed this complex computer in less than a year.

The group built the Eagle by themselves. Tom let all of the engineers believe that they invented it. He said, "When this is all over, there are gonna be thirty inventors of the Eagle machine." These inventors didn't have much hope of monetary rewards, but they enjoyed playing the game immensely. It's like playing pinball. "You win one game, you get to play the next." "West . . . gave enough freedom to invent, while at the same time guiding them toward success." There was romance in putting out "a seemingly endless series of 'brush fires.'" West made this project "the most exciting thing in our lives . . . ," said one team member. "West never bored us."[5]

People Treating Others As They Want to Be Treated

Mary Kay Cosmetics: Mary Kay starts right out by training all of her Beauty Consultants to go by the Golden Rule: "In everything, do to others what you would have them do to you."[6] She also believes in a constant climate of sincere praise. All of us want to be praised for what we do. She points out that beauty queens and movie stars often seem to be the only women that are appreciated. If a woman works day and night in her home, she receives a comment "only if she *stops* doing it."

She also believes in accountability and excellent performance standards. In fact, people don't perform with excellence unless you appreciate them and tell them often how well they are doing.

One day she overheard Helen McVoy, one of her associates, enthusiastically telling a new Consultant, "You had a thirty-five dollar show? Why, that's wonderful."

Mary Kay wondered what was going on.

Helen presented the new recruit to Mary Kay and said, "Last night she had a thirty-five dollar show!" She lowered her voice and said, "At her first two shows she didn't sell anything — but last night she sold thirty-five dollars! Isn't that terrific?"

Mary Kay saw immediately that without praise the new recruit might quit. Helen gave her the praise she needed to become successful. We all need to become winners gradually. We get confidence each time we have one small success and that leads to bigger ones. It's like a parent encouraging a small child to try again when they first start to walk and keep falling down. "Without praise from our parents, a lot of us might still be crawling!"[7]

So, living by the Golden Rule and praising people enables them to achieve great things. Excellent organizations love people and encourage healthy relationships. These companies discover people's needs and set high standards to meet them.

Johnsonville Foods: Excellent companies know that people want to be treated as adults. They don't want supervisors telling them what to do and when to do it, especially when they often know better than the supervisors. In America each supervisor covers about ten employees. In Japan it's about 200. When workers own their jobs and their minds, they can do without much supervision. It's a matter of creating a trust climate. People work most productively and resourcefully in teams. They weed out those who won't adopt a standard of excellence. Good companies decentralize and delegate responsibility to project teams. They and their people reap great benefits. It's not easy working in Johnsonville Foods, HP or 3M, but a challenging job rewards and inspires. People have fun, too. The workers at Johnsonville Foods own their jobs and love it.

Johnsonville Foods produces sausages in Sheboygan, Wisconsin. Their revenues grew from $7 million in 1981 to about $130 million in 1991. CEO Ralph Stayer liked the growth. He said, "watching people grow is my number one joy."[8]

Johnsonville stresses "lifetime learning." One worker (called a "Member") said, "Look, anything you learn means you're using your head more. You're engaged. And if you're engaged, then the chances are you'll make better sausage." Each team works on projects. Everyone generates projects. Teammates make it hard for those who don't want to be involved in the "personal growth business."

The Plant Manager considers himself to be a teacher and coach. He leads people to manage themselves. He said, "These people are industrial engineers. Farmers are engineers, they're businessmen, they're economists. They own and operate their own business. Each person at Johnsonville can do the same thing . . . ."[9]

What he called "Pride Teams" talked about situations that they could make better. Those who didn't like it got out or were voted out. Peer pressure took the place of control by supervisors. People right out of high school learned to do scheduling. They could understand inventories, profit and loss, and budgets. This Plant Manager felt like the same thing could be done any place. People must trust your motives and know that "you're in it for them, not just for yourself."[10]

According to the Executive VP of operations, they made a big move when they did away with front-line supervisors and dispersed all their activities to people working on the line. Some of the supervisors stayed around and found other jobs, in production, purchasing, and engineering. He said, "It's part of being yourself, twenty-four hours a day . . . . We ask ourselves frequently, 'What do you want to be when you grow up?' . . . I'm still growing up, and I want to continue to grow. I want to be productive forever."[11]

CEO Stayer told how their standard of excellence made their company a more difficult place to work than other companies. Only people who really want to excel stay at Johnsonville, "nothing else is accepted . . . . This is a way of life . . . ." They don't really put in the right programs and "fix" their people. "It's just the opposite. We fix *me* and our values first, then all the rest happens."[12]

Honda Motors

We highlight Honda as an excellent company to illustrate what kind of philosophy and energy it takes to achieve a standard of excellence on our four major points: customer attention, effective innovation, putting people first, and top quality leadership.[13]

The Standard of Excellence in Leadership: Soichiro Honda started his company in 1946 to produce internal combustion engines and machine tools. In 1948 he incorporated the company as Honda Motor Company Ltd. In the next year Takeo Fujisawa joined Honda as cofounder in charge of financing and marketing. Honda took charge of technology and he described their working relationship as an excellent one:

> Fujisawa would say to me, "I am at such and such a place, and I see a storm coming. So be careful!" Then I would be careful. We had heart-to-heart communication, although we were at different places and acted differently. Yet, we had the same goal of reaching the top of that mountain.[14]

Both men dreamt of producing the most excellent products and selling them worldwide. Neither graduated from college, or ever worked for the large family-dominated business establishment that controlled Japanese industry before the end of World War II. The powerful Ministry of International Trade and Industry treated his start-up company as a second-class citizen and gave it little encouragement. Because of this it took considerable time and effort to get approval and construct Honda's Tokyo factory.

Intense Listening to and Close Cooperation with Customers: Honda listens to the American consumer and builds the kind of car that the customers want. When gasoline prices skyrocketed during the oil embargo of the early '70s, the American auto producers refused to downsize or design fuel-efficient cars. In 1975 Honda introduced its CVCC engine that didn't require unleaded gasoline and gave over 40 miles per gallon fuel efficiency.[15]

On the Accord, how did Honda come up with their trunk design? Their own design team spent one afternoon in a Disneyland parking lot. They watched how and what people put into and took out of their car trunks. Because of these design changes, Honda Accord owners can fold down their back seats and use their sedans as pickups.[16]

Most automakers depend strictly on design engineers to develop their automobiles. At Honda, people from sales, engineering, and R&D cooperate from start to finish. They consider all conceivable ideas and end up building cars that the customers want and buy. American car-buyers responded well to the excellence of Honda's quality. Headquarters in Japan asked American marketing executives, "How many cars do you want for next year?" Sales for 1974 had been 43,000. One of the American marketing executives said, "We want 150,000 cars." This amazing jump in one year from 43,000 to 150,000 stunned the headquarters people. They had expected a request for about 59,000.[17]

Dealers say, "Honda always is trying to create a better product. They keep striving for perfection." Honda typifies the best in American success stories. In every way this young company illustrates what it takes to have a visionary standard of excellence and to achieve even more than what was initially dreamed. The company believed that it could accomplish its standards with an outstanding degree of excellence.[18]

Honda focusses strongly on long term service in addition to its original excellence in product quality. Perry Rutan, senior vice president of service, said of a service problem, "It won't go away by itself, so we want to fix it immediately. The sooner we can take care of it, the better off we are." He emphasized the fact that with top leaders that are engineers Honda stresses standards of engineering excellence more than other automakers. Honda's main concern is what happens when the customer drives their Honda car.

In fact, dealers report how much most customers love their cars' performance. At the 7,500-mile checkup, owners of Honda often say, 'I don't know what you're supposed to do to my car, but *please* don't mess it up. It's running great just the way it is.'

"Now that's a welcome sound to hear from customers. With other car manufacturers, we've had customers come in with what we call 'the laundry list.' . . . With a Honda, there isn't a list, and if something is wrong, it's fixable. We get the car fixed, the customer is happy, and quickly back on the road."[19]

Innovation with Excellence: At the very beginning, Honda decided to make the most excellent machines in the world. By 1955 Honda led in Japanese motorcycle production, and by 1964 they had almost fifty percent of the American motorcycle market and had revolutionized the industry. They tried hard to be number one in the world. In 1966 Honda racing teams won five classes in the World Motorcycle Championship Grand Prix race, the first time this had ever happened. In 1984 the company won ten major U.S. race championships. Incredibly, the first fourteen motorcycles to cross the finish line in the Daytona were Honda's new Hurricane 600 motorcycle. This kind of performance gave the consumer a great message about Honda's excellence. To maintain this standard and stay on top, John Petas, senior VP of the U.S. motorcycle division says, "We must remain innovative . . . . We must never become complacent or satisfied." It's no wonder that Honda leads all the world's motorcycle producers, with more than a fifty percent share of the world market.[20]

Honda developed all the company's engineering technology in-house and did not depend on any other company. They produced a world-class motorcycle and later a world-class automobile. And they did it first in Japan, second in America, and finally in countries all around the world. Honda started exporting automobiles to the U.S. in 1966. In September 1966 their F-2 car set a world record of eleven consecutive victories. They announced the CVCC engine in 1971, the first engine to meet the standards of the Statutory Clean Air Act in the U.S. This engine won the Society of Automotive Engineers' Prize for 1973 and passed the EPA's exhaust emission test in 1974. The first Accord hatchback won *Motor Trend* magazine's "Import Car of the Year" award for 1975. In 1982 Honda produced the first Accords in America, and U.S. workers matched the quality of Japanese workers. Honda trained the workers from Ohio in Japan until they were able to assemble the cars themselves and train others. They allowed off the production floor only cars that matched Japanese quality standards.[21]

Treating People as Associates: When Soichiro Honda decided to make motorcycles (and later automobiles) in America even his dealers here did not believe that Americans could match the superb quality of machines produced in Japan. But Honda believed that Americans and Japanese could meet the same standards. He overcame powerful forces to design and produce the most excellent motorcycle in Japan, and he knew that "nothing was impossible" if he could get people with excellent attitudes. According to Honda, innovation "doesn't just happen." Innovation occurs when "you think people are important and you want to improve their lives."[22]

The huge majority of associates that work for Honda have had little or no manufacturing experience. Public opinion figured that local labor in Ohio could not match the quality standards of the Japanese. But the company recruited "the best available people." Al Kinzer, Honda VP, considered lack of experience an advantage. "We didn't want people with bad habits." People who had never built an automobile "probably will accept our high standards for doing the job." Honda considered "one's attitude about work" most important, not previous job experience. They were "looking for team players, not superstars." They knew that they could find them by hiring, not the smartest people, but those with the best attitudes. They would rather train them their way than be defeated by conventional wisdom and traditional habits. Honda used extensive interviews rather than intellectual testing, considering personal relationships most vital. Honda didn't "believe in treating people like cattle." They did it "eyeball to eyeball."[23]

Honda calls their workers associates. They create a family climate. Everyone gains by maximum cooperation and respect for each other as people with dignity and value. Honda's associates think and react quickly to emergency situations. Their standard is excellence.[24]

Honda provides the best training possible for all associates regardless of cost, and they face the greatest challenges first rather than putting them off into the distant future. Advised to produce in other countries before trying the highly competitive American market, they chose instead to produce in America first after Japan. Mr. Honda originally dreamt that his company would be a global one. He wanted to "expand into markets in far away places."[25]

What Did Jesus Teach and Do with Excellence?

He related to people as if they were God's "customers": He treated sick people in Palestine better than any doctor treats his patients today. In the parable of the wise and foolish builders He supplied the rock foundation that the wise man built his house on, so in a sense the man was His "customer" (Matt 7:24-27). He listened with a tender heart to sinners and discovered their real needs better than any psychiatrist counsels his or her clientele. He exalted the humble and He lifted up the least of people. (See Luke 18:9-14.) At the same time He humbled the proud and said, "The first shall be last and the last first" (Matt 19:30). He confronted His enemies with tough-minded warnings, for their own good and the good of their followers (Matt 20:18; 23:1-39).

He showed that His Father and He cared for the practical needs of all people. As Savior of the world, He provides the hope of eternal life for every person even though many people don't know it yet (John 3:16-17). He gave excellent training to His followers, better than college professors or seminar leaders could provide for their students (John 1:18). He displayed the excellent greatness of God, Creator of Heaven and earth (John 17:26). He revealed Himself as co-Creator (John 1:3). Everything was made for Him, through Him, and by Him (Col 1:16). He made it plain that all nature, technology, and science comes ultimately from God, even though people do the work of experimentation and discovery (Heb 1:2,10).

Jesus revealed that God supplies everything we have, the air we breathe, the food we eat, the children we bear, and our very lives (Acts 17:24-29). Every good gift comes down from the Maker of Heaven and earth (James 1:17). He created everything by wisdom, knowledge and power. What can be known about God is plainly understood because of His Creation (Rom 1:18-20). Christ makes God known to all who will believe, listen to His word, and obey what they learn. We understand His gifts to us best by closely studying His parables, His miracles, His relationships, and His teachings (Mark 4:33-34).

What did Jesus do? He met the needs of those God loves, God's "customers." He warned His enemies in no uncertain terms (John 9:41). He exposed the corruption of religious hypocrites, not those they condemned as "sinners" or "outsiders" (Matt 7:15-23).

Innovation — Making needed changes in our hearts and lives: Jesus announced the kingdom of heaven and asked all who heard Him to change their hearts and lives. This is innovation — a challenge to the existing process. People addicted to the comfort of human traditions wanted no change. They wouldn't let even God make changes, nor His only Son. Jesus challenged the status quo and the corruption of the establishment, and this takes the best kind of innovation — tough-minded commitment to eternal standards, values, and goals.

He did excellent miracles and wonders never seen before or since. Even His opponents admitted that He had great power and wisdom. He taught His disciples how to grow spiritually, and He demonstrated the kind of changes they had to make. He expected them to change gradually and be transformed into His likeness. This pleases God the most. Bearing spiritual fruit requires steady change, and change for the better leads to excellence. What about mistakes and sins? Jesus forgave them quickly because he knew that we learn best by making mistakes and then correcting them. He treated Peter with great patience and had confidence that Peter would develop his gifts (John 21:15-19). Jesus transformed John the "son of thunder" into the humble "apostle of love" (1 John 4:7-21). His small, hands-on group learned innovation in their hearts by daily practice.

The Importance of People: God loves little children. He designed and created the human body, spirit, and mind. He made the natural world to train people for the kingdom of heaven. Jesus taught in a way that could be understood by children while educated people couldn't always understand Him. He taught in stories and parables that could be easily remembered. He avoided technical jargon and abstract technicalities (Matt 11:25-30). He revealed things about heaven much too important to entrust to a heartless, intellectual elite. They didn't have much respect for crowds, "sinners," or "aliens." Jesus "leveled the playing field" (John 7:45-52). He behaved with fairness and impartiality. He wanted the world to know that God loved all people, that God did not play favorites. He expected all people to develop discernment and not judge by mere appearances.

Jesus organized His disciples into an intimate family. He spent three years in such a relationship with the twelve disciples. He wanted people to own their faith, take responsibility, and grow into loving relationships. People meet needs in relationships, and we must develop sensitivity to the needs of people around us in our natural networks. The tradition-bound people of His day didn't have this kind of intimacy with each other, or with God (John 13:1-17:26).

Leadership Excellence: Jesus provides the best model. He showed the world a perfect example of love. When the established religious leaders forgot the value of people, Jesus opposed their hypocrisy to their faces. He defended those who needed a supporter. Read Matthew 23 and see how Jesus looked at the leaders who failed to love and respect the dignity of every person no matter how weak, sick, or outcast.

Jesus Himself accepted no special privileges. He came down from Heaven to serve, not to be served (Matt 20:24-28). At first John objected to Jesus' request for baptism (Matt 3:14). Peter objected when Jesus started to wash his feet (John 13:8). Peter also objected when Jesus predicted that He would be tortured and killed in Jerusalem (Matt 16:22). The disciples didn't always understand the servant role that Jesus modeled for them. Even as He prepared to ascend into heaven they asked, "Are you at this time going to restore the kingdom to Israel?" (Acts 1:6). They had tunnel vision. It would take time for them to understand the excellency of God's worldwide, all-time goal. Jesus expected courageous loyalty to God's standards but allowed great freedom of judgment for practical application.

Jesus led instead of driving. The "Good Shepherd" walked ahead of the flock (John 10:3-4). He knew what He was talking about and what He had come to do. He did exactly what His Father had taught and shown Him (John 5:16-27). He fulfilled all that the Prophets taught about Him. What would Jesus say and do today? He would ask us to recognize the simplicity of God's revelation. He would tell us to be thankful and wonder at the excellency of the Creation. We can learn from anyone who has wisdom, and Jesus would tell us to be wiser than those in our society who have also discovered His principles (Luke 16:8-12; 10:3). As His followers we need to be as wise as serpents and as harmless as doves. Nothing can overcome or defeat God's plan for excellence (Matt 21:42-44).

What Do Churches Need to Discover about Excellence?

Treat People as "God's Customers": If Jesus taught against any one thing, He taught us not to be snobs. God shows no partiality and we must not make Him look like a snob. This means that we should follow Jesus in exalting the humble. We need to help the last become first, the most excellent to serve the least excellent. (See Matt 5:1-12.)

If we accept God's plainly stated priority to save all people, we will love the people in our circles of influence, our natural networks of family, relatives, neighbors, friends, fellow workers, and acquaintances. Meeting the needs of those around us takes time, and it's risky. We have to learn something about them to feel their needs and to know their problems. Jesus didn't come to judge, and He warns us not to be critical of others. Cynics and critics seldom understand the needs of others and almost never make many intimate friends.

Secular organizations don't make enemies of their customers, and we need the wisdom to love the "customers" that God brings into our lives. In a sense we are "selling" the goodness and greatness of God. We glorify Him when we seek to understand and help meet the needs of people. We can do that best when we who believe in Christ unite in Him. We need to cultivate the same mind and attitude, but accept variety in opinions (1 Cor 1:10). He prayed in John 17 for perfect oneness with God and Himself. Our unity will cause the world to believe that God has sent Him (Eph 4:11-16). By uniting in love we can persuade others to believe in Him (John 6:29).

Innovate Towards Excellence: We need to test what we are doing and explore better ways. Do we stress comfort and pleasure above courage, truth, and obedience? Do we ignore the battles that Jesus had to fight against corruption, snobbery, and hypocrisy? In other words, are we in danger of repeating history, making the same mistakes as those who rejected Jesus?

God gives us all a lot of time to learn His will. We should desire a life of continuous learning. We need to use our talents, so we need to learn how to develop them through practice. How will we grow if we risk nothing for Jesus, and for His "customers?" (Matt 25:14-30). Test all things, and accept only what is good (1 Thess 5:21). Are change and innovation bad words in your congregation? How can we test, and how can we improve, if we can't get closer to Jesus by loving His word? It's hard to bring about change even if we encourage it. We have to free up members to follow Jesus by their own study. We all have to work out our own knowledge of God's will in order to have a living faith that we can call our own (Phil 2:12-13).

Excellence Comes From People Participation: Christ gives us the responsibility to love our neighbor. It goes right with loving God. We can't even love God, whom we haven't seen, if we don't love those we do see (1 John 4:20-21). What could be simpler than that? Almost all of Jesus' parables compare those who didn't listen and didn't love with those who did. Once we get the meaning of a parable, it's hard to forget it. That's how Jesus makes His will known to child and genius alike. He doesn't play favorites. He treats all people alike, and that's not always how society does it (Rom 2:11).

Churches need to encourage participation in life, not spectator Christianity. It's not easy with our church culture so comfortable, sitting, listening, and often leaving it at that. We have become accustomed to letting the experts preach it and teach it with little power to implement it. And the experts often accept this role. Their body language and sophisticated use of words and stories can lull us into believing, "It's their job to do the thinking. The Pastor is to do the work of God. Our job is merely to show up on Sunday." (See 1 John 3:17-18.)

How Can We Lead With Excellence? Our leaders need to be honored for what they do, but we need to avoid inadvertent hypocrisy. If we members don't study the word enough to see the simplicity of God's priorities, how will we be able to keep our pastors humble? Even secular organizations expect integrity, visionary thinking, fairness, and competency from their leaders. We should excel in these same leadership characteristics.[26]

Do our leaders delegate to members the responsibility to grow spiritually? Or, do we consider the word "spiritual" undefinable, like Pilate thought of truth? (See John 18:38.) Does the vision of our church match God's vision? Do we realize that His principles are simple to understand but hard to achieve? The complexity comes when we apply God's principles to specific life situations with particular people (1 Cor 9:19-23). There is plenty of mystery and complexity, but not with Christ's priorities.

Jesus trained His disciples in a small, on-the-job group. He didn't choose many who were noble, rich, educated, or powerful (1 Cor 1:26-31). He chose those with teachable hearts. If the heart is healthy, Christ has no trouble training our intellects. Exalting the intellect does not guarantee that the heart can be changed. Isn't that one of God's biggest problem with us? If He can convert our hearts, then He has our minds too. Then He can get us to understand His point of view. Our leaders need to understand God's priorities for excellence in servant-leading (Matt 23:8-12). We all lead in some way. Parents lead children. Older people lead younger people (Titus 2:1-10). Mature people guide those who are weak. In small groups leaders and facilitators surface naturally (Gal 6:1-5).

Leaders in excellent organizations have discovered that small project teams produce better results than specialized staff experts. Churches are learning the same thing. Small intimate groups experience more of what the first century believers experienced. We need to see the wisdom of decentralizing control and freeing up Christians to follow Jesus. *Be loose on controls*: give people freedom, space to grow, and encouragement to follow Jesus by their own effort. *Be tight on character standards*: committed to growing people mature in Christ.

What Can the Grassroots Christian Do?

The Wisdom of Treating People As God's Customers:

◆ What have we learned from our experiences in excellent secular organizations?

◆ What do we learn from our personal study of Jesus and the Bible?

◆ Do we take advantage of every opportunity that we have to teach or lead, especially in small groups and ad hoc task forces?

◆ Do we really understand why people may reject "churchianity" but not Christ?

◆ Can we think up our own parables of how Christ would describe His "customers?"

The Way to Grow Like Jesus Through Innovation:

◆ We have to work our way through long-standing human traditions carefully.

◆ We really need to investigate and experiment with small groups, just because the New Testament clearly reveals their importance and usefulness.

◆ We need to center on what Jesus taught, see His priorities, and not dwell on the fringes. (See Rom 14:1-13; 16:17-19; Matt 7:24-27; Titus 3:9-11.)

◆ We need to be patient with tradition-bound people, but tough-minded in following the standards of the apostles and Jesus. The havoc worked by false leaders certainly concerned Jesus. (Read 2 Peter 2:1-22; Jude 1:3-25; 1 John 2:18-27.)

God Loves Participating People:

◆ Be aware of the people in your circle of influence.

◆ See God's kingdom as a family like Jesus did (cf. Mark 10:29-31; Luke 12:32-34; John 13:34-35; 15:9-17).

◆ Consider God's priority for meeting the needs of people (Matt 6:33).

◆ Learn to love first those who are nearest, those God brings into our lives.

◆ Cultivate intimate, living relationships at all costs.

◆ Encourage people to work at maturing their own relationship with Christ (Eph 3:14-21).

How We Can Learn to Lead:

◆ We can start on a low key. Grow with the exercise of our gifts (1 Cor 14:12; Eph 4:11-5:21).

◆ Be careful not to become entangled with and defeated by dogmatic leaders (Mark 7:1-23; Matt 16:5-12).

◆ Become an independent thinker and work out our own faith from our study of God's word as the Holy Spirit teaches and leads us (John 15:1-17; 1 Cor 2:9-16; 1 John 2:24-27).

◆ Be patient and loving with our leaders, but hold them accountable to God's standards (1 Tim 5:19; 2 Tim 2:16-17; 4:2-5).

◆ Learn to confront in love where it is necessary.

◆ Learn to deal with determined opposition. Jesus and His disciples had to do it (John 5:31-47; 8:12-59; Matt 23:1-39).

◆ Lead by example and with integrity.

◆ Develop an accurate vision of what Christ does as head of His body (Eph 1:15-23).

Ways for Small Groups to Study Excellence

Here is a series of agendas for small group meetings:

God's Customers:

◆ Icebreaker: Describe how you experienced excellent treatment by a loved one, teacher, or neighbor when you were a child (30 minutes).

◆ Study how Jesus initially approached people to tell them the good news and help meet their needs (30 minutes). Read and discuss Matthew 4:17-5:16; 6:19-34 and 7:1-12.

◆ Discuss your present relationships and allow time for each one to pray for needs (20 minutes).

◆ Describe how small groups can bring about God's vision for the oneness of His church on earth (10 minutes).

Innovation and Its Role in Small Groups:

◆ Icebreaker: Describe a big change in your earlier life that turned out for the better (30 minutes).

◆ Study the changes that Jesus came into the world to bring about (30 minutes). Read and discuss John 9:1-34 and 10:1-18.

◆ Discuss each person's need for continued growth, and pray for individual needs (20 minutes).

◆ Describe your church's vision for change and growth through small groups (10 minutes).

God Loves Participating People:

◆ Icebreaker: Describe an early experience of how you treated another person and how they treated you in return (30 minutes).

◆ Study how Jesus treated the sinners and the sick. How did the

Jewish leaders treat them? (30 minutes). Read and discuss Luke 15:11-32.

◆ Pray for each other's needs, especially for sickness and difficult experiences (20 minutes).

◆ Describe God's vision of His word leavening the whole world (10 minutes).

Leadership in Small Groups:

◆ Describe the earliest time you had an opportunity to be a leader (30 minutes).

◆ Study Jesus' leadership style with His disciples (30 minutes). Read and discuss Matthew 13:8-12; John 13:1-17 and 17:20-26.

◆ Pray for church leaders, small group leaders, and other needs (20 minutes).

◆ Describe your vision of how God will raise up true leaders (10 minutes).

RECOMMENDED READING

Wolfe J. Rinke, *Winning Management: 6 Fail-Safe Strategies for Building High-Performance Organizations*, (Achievement Publishers).

REFERENCES

1. Tom Peters and Nancy Austin, *A Passion for Excellence*, (New York: Warner Books, 1985), xvii.

2. Joe gave Martin Luther King the title of one of his most famous sermons in 1963. It was "A Tough Mind and A Tender Heart Are One."

3. Peters and Austin, *A Passion for Excellence*, 111, 512-513.

4. Ibid., 154, 157.

5. Ibid., 190-194. Based on Tracy Kidder, *The Soul of a New Machine*, (New York: Little, Brown & Co., 1981 in association with the Atlantic Monthly Press).

6. Mary Kay Ash, *Mary Kay on People Management*, (New York: Warner Books, 1984), 1-10. Matthew 7:12.

7. Ibid., 21-32.

8. Peters, *Liberation Management*, 238.

9. Ibid., 239.

10. Ibid., 240.

11. Ibid., 241.

12. Ibid., 242.

13. Shook, *Honda*, 8-12.

14. Ibid., 9.

15. Ibid., 61.

16. Ibid., 64-65.

17. Ibid., 63.

18. Ibid., 67.

19. Ibid., 79.

20. Ibid., 58, 217-220.

21. Ibid., 49, 187-189, 221.

22. Ibid., xv, 166.

23. Ibid., 167-169.

24. Ibid., 125-128.

25. Ibid., 5.

26. Kouzes and Posner, *The Leadership Challenge*, 16.

CHAPTER SIX
TIMETABLE

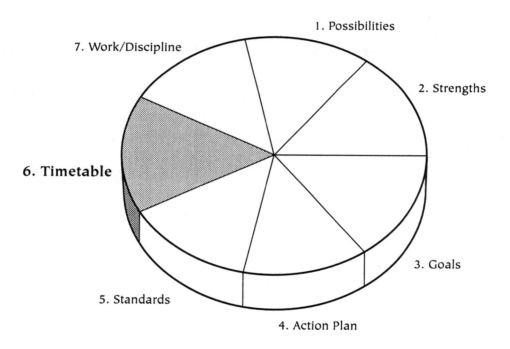

1. Possibilities

7. Work/Discipline

2. Strengths

6. Timetable

3. Goals

5. Standards

4. Action Plan

6

HITTING TARGETS OR TAKING THE EASY WAY OUT?

So do not worry, saying, 'What shall we eat?' or 'What shall we drink?' or
'What shall we wear?' . . . But seek first his kingdom and his righteousness,
and all these things will be given to you as well.
Jesus (in Matt 6:31, 33)

You have been raised to life with Christ. Now set your heart on what is in heaven,
where Christ rules at God's right side. Think about what is up there, not about what
is here on earth. You died, which means that your life is hidden with Christ,
who sits beside God. Christ gives meaning to your life,
and when he appears, you will also appear with him in glory. . . .
Yet Christ is all that matters, and he lives in all of us.
Paul (in Col 3:1-4, 11 [CEV])

Most people are constantly trying to find time for the "important" activities in their
already overflowing . . . schedules. They move things around, delegate them, cancel
them, postpone them — all in the hope of finding time for first things. The key,
however, is not to prioritize your schedule, but to schedule your priorities.
Stephen Covey[1]

Key Points

To follow our plans with vision and integrity, we need to be sure of our priorities. The prophets constantly exposed the lack of vision and integrity in God's people and leaders. Jesus "fought" constantly with the leaders of His own people to get them to see how their foolish priorities and inappropriate traditions nullified God's Word.

Effective people and organizations schedule their priorities rather than prioritizing their schedules. Jesus put relationships, seeking and doing God's will, and great possibilities at the top of His priorities. Churches need to recognize the simplicity of Jesus' priorities. Christians with experience in secular organizations can help greatly in church leadership roles. Those involved in small groups get to know each other intimately and can learn to develop the most appropriate priorities.

****

We need to *revolutionize what we do and how we do it*. We need to set tough-minded priorities and spend our time working on the most important things. We don't need to prioritize our schedules and timetables, always struggling to get a larger number of unimportant things done faster. That's a formula for frustration and mediocrity. We must learn to center our minds on the most important priorities.

According to researchers Stalk and Hout (Boston Consulting Group senior partners) we waste 95 to 99.95 percent of our time on things that aren't as important as the things we fail to do at all. We need a more exciting and more meaningful set of priorities than that.

How can we improve our approach to setting priorities and spend more time on the truly important opportunities?

Peters and Austin recommend that leaders should "live your vision, values, and priorities in your scheduled meetings, visits, and in the minutiae of your daily routine. If you are in your office more that 35 percent of the time, ask yourself why. . . . Miss no opportunity to signal your abiding concerns."

They ask all leaders to review and modify their daily calendars to include a very small number of highly effective priorities. Leaders signal their abiding concerns by spending time with the right people. They can show others what's important only if they get out and talk with those who know what's going on; i.e., their front-line workers, their customers, and their suppliers. They get their innovative ideas from these people; not at desks or from analyzing reports by those who write well but may not know what's happening in the real world.[2]

What Are Secular Organizations Doing?

Allergan: About one-half of the company's revenues come from ointments that help people with eye problems. In one major breakthrough they developed "a product to help contact-lens users." Data overwhelmed the whole industry. They read reams of prescriptions and listened to boring professional jargon from doctors. In order not to miss the consumer's point of view, their Chairman, Gavin Herbert, insisted that his people get information directly from patients. When they did, one problem surfaced constantly: "itchy-scratchy eyes." He said, "Now you know no ophthalmologist, after twenty years of professional training, is going to write down as his diagnosis 'itchy-scratchy eyes.' It's just not professional language. Yet it was the problem." When they started working on something to help "itchy-scratchy eyes" they ended with a very successful product line.

Excellent companies listen to their customers. They give a much greater priority to *naive listening*. They tell their people to spend much more time with the end-user and really observe what they experience, say, and do. Peters and Austin keep finding that people with hands-on experience lead hands-on companies. The chairman of Allergan worked in his father's pharmacy, and the family lived above the store. His father founded Allergan.[3]

What Tough-Minded Means

The tough mind is resilient. It expends the energy to set and maintain reasonable boundaries while allowing room for growth — inside a framework of clear values. We believe deeply that a tough mind and a tender heart are one and that a transcendent faith — a living and growing belief in God — is crucial to tough-minded family living.

The term "tough-minded" refers to a quality of quiet, confident resilient strength that enables the person who exemplifies it to lead others to become the best they can possibly be. When practiced in the business world, it has led to high productivity, motivation, and enhanced satisfaction for both the team and the consumer. The tough-minded person loves life, builds people, is excited about starting each day, is an actualizer![4]

Milliken & Company: Roger Milliken spends 80% of his time on customer issues. While he lectured at the Milliken Customer Service Center, one customer asked, "Who's minding the store while you and Tom [Milliken President Malone] are doing this?" Roger said, "But what could be more important for me than to spend time with customers?"

One of his marketing directors spent two weeks working on the second shift in a customer's hospital. He said, "What an experience . . . to actually maintain your products . . . in the environment where they are used." He cleaned carpets using the machinery they used. He handled the same problems that they faced. He cleaned up stains, urine, and stuff he couldn't name in public. Two weeks of this wore him out, but he planned to do it every six months. What resulted? He said, "I'm learning . . . exactly what our health care customers require. . . . I guess if we will just follow the Golden Rule — 'Do unto others as you would have them do unto you' — we will become more efficient in our dealings with all people, including our customers."

Many of Milliken's programs have come from a passion for naive listening to customers. They get their first-line people to meet with first-line people in their customers' factories. Factory people know the practical problems better than salespeople. Milliken gives all salespeople an internship in manufacturing. They also give "bring customers to life" videotapes to provide a "stand-in-the-customer's-shoes" training program for their service people. They want all hands, including hourly people, to get a "feel" for major customers.[5]

It's no wonder that Milliken is tops in the textile field. They have revolutionized the meanings of timetable and priority. With 80% of their top man's time and effort used for their customers, how could they fail? Everyone in the whole company gives quality and customers top priority. And they do much the same thing with their suppliers.

The Challenge of Your Most Important Priorities

Commit yourself to a growth-producing set of top priorities. Chart and carry out self-generated priorities rather than simply responding to directives laid on you by someone else.

Priorities are not promises to be kept at all costs. They are the best estimates that could be made at the time. Allow modification of priorities and allow mistakes. You cut off innovation and discovery when a person feels guilty for normal mistakes, failures and changes in plans and forecasts.

"Thomas J. Watson, former president of IBM, had a simple formula for achieving success: *Double your failure rate*. He knew that one crucial need in blasting your way out of the twilight zone of mediocrity was to dare mightily, to dip into your physical, mental, and spiritual reservoirs until that supply of strength has grown and grown."

Joe Batten[6]

Hewlett-Packard makes Management By Walking Around (MBWA) a top priority. All of the excellent companies do this in one way or another, but HP excels at it. Barney Oliver, former head of HP's Research and Development, wandered regularly. He asked very tough questions. He spoke with candor. But he left people with their own initiative; he didn't take it away even though he could terrify young engineers. But people got used to having him around since he wandered part of every day. Barney demanded intelligence but he also encouraged open participation and tough-minded wisdom. Those who knew him agreed that you learned a lot and he "had not taken away space, had not in any sense told you what to do or what the next steps should be." He enhanced the performance of those he came in contact with.

Bill Hewlett and Dave Packard initiated MBWA early in the company's history along with Management by Objectives and what they called the "open door policy." They wanted to build trust and release people so they would freely express "ideas, opinions, problems, and concerns."

Why wander about and communicate? Primarily "to find out what's going on, to find out what's bugging people," and to reveal your priorities to them. Excellent companies make MBWA a vital priority. But it's hard to do, because it's the opposite of looking busy. Unfortunately, the keep-them-looking-busy syndrome prevails in many mediocre and ineffective companies.[7]

Mervyn's: They stay ahead of competition by remerchandising their billion-dollar-plus operation once a week. Mervyn's does every week what others do about every 13 weeks. The people in the company keep in touch. Their top merchants and executives get together for a Weekly Store Check. They redo everything and create the Ad Supplement. This group goes together through a single store for four hours once a week. They examine the store's live format closely and ask, "What does it feel like?" They decide to do *what makes sense* for the next week.[8]

How Do We Actually Focus on the Most Important Priorities?

Knowing how to say "No.": In our professional experience we have found this to be one of the most important keys. Often people know what's important and yet spent more than 95% of their time on what is not important. Why?

1. Many of us act busy and stay busy, because we worry too much about what others think of us. We should do what produces the best results, not just try to look busy. Excellent leaders want people to spend their time on important priorities.

2. Maintaining the status quo and following obsolete traditions take time. We must say "no" to these and give top priority to the most important things. Again, excellent leaders don't want their people wasting time on things that have little or no value.

3. We have tunnel vision. Old habits may be nonproductive but we fall into them without thinking. They feel comfortable. Other people accept them. We've gotten by with them for a long time. In order to change things and make good things happen, we must abandon bad habits and learn to prioritize and do what actually works best.

4. We have to discipline ourselves to perceive a broader point of view. Do we see the opportunities coming our way? Do we look at the actions and listen to the words of our customers, our suppliers, and those around us?

5. We don't delegate all that we can to others. Do we trust others to learn and do new things? We honor people when we expect and ask more from them. The more we delegate the more our time will be free to use on top priorities.

What is important? The previous chapter covered the four most vital standards of excellence. These require top priority attention:

1. Listen closely and openly to customers: They know what needs changing, where to find the best opportunities. This accounts for more than 60% of all excellent innovations.

2. Work at innovation: Encourage many experiments, make small changes constantly. Combine this obsession for experimentation — trying things constantly — with close contact and cooperation with customers and you'll find many vital priorities. Roger Milliken spent 80% of his time on customer attention.

3. Spend time with people: They know the most about things going on around them. Important priorities come from encouraging

people to take more responsibility, and do excellent jobs. Things can be done best by letting teams of workers set their own goals, and do their own planning and implementation. Remember the example we gave of Johnsonville Foods.
4. Develop leaders: to be coaches, facilitators, and visionaries. Why? Because this works best. Excellent leaders make it their top priority to encourage their people to be competent and see the opportunities ahead. They don't drive them or support inappropriate traditions that no longer produce results.

The Advantages of Keeping a Personal Journal

In living, leading, and consulting the authors use a bound log book as our basic prioritizing instrument. We use it for daily, weekly, and longer range planning. It has been extremely valuable for collecting important data while walking around (MBWA), visiting customers, suppliers, clients, and in our personal lives. We've designed critical experiments, started collecting data, immediately discovered problems no one knew were there, and made breakthroughs in record time.

Log book or journal records can be very flexible. We placed top priority on measuring the right things, not measuring things right. We collected data that revealed what needed to be known, and we analyzed these with powerful computer programs to draw the conclusions that we needed to make. We were able to innovate constantly, delegate to others in the organization, and discover which goals should have top priority.

Stephen Covey points out,

Keeping a personal journal is a high-leverage [important long-term] activity that significantly increases self-awareness and enhances all the endowments and the synergy among them. . . .

If you're not sure why you still do some things that you know are harmful or self-defeating, analyze it, process it, write it down. . . . It helps you to make wise choices.

Keeping a personal journal empowers you to see and improve, on a day-by-day basis, the way you're developing and using your endowments. Because writing truly imprints the brain, it also helps you remember and apply the things you're trying to do. In addition, it gives you a powerful contextual tool. As you take occasion — perhaps on a mission statement renewal retreat — to read over your experiences of past weeks, months, or years, you gain invaluable insight into repeating patterns and themes in your life.[9]

Just plain common sense: The ideas and principles that we've covered in our first five chapters show that the excellent organizations use their common sense. There is really nothing mysterious about success. It takes tough-minded discipline, but that discipline improves with practice. Inspiration comes from living examples. Good companies keep revolutionizing and prioritizing how they do everything. Study the companies that do the things we've written about. You'll get plenty of ideas for your own priorities. What do some of the experts say?

◆ Mary Kay Ash: We're not in the cosmetic business — we're in the people business.

◆ Warren Bennis: Leaders do right things; managers do things right.

◆ Stephen Covey: Work on important priorities; say "No" to the lesser good.

◆ Peter Drucker: Elephants have a hard time adapting. Cockroaches outlive everything.

◆ Michael Hammer: Obliterate the organizations that aren't working. Re-engineer.

◆ Laurie Beth Jones: The self-mastery, action, and relationship skills that Jesus used to train and motivate his team . . . can be implemented by anyone who dares.

◆ Tom Peters: Move faster and listen to the fanatics. Experiment, experiment! Wow!

◆ Bob Waterman: Organizational renewal must be our top priority.

◆ Jesus: Center your priorities on God's kingdom and righteousness.

On this last point C.S. Lewis once wrote that focusing on Heaven made people much more effective in human society. Being Heavenly-minded makes us of greater earthly use.

What Did Jesus Teach and Do about Priorities?

1. Our Father created everything through Jesus for a definite purpose and for our good. (See John 1:3; Col 1:15-20; Heb 1:1-2,10):

    ◆ We live here on earth to learn something important for our future life in Heaven. (See 2 Cor 4:16-18; Phil 2:12-13.)

    ◆ God supplies everything we need, but we have to work by "the sweat of our brow" to get and use what we need. (See Matt 6:33.)

    ◆ God tests us as well as training us; He uses both good things and adversity. (See Rom 8:28; 2 Cor 1:3-7; Heb 12:4-11.)

    ◆ His Holy Spirit lives in us to encourage us, teach us, guide us, protect us, and pray for us. He engineers circumstances and even helps us to learn much by our mistakes. (See 1 Cor 2:9-16; Rom 8:28.)

◆ God has done everything well no matter how it looks to cynics or the faint in heart. Everything that He created is good; every good thing has come from Him. (See James 1:16-18.)

2. Jesus revealed the simplicity of God's priorities, but many of the religious people He came to teach did not want their human traditions and interpretations changed or made simple. Their leaders didn't really want the sick, insane, and uneducated people to know everything that they needed to know. (See Matt 11:25-30; Mark 7:1-13.)

◆ Jesus told us to treat others as we want to be treated by them (Matt 7:12). This principle fulfills the teaching of the Law and the Prophets. The Golden Rule includes loving God with all your heart, soul, mind, and strength; and also loving your neighbor as you love yourself. What could be more simply stated, but then, what could be more difficult to apply to our daily lives? (Matt 22:37-40).

◆ According to Jesus and the Prophets, we create our greatest problems by shutting our eyes, stopping up our ears, and hardening our hearts. (See Matt 13:11-15.)

◆ We often would rather fight than cooperate. Just look at the simplicity of Jesus' words: "I pray also for those who will believe in me through their message, that all of them may be one, Father, just as you are in me and I am in you. May they also be in us so that the world may believe that you have sent me" (John 17:20-21). How can we be part of the answer to Jesus' prayer?

◆ Common sense teaches us plainly to give a higher priority to long-term survival than to short term. Seeking God's kingdom and righteousness should take priority over care for food, body, and clothing. Jesus spoke pretty plainly of spiritual priorities when He told His disciples that they would have to lose their lives in order to find them. Their souls were worth more than the whole world (Matt 16:25-26).

◆ Only through practice and perseverance do we grow in wisdom, love, and forgiveness. Check out Jesus' priorities in the Lord's Prayer (Matt 6:9-15) and in the Parable of the Unmerciful Servant (Matt 18:21-35).

3. By setting priorities and working out our most important goals, we discover new important opportunities and goals. Jesus

worked constantly toward goals. He "walked" His priorities more than He "talked" them. He revealed God's nature to His disciples and to us by living and doing what His Father had shown Him and told Him. He associated with those He came to save, even though that wasn't very popular with many dogmatic religious leaders (see Matt 11:16-19; John 12:49-50; 18:24-25):

◆ He attended a friend's wedding with His family and His disciples, and He even supplied the best wine when the host's wine ran out (John 2:1-11).

◆ He went into the temple at age twelve and amazed the teachers of the law by His questions and by His answers (Luke 2:41-52).

◆ He asked twelve men from very common occupations to *Learn By Walking Around* with Him, and then to *Lead By Walking Around*. (See Luke 6:12-16.) He used this leadership principle that is so important to the success of modern excellent organizations, *Management By Walking Around*, or simply *Keeping In Touch With People*.

◆ He identified with the poor, sick, and sinful. He helped them effectively by avoiding the practice of corrupt luxury and ruthless power. (See Matt 8:18-22; 9:10-13; Phil 2:4-11.)

◆ He did associate with the rich and powerful by accepting invitations to dinner, but He never failed to tell them the tough-minded truths that they needed to know (Luke 18:18-22). They played key roles in His most memorable parables: the Tenants (Matt 21:33-46), the Good Samaritan (Luke 10:26-37), the Rich Man and Lazarus (Luke 16:19-31), the Great Banquet (Luke 14:15-24), and the Rich Fool (Luke 12:13-21).

4.   Jesus brought needed innovation and change to the traditional way of practicing religion, by revealing God's true priorities, people's wrong-headed loyalties, and the religious leaders' addiction to foolish goals and priorities:

◆ He deliberately broke false and blinding traditions. These were deceiving everyone and nullifying what God actually wanted believed and done. (See Mark 7:1-13.)

◆ He gave a true perspective of God's will and God's kingdom by performing astounding miracles, speaking with obvious wisdom, and telling dramatic and easily-remembered parables and stories. (See Matt 4:23-25; 7:28; 13:1-57.)

◆ He infallibly demonstrated the love of God by allowing His enemies to kill Him. He used the ultimate weapon of love to defeat their insane jealously and ambition. God completed the victory by raising Jesus from the dead and exalting Him to rule over Heaven and all the kingdoms of this world. (See Matt 27:32-61; 28:16-20; John 3:16.)

♦ We have a fundamental responsibility from Christ: Make our priorities agree with His priorities. (See Matt 7:24-27; John 6:29; 7:17.)

5. How does Jesus' tenderness and gentleness fit in with His tough-mindedness? He treated the weaknesses and mistakes of His disciples with patience. He asks us to love our enemies, because God gives sunshine and rain to both the righteous and the unrighteous. It takes great courage and strength to win people over by love and humility. It's not cowardly to turn the other cheek, go the second mile, and pray for those who mistreat us, not if we do these things for Jesus (Matt 5:38-48). He even asked God to forgive the people who put Him to death for this reason: "they do not know what they are doing" (Luke 23:34). He used tough-minded discipline with those who were blind, stubborn, and needed a radical change of attitude. He modeled tenderness and gentleness with those who needed encouragement:

♦ Jesus wept and was deeply moved by the grief of Mary, Martha, and their friends at the death of their brother Lazarus. He knew that death had no power, but He still showed great tenderness with those overcome by death's horror. (See John 11:17-44.)

♦ He stopped the funeral procession for a young man. His heart went out to the man's mother, a widow, and he told her, "Don't cry." He said to the young man, "Get up." The man sat up and Jesus gave him back to his mother. (See Luke 7:11-17.)

♦ Peter got himself into trouble constantly, but Jesus always forgave him. We need to realize that God uses our whole lifetime to mold us into the likeness of Christ. We can read how hard it was for God's people, Israel, to obey. The prophets were continually warning them of dire consequences, but they had to learn the hard way. God usually ended His messages with hope for the future when He would bring His dispersed children back from the ends of the earth.

How Can Leaders Improve Priorities?

We develop the most excellent priorities when we open our hearts and minds to the best possibilities and build on people's strengths, not focusing on weaknesses. We need excellent character standards and wisdom to work effectively toward the highest quality goals. That's what it means to schedule our priorities effectively. Instead of letting others do it, we choose what's most important from the various possibilities:

◆ God's "customers" are those He wants to reach with His good news. We need to hear what they say and understand their problems. If we have self-righteous tunnel vision, if we have a fortress mentality, we will be more interested in spoiling the saved than saving the spoiled. God wants us to reach out to everyone, to approach people the way that Jesus and the disciples did. We can see His priorities if we will open our eyes, ears, and hearts.

◆ Do we see the need to make changes? What improvements can we make if we examine our traditions and habits? This takes great courage and wisdom. We all resist change, *especially when it's for our own good*. Will we make innovation a top priority and a good word? We can't grow toward the perfection that God wants without constant change for the better. That's positive innovation, not negative or destructive. Even good changes upset people, so churches need to make them with wisdom and patience.

◆ Jesus honored people, even weak people. Will we see people's potential strengths? We need to help the last become first, because God loves all people, especially the less fortunate. Jesus certainly showed us this in the way that He dealt with "outsiders" and "sinners." We need to give top priority to what we are for. Let's stop focusing on what we are against. It's very easy to fall into the trap of unfairly judging and criticizing others. We often overlook and discount the marvelous changes that Christ can and will bring into the lives of the people we look down on. (Please read Romans 2 and 3.)

◆ In choosing the highest goals we need a standard of excellence for serving our fellow human beings. That's how we'll end up serving God according to His will. Will we study and learn from Jesus' daily habits and priorities? His priorities can be understood. John put it plainly when he said,

> Dear friends, if our hearts do not condemn us, we have confidence before God and receive from him anything we ask, because we obey his commands and do what pleases him. And this is his command: to believe in the name of his Son, Jesus Christ, and to love one another as he commanded us.

> Those who obey his commands live in him, and he in them.
> And this is how we know that he lives in us: We know it by
> the Spirit he gave us (1 John 3:21-24).

How about Grassroots Christians and Small Groups?

Excellent organizations decentralize and delegate everything feasible to front-line workers. They reduce the hierarchy and flatten the organization. They take people out of functional departments and assign them to small teams. This eliminates the handoffs from one department to another which delays projects so much.

The small group structure in the church puts ministry into the hands of the people. Small task forces function better and faster than big committees. But the real advantage of small groups come from people meeting weekly in homes where it's easier to invite others in their normal networks of relationships. Oscar Thompson called these relationships Concentric Circles of Concern. These circles radiate out as follows:

1. Self: Where we all start and where we all are most of the time (the smallest circle).

2. Immediate Family: Our spouse, children, and relatives living with us.

3. Relatives: All those we have some contact with.

4. Close Friends: These know us pretty well and love us.

5. Neighbors and Business Associates: We see them quite often.

6. Acquaintances: We see these occasionally.

7. Person X: The stranger (the outside circle).[10]

In his excellent book on priorities, Stephen Covey develops a similar approach "that encompasses everything that we are concerned about — our health, a meeting with the boss, a teenage son's plans for the weekend, offensive magazines on display . . . , the threat of nuclear war." He pictures our priorities in three concentric circles:

◆ The Circle of Concern: This includes all our concerns (the outer circle).

◆ The Circle of Influence: Here we can actually make a difference.

◆ The Circle of Focus: This is where our time and effort is used most effectively (the smallest circle).[11]

Both of these ways of portraying how we relate to those around us help us to see why small groups help build relationships. God's family thrives on relationships. We meet needs in these, our needs and those of people we know. God meets our needs constantly whether we acknowledge Him or not. Every perfect gift comes down from Him. As the Lord's Prayer reveals, our Father in Heaven hears us and provides what we need.

We also relate to people around us on a personal level even more often than we do in small groups. Here we can make relationships our top priority. Oscar Thompson tells the story of Brenda, who came to see him because she was so unhappy and felt like, "Nobody loves me." He knew that her parents loved her, but they were also very busy in their new business. She said, "I could die and nobody cares."

He asked her, "Who told you someone was supposed to love you . . . ? You have been created . . . as a channel for love to flow through you to others. . . . You want the flow to go the wrong way." No wonder Brenda was miserable. Oscar told her to make a commitment from the heart to "meet the needs" of whoever God brought into her path.

She told Oscar, "Judy is a freshman. . . . She is just dumb. . . . She rides on the bus with me, and . . . she just bugs me." Brenda was a senior and had to ride forty-five minutes on the bus with Judy every day. Thompson challenged her: "Why don't you meet some of the needs of this lowly little freshman's ignorance."

Several days later Brenda came back to Oscar's office. She told him how Judy sat down right beside her on the bus. It really bugged her, but she prayed, "Lord, I'm going to meet her need if it kills me." She turned and looked right at Judy while she was talking. She noticed by Judy's face that "underneath all that chatter was a hurting little girl." Brenda asked her to tell her about her brothers, sisters, mom, and dad. Judy was quiet at first but then said, "Brenda, my mom and dad are getting a divorce, and I am so scared. We are going to have to move, and my whole world is coming apart."

Brenda told Oscar, "I just listened . . . . I felt the love of God wanting to meet that little girl's needs through me. I put my arm around her, and we talked until we arrived at school. . . . After getting off the bus, Judy . . . put her arms around me and said, 'Oh, Brenda, I just love you.'"

Brenda started looking outside of herself more and more. She even started helping her little sister, Kim, with her homework. At first Kim said, "I don't believe this!" But Brenda helped her solve her algebra and then helped clean Kim's room and prepare the evening meal for their parents. Her mother came into her room later and said, "Honey, I do not know what changed your attitude today. . . . Your little sister came in tonight . . . and said that she really did love her big sister . . . we just wanted you to know that we love you too."

Brenda finally told Oscar, "All this time it has been *me, my, mine.* . . . I have learned that . . . I am meeting the needs of others, and my own needs get met too."[12]

Things work like this in *circles of concern and influence* and especially in the inner circle, *the Circle of Focus.* It happens in individual relationships, like with Brenda and Judy. And it happens in groups of 10 or 12. Relatives, close friends, neighbors, and business associates may come with us to a small group meeting in a home but not to a church building.

Jesus sets our priorities, and these produce the fruit of the Spirit in our relationships. God wants to produce the character of Jesus in our lives. This means bearing the following fruit:

◆ "Love — the relationship"
◆ "Joy — the result of the relationship"
◆ "Peace — the result of the correct relationship"
◆ "Longsuffering (patience) — the maintenance of the relationship"
◆ "Gentleness — the attitude of the relationship"
◆ "Faith — the means of the relationship"
◆ "Meekness — the submitted will in the relationship"
◆ "Self-Control — the control of the relationship"[13]

A Cell-Group Agenda on Priorities:

◆ Icebreaker (30 minutes): What was an important priority on your agenda when you were in Grammar School, Intermediate School, or High School.
◆ Discuss Jesus' priorities (30 minutes): For individual Christians, our leaders, and for the people of the world. Use what Jesus said in Matthew 6:25-34 and 16:21-28.
◆ Discuss needs and pray (20 minutes).
◆ Vision (10 minutes): The leader presents an inspiring statement on how our priorities enable us to please Christ and serve others.

REFERENCES

1. Stephen R. Covey, Roger and Rebecca Merrill, *First Things First,* (New York: Simon & Schuster, 1994), 88.

2. Peters and Austin, *A Passion for Excellence,* 539.

3. Ibid., 16.

4. Batten, Havemann, Pearce, and Pedersen, *Tough-Minded Parenting*, (Nashville: Broadman Press, 1991), xii, 49.

5. Peters and Austin, *Passion for Excellence*, 18-20.

6. Adapted from Joe Batten, *Building A Total Quality Culture*, (Menlo Park: Crisp, 1992), 40.

7. Batten et al., *Tough-Minded Parenting*, 448-449, 450-451. David Packard, *The HP Way*, 155-157.

8. Peters and Austin, *Passion for Excellence*, 33.

9. Stephen Covey, *First Things First*, 63-65.

10. W. Oscar Thompson, Jr., *Concentric Circles of Concern*, (Nashville: Broadman Press, 1981), 21, 68.

11. Stephen Covey, *First Things First*, 150-151.

12. Thompson, *Concentric Circles*, 94-99.

13. Ibid., 143.

CHAPTER SEVEN
WORK/DISCIPLINE

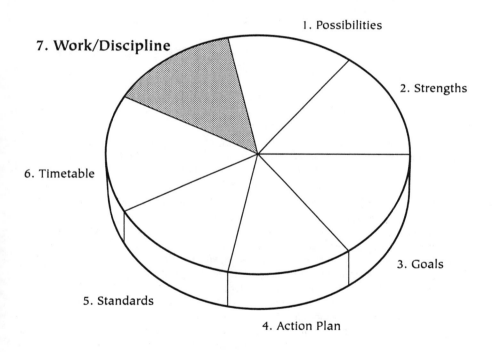

7

ISN'T IT STRANGE . . . ?
WHEN YOU LOVE LABOR,
YOU LOVE LIFE!

Need and Struggle are What Excite and Inspire Us.
William James

Whatever you do, work at it with all your heart, as working for the Lord, not for men, since you know that you will receive an inheritance from the Lord as a reward. It is the Lord Christ you are serving.
Paul (in Colossians 3:23-24)

The key to bringing the culture and the Church back together; to renewing the workplace and reforming the Church; to choosing Christ as the Lord of life, rather than leaving Him out of the system — may well be a movement of people who are known for their hard work, for the excellence of their effort, for their honesty and unswerving integrity, for their concerns for the rights and welfare of people, for their compliance with laws, standards, and policies, for the quality of their goods and services, for the quality of their character, for the discipline and sacrifice of their lifestyle, for putting work in its proper perspective, for their leadership among coworkers — in short, for their Christ-likeness on and off the job.
What could an army of such workers accomplish?
Doug Sherman and William Hendricks[1]

Key Points

Tough-minded faith in God's discipline enables us to work His plan and realize His and our dream. We point out in this chapter the importance of hard work and obstacles to overcome. Hard work at what our hands find to do succeeds dramatically. Faith working through love matters to God. He motivates us and works in us according to His good pleasure.

Secular organizations have learned that work and discipline prepare them for unexpected opportunities. The most excellent ones prepare best for whatever comes along. Jesus preached *preparation*, *responsibility*, and *accountability*. Churches can improve in using wise discipline and works of love. Christians who have learned work and discipline as habits find them rewarding and even fun. Small groups help all of us to pool ideas for effective achievement and necessary discipline.

✳✳✳✳

THIS chapter on work and discipline completes the circle with chapters one through six. All of the first six steps to achievement require disciplined work. All great achievement comes from a love for work and discipline. Work itself needs motivation from still deeper attitudes and principles. We will cover these in part two on the Dynamics of Motivation.

The excellent companies inspire workers and leaders to work and discipline themselves in the areas covered in our first six chapters:

◆ *Discover the best possibilities and opportunities*: What seems to be luck comes to those who prepare creatively and wisely for opportunities.

◆ *Develop strengths, talents, and gifts* to optimum levels: People achieve much more than many leaders expect from them. We all need to learn the tremendous value of *focusing on strengths* and not on weaknesses, what *can be done* and not on what won't work.

◆ *Set goals and organize them* in bite-sized chunks: People working together in teams respond best to the needs of markets and customers. They can make constant change work in their favor and diffuse the retarding force of bureaucracy.

◆ *Take effective action*: Experiment constantly with possibilities, strengths, and goals. Action-oriented people produce ten times as much value.

◆ *Make excellence the standard* for all planning and work: Look and listen for a better way, challenge the status quo, watch the markets not the hierarchy, and resist the pressure to conform and be polite where these undermine teamwork and group success.

◆ *Do first things first*: Base timetables on the most important priorities. Focus on *Toughminded Optimism* and *Total Quality*, not on politics, fear of change, and the negative thinking of *naysayers*.

What Are Researchers Discovering?

Scott Peck describes vividly the connection between discipline, work, responsibility and love:

> I can solve a problem only when I say "This is my problem and it's up to me to solve it." But many, so many, seek to avoid the pain of their problems by saying to themselves: "This problem was caused me by other people, or by social circumstances beyond my control, and therefore it is up to other people or society to solve this problem for me. It is not really my personal problem. . . ."
>
> The will to extend one's self for the purpose of nurturing one's own or another's spiritual growth. . . . When we love someone our love becomes demonstrable or real only through our exertion — through the fact that for that someone (or for ourself) we take an extra step or walk an extra mile. Love is not effortless. To the contrary, love requires great effort.[2]

We stress in these pages hard work and overcoming obstacles. Often, those people who appear to have it made from childhood by birth, rank, and perquisites do not make it in the end, whereas good old American hard work succeeds dramatically for other people with few advantages at the start.

Strangely, the majority of people on the planet have no idea of their possibilities. Our free enterprise system provides for freedom of economic, social, political, and spiritual enterprise. It offers us one of the most precious gifts human beings can have: the opportunity to choose from our possibilities. We are one nation under God . . . .

The Joy of Work and Discipline

The joy we receive from work and discipline is a direct product of how we perceive their meaning. Is work "keeping a stiff upper lip" and making a vow to work *hard*? Is *discipline* "facing up" heroically to a difficult task? Does that sound inviting, energizing, stimulating? Do these thoughts free you up, make your heart sing? I doubt it.

The most successful people achieve enormous results, but this is not because of rigid commitment or an obsessive approach to work. They *enjoy* work itself. All the great achievers see work as a privilege, an opportunity, a gift. They see

work and *discipline* as the only sure road to growth, joy, and fulfillment.

    Discipline is defined as "training which builds, molds and
strengthens." It produces a zestful concept of work. It has little
relationship to what is rigid and painful. Discipline and its
expression, work, will be joyful and rewarding only if nourished
by a transcendent goal and by a viable faith in God, yourself
and those around you. Your personal reality is tied directly to
your *perception* of work and discipline.

Joe Batten[3]

They Found the Truth To Be the Opposite of Traditional Wisdom

    Dr. Henry Link's professional group of researchers spread out
across the country to determine what a cross-section of Americans
of all types, at all levels of our society, could tell them about a life of
fulfillment and effectiveness.

    They found that *happy* people do *something difficult* virtually every
day, something which makes them reach down within themselves
and find a new kind of strength, a new capacity for coping, new
answers, new staying power.

    On the other hand, most unhappy people do precisely the oppo-
site. Over many years these people have developed an expedient set
of attitudes of avoiding anything very difficult. Consequently, as the
years go by, they build up feelings of inadequacy and self-loathing.
Such "unhappy" people forge a vicious circle which becomes
increasingly hard to break out of.

A Girl Who Wouldn't Be Stopped

    Dr. Eisenberger reports on people who work hard, and he calls
them America's industrious minority. He writes of Sandy's doctors
and teachers who told her that she had subnormal intelligence and
couldn't do normal tasks. She responded by trying all the harder:

    "When I wanted something, I just never gave up, ever. Especially if
    I thought my parents were holding me back because I couldn't
    handle it. Everybody always said, 'Look at little Sandy with the
    skinny arms. She's so weak.' In high school in my senior year they
    had a competition to see who was the most physically fit. I did 364
    push-ups, girl's push-ups, not guy's push-ups. But I was dying. I

said there's no way I am giving up. I did push-ups all through my gym class . . . and . . . English class. . . . I was jello the next day."

Sandy Roca's remarkable success overcoming her childhood disabilities shows that industriousness can be learned outside the home. Unfortunately, schooling and jobs in contemporary America have rarely been the source of strong work values.[4]

Eisenberger also gives us important evidence and recommendations concerning the work ethic in youth:

To ignore whether a child works hard to complete his chores or homework nurtures the child's laziness... Most adults with strong work values were frequently praised as children by their parents for high effort, were told of the importance of industriousness for a worthwhile life, and observed their parents practicing what they preached. Crucial to the child's acceptance of positive parental work values over the popular culture's glorification of indolence and sensuality is the existence of a strong emotional bond between child and parent. . . .

Parents who wish to instill strong work values in their children should bite the bullet; beginning when children are young, parents should take an active role in limiting youngsters' total daily [TV] watching time and the proportion of that time involving programs most damaging to the work ethic. . . . They [Children] could be encouraged to spend more time on homework and chores and more time reading books, getting out of the house to see friends, and chatting with parents.[5]

Life's Inmost Secret

◆ Charles De Gaulle shares a powerful message:
"A man of character finds a special effectiveness in difficulty, since it is only by coming to grips with difficulty that he can realize his potentialities."

New Obstacles and Difficulties

"My secret is that every morning I ask the Lord to provide me with new obstacles and difficulties." . . . She explained the meaning of her brief and sprightly remarks.

When Frank died, I had some moments of despair and my first thoughts about my family, of course, were for their security. I decided that I just might make a go of the consulting firm and slowly built it toward a satisfying level of profitability. Somewhere along the way I began to realize, as a result of the research I'd carried out, the exciting life Frank and I had together, and other factors, that boredom and lack of challenge were the chief enemies of a long, happy, and productive life.

As I steadily evolved toward a practice of actually seeking out challenges and tough situations to research and solve, I came to realize more and more that those were the moments in which I truly felt totally alive, creative, healthy, and happy. I began to notice as the years went by how many of my friends and colleagues lost their health and productive ability in direct proportion to the extent to which they avoided tough and exciting situations. Many of them who played it safe and secure just lost their basic zest for living.

Lillian Gilbreth[6]

◆ John W. Gardner said, "The best kept secret in America is that people would rather work hard for something they believe in . . . than enjoy a pampered idleness."

◆ Kahlil Gibran wrote,
Always you have been told that work is a curse, and labor is a misfortune. But I say to you that when you work you fulfill a part of earth's furthest dream, assigned to you when that dream was born. And in keeping yourself in labor you are in truth loving life. And, to love life through labor is to be intimate with life's inmost secret.[7]

Both young and old need to test the truth of Gibran's words for themselves, discovering the relationship between dreams, desires, and disappointments on the one hand and the realization of universal goals and values on the other.

What Are Secular Organizations Discovering?

The Role of Leaders: Leaders need more than integrity, competence, vision, and fair-mindedness. They need the discipline and wisdom to put adventure and excitement into the work of their people.

◆ Develop a vision consistent with the shared values of the company and the workers. It should not be at odds with the dignity of individuals.

◆ Inspire people to be and do the best that they can, and develop in them a winning attitude. Select inspiring and exciting goals, unique opportunities, and solvable problems. Get people working toward goals that give them the habit of winning.

◆ Encourage naysayers to change or "allow" them to find another job. The leaders in excellent companies employ only people who share enthusiastically in the vision, mission, and work of the organization.

◆ Give everyone a chance to contribute their personal share of work, and receive rewards according to their achievements. Don't perceive workers as "stupid."

Porsche: Bob Waterman tells how Peter Schultz, the head of Porsche, rejuvenated the company's winning spirit. Dr. Porsche designed both the Volkswagen Beetle and the Porsche sports cars. Soon after Schultz took over, he asked Dr. Porsche to describe his all-time best car, and Porsche answered with, "We haven't built it yet." He showed a winning spirit.

His managers told Schultz that they couldn't win the over-all 24-hour Le Mans Grand Prix, but they might win in their class. Schultz wouldn't hear "talk about not winning."

The next day he called another meeting to discuss "how they could win." They really got excited. They actually thought they could win if they had the chance to try. They put parts from a 917 Porsche into a 936 and made other improvisations. A retired race driver heard about it through word of mouth and volunteered to drive the car. They *won that race* and regained both their winning spirit and profitability.

According to Schultz, you can't teach people courage, you have to hire people with it. Good people won't stay for money alone. They want interesting work. Porsche kept the interest up by doing contract design work for other companies: the airbus, small cars for the Russians, and a formula 1 racing car.[8]

Give people every opportunity to be successful. Front-line workers know the most about their jobs. Make the work as interesting as possible. Give them freedom and expect them to do their best, and they will do great things without supervision.

◆ Give people opportunity on the job to experiment, learn new skills, and be cross trained. The best companies encourage and even require that their workers take outside courses. Many companies operate their own schools, because they know best how to train people to excel.

◆ Delegate a maximum of authority and responsibility. People work best with all the facts in the company available to them. People do marvelous work when they are given the tools they need and the freedom to do whatever they have to do. In our personal experience disciplined and highly motivated workers accomplish miracles. They come up with innovations that no one else would ever discover.

Humana took over the management of Louisville's General Hospital. It had lost $3.6 million in 1981 and could lose $10 million the next year. It had reduced its services to the bare bones and ran out of needed supplies daily. They called the Intensive Care Unit "pre-mortem," and during the summer, temperatures in some wards got up to 105 degrees.

Within three years Humana increased their care, put patients in double rooms instead of wards, gave the nurses flexible hours, and completely turned around the life of the hospital. They did the things they knew how to do best. The manager of the hospital, Gary Sherlock, listed four factors: (1) They copied what they had done elsewhere, better service at lower cost. (2) They treated people with dignity. (3) They insisted on good communications in both directions. (4) They motivated people with an inspiriting vision.

They started out with the adventure of turning around a terrible situation. They ended up by improving service to patients drastically, making a profit, increasing medical education and research, and cutting costs. Mary Powell said, "We've got a happy bunch of people around here."[9]

Project Teams (Possibility Teams): These break down the barriers that stifle and slow down needed action. Autonomous teams carry out work many times faster (10 to 30 times faster) and with far less cost than the traditional hierarchal organization does. Handoffs among several departments increase cost and create terrible delays and snafus. Teams working in the same location with one leader work best and have better discipline:

◆ Include people with the necessary expertise on the team full time. Reduce functional departments to the bare bones or eliminate them entirely.

◆ Allow teams to work together as a unit, set their own goals, and even choose their own leader. Then they own the project, and make it their job to reach the goals. Make them accountable to report periodically. Leaders should coach them rather than supervise.

◆ Choose team members from volunteers and expect them to cooperate fully with each other. Make open communication the standard with essentially no company data withheld. Creative freedom produces far more advantages than secrecy.

Tom Peters in *Liberation Management* tells his favorite story of a company completely changing its work-style to "self-managed cells/clusters/teams/businesses of 2 to 35." *Titeflex of Springfield, Massachusetts* makes fluid and gas holding hoses.

Before changing to small teams they made *300-400 pieces per month* and took from *9 to 11 weeks* to fill their orders. To process a new order Titeflex took numerous meetings and three to five weeks before any product got to manufacturing. Altogether ten different departments took part in some phase of the manufacturing and quality control before the order was delivered to shipping.

After President Jon Simpson organized Titeflex into cells of 5 to 10 people each, three such teams handled each order, the Genesis Team, the Business Development Team, and the Final Assembly Team. The workers themselves created the first self-managed team between Friday and Monday. The whole Industrial Products Division completed the change less than one month later. No real problem surfaced.

Simpson visited each of the three shifts and talked to people one on one. He learned their names, and this made a major impression on the workers. They opened their accounting books and gave people unlimited access to them. One old-time Teamster found the changes easy to accept because the workers had already asked for such changes.

Instead of *9 to 11 weeks* deliveries now took only *2 to 5 days*.

Productivity went up from *300 or 400 pieces* per month to *9,000 to 10,000 pieces* per month, a *thirty-fold increase*.

These "miraculous" improvements dramatically increased sales and profits.

Crash orders went to a two-man Rapid Deployment Team. Teamsters John Strange and Joe Tilli handled everything from order entry to shipping in *three to four hours*. For example, one aerospace customer came in with a rush order and left the same day at 1 p.m. with the part completed.[10]

We believe in small groups, not only in manufacturing and service organizations, but in the way Christians build relationships with each other and spread the wonderful news of Christ to the people they meet and know as friends and relatives. *Small cell groups work extremely effectively in virtually every circumstance.*

Freedom in supervision goes along with *tight controls on values*:

◆ Expect everyone to work and discipline themselves. Commit people to whatever it takes to get the best possible results. Expect failures that teach necessary lessons, but not foolish repetitive mistakes. Encourage and insist on continuous experiments.

◆ People learn to work smarter not harder. Make their jobs fun and rewarding. Enthusiasm leads to higher productivity, much faster deliveries, and more effective decisions.

◆ Important goals give jobs meaning. Involve the workers setting their own goals, working towards them, and receiving the rewards that come with victory.

◆ In many companies the Golden Rule makes their teams successful. People learn the importance of giving as well as receiving. People develop close relationships and love working together.

◆ Stress courage and integrity. Encourage people to work hard at learning, and support them in the work of continuous growth. Learning companies operate this way, and they move faster and serve better than companies that don't encourage constant learning.

People at Honda have a lot to say about their jobs. One manager said, "We want associates to use their heads . . . when the company solicits their thoughts, their hearts eventually are won . . . people have a total commitment to their company."

Department heads give associates control because "to do their best work they must fully understand their jobs and give their full commitment."

Honda wants workers to be innovative, improve quality, work more efficiently, and solve problems. They want people who can think and act in emergencies. Honda has respect for the individual; they develop a thinking workforce. They treat their workforce as their most valuable asset.[11]

How Jesus Viewed Work

Real work: It takes work to believe in Jesus as the One who came down from heaven and went back into heaven. God sent Him, but we often ignore what Jesus said and did. We put Him to death, because we loved our traditions, wanted nothing to change, and focused everything on "making it" in society. Jesus thrilled the common people who saw and heard Him, but when it came to risking everything for Him many turned from Him to save their own skins. They and we don't always want to work when it's hard and when it means

risking all that we have. We can know that Jesus' words are trustworthy, if we choose to do His will. We will find out eventually that
His teaching comes from God (John 7:17).

It takes commitment, discipline, and work to want to do God's
will. If the Bible teaches anything at all, it teaches us that working
towards a great, eternal vision may be thrilling, but it's a lifelong
work. It takes risk, and we will be criticized by those who focus only
on power, pleasure, and riches. In another example Jesus praised
Mary when she sat at His feet listening to His exciting stories. She
didn't want to lose any opportunity to learn great and eternal things
from Him. But how did her sister Martha feel about that? She not
only felt angry with Mary but she also blamed Jesus. Concerned primarily with many chores, she came to Him and asked, "Lord, don't
you care that my sister has left me to do the work by myself? Tell her
to help me!"

Jesus responded with discipline and tenderness: "Martha,
Martha, you are worried and upset about many things, but only one
thing is needed. Mary has chosen what is better, and it will not be
taken away from her" (Luke 10:40-42).

Jesus showed Martha that Mary had focused on the higher priority. If we put His message into perspective, everything else will fall
into place. Jesus definitely favored hard work, and we need to work
hard and discipline ourselves to do what really matters to Him? We
must properly integrate the secular with the eternal.

When Jesus began healing people who were insane, the religious
teachers said, "He is possessed by Beelzebub! By the prince of
demons he is driving out demons."

Even His family said, "He is out of his mind."

When Jesus found out that His mother and brothers were looking
for Him, He asked, "Who are my mother and my brothers?"

Then He shocked those sitting around Him with this surprising
answer: "Here are my mother and my brothers! Whoever does God's
will is my brother and sister and mother" (Mark 3:20-22,31-35).

Here we see the same distinction that Jesus made in all His
teaching and actions. We must seek to do God's will first, then we
can get everything else into the right framework. But we must work
to discover what pleases God. We must present our bodies to Him as
a living sacrifice. Only then will we be able to find out and know
what God's will is, what is good and pleasing to Him. We must work
hard to avoid the futility of this world's thinking, and allow God to
transform and renew our hearts and minds (Rom 12:2).

Work and money as ends in themselves: The Pharisees loved money, praise, and power as ends in themselves. Jesus offended them when He said, "You cannot serve both God and Money." The Pharisees, who loved money, sneered at Jesus, and He said to them, "You are the ones who justify yourselves in the eyes of men, but God knows your hearts. What is highly valued among men is detestable in God's sight" (Luke 16:13-16).

Money is important, but serving God is much more important. This higher priority makes all work exciting. Serving God brings great adventure, but it takes risk. People and leaders who worship money like the Pharisees did will sneer at us and write us off as fools. Excellent organizations know that many other priorities motivate people more than money. If we get our priorities right, treat people right, and work smart, then profits will result.

When Jesus told His followers to lay up treasures in Heaven He didn't promise ease. He did say, though, that robbers couldn't steal, rust couldn't tarnish, and moths couldn't eat up the treasures we build up in heaven. But these things certainly happen to treasures accumulated on earth. He taught the same lesson in the story of the *rich ruler* (Matt 19:16-30) and His parable of the *rich fool* (Luke 12:13-31).

How do we keep our hearts and minds on the great lessons that Jesus taught? Why preoccupy ourselves with money, power, and our reputations? Why fear losing what we have and being looked down on as fools? It's not easy to follow Jesus. It's hard work, and it takes lifelong discipline. Even our own families may think that we're out of our mind.

Churches need to put first things first, make church work exciting, and expect the best from their leaders and their people. We will commit ourselves to Christ's high principles and become what He wants us to be.

Work in the parables:
We have stressed parables as the backbone of Jesus' teaching. We described the parables as secular stories that reveal higher spiritual truths, truths of eternal importance. Most of the parables deal with work, and many of them involve money. In the parable of the vineyard (Matt 21:33-46) the owner expected the *wicked tenants* to work as if the vineyard were their own. And he expected them to give him a reasonable return on his investment. What did they do? They saw an opportunity to take over the vineyard and keep everything for themselves. First they beat up the owner's servants who were sent to

get his share of the production. Next they killed some of his servants. Finally, they killed his son, because they thought they could grab ownership of the vineyard.

Don't we do the same thing when we live our lives to make money, get rich, own property and businesses, and feel no obligation to God? Who gives us the air we breathe and the lungs we breathe with? Where do we get our food, our mouths and stomachs? Who designed our hearts to beat 60 or 70 times per minute? Who made our blood, arteries, and veins? God made our lives like the vineyard, and God expects us to use our lives to serve Him. Do you see the importance of work and discipline in choosing to do His will? *Do you see the connection between Jesus' lessons and the discoveries of excellent companies.* They learn to do what serves their customers the best and motivates their people to the highest achievements. He wants us to work wisely and grasp the opportunities He provides.

Jesus taught another amazing parable on work. In this story, people who really wanted to work for the owner got the same wages no matter how long they worked. Normally those who work the longest should get more than those who start working later. But God treats *right attitudes as important as long hours.* He values only work based on the best values and attitudes. In teaching English to Cambodian refugees Warren paraphrased the Parable of the Workers in the Vineyard (Matt 20:1-16) to show them that God accepted them even though they came from a foreign country and hadn't been Christians very long:

> *Jesus loves even those who start working late.* He told a story that shows how God treats poor and weak people. It's called the parable of *"The workers in the vineyard."* In the story a landowner hired men to work for him. Some he hired early in the day. Others he hired a little later. Finally he hired some people who worked for only one hour. When it came time to pay everyone, he paid those who went to work last the same amount as he paid the first ones.
>
> The people who worked all day got angry and grumbled, "These people who were hired last worked only one hour, while we did a whole day's work in the hot sun. Yet you paid them the same as you paid us!" The boss reminded them, "I haven't cheated you. You agreed to work all day for the amount that I paid you. Now take your pay and go home. I want to give the people who were hired last as much as I gave you. Don't I have the right to do as I wish with my own money? Or are you jealous because I am generous?" Jesus told his disciples the meaning of the story: "So

those who are last will be first, and those who are first will be last. This is how it is in the Kingdom of heaven."

At first I found this story hard to understand. As I learned more about God, I came to understand how wonderful this story is. In our society companies pay people by the hour and how much they do. In heaven God welcomes people there because they believe in Christ. Remember the story of the thief on the cross? And remember what Jesus said about the tax collectors, the prostitutes, poor people, and little children. God accepts people who the rich, the powerful, and the educated sometimes despise and look down on. They worked only a short time in the vineyard. The rich and powerful often think that they do all the work. They expect to get the best and the most. But God honors the humble person, the one who has good attitudes and also works. God can use humble people in heaven, but he can't use the proud who demand that God honor them. Another way to look at this story is this: Jesus' own people thought that they should be first and the Gentiles last. God accepts both Jew and Gentile because of their faith, a faith that works through love. (See Gal 5:6.)

God pays the workers who come to work last the same as the workers who come to work early. All get rewarded for obeying the Master, not for how much work they did. Since God wants to save all people, he does not show favoritism to the powerful, educated, and rich. In all societies these people come in first and make the most money. These people have an advantage over weak and poor people. God treats all people fairly and yet, He doesn't show favoritism to the poor and weak people.

Please notice this about the above parable: it's very similar to Jesus' famous parable of the *Prodigal Son* (Luke 15:11-32), only the prodigal son story is better understood and more loved. The *father* who welcomed the prodigal boy back home was like the *landowner* who gave as much to those who worked only one hour as those who had "borne the burden of the work and the heat of the day." The *wayward son* was like the *people who worked only one hour* but got a full day's pay. Just as the *older brother* complained bitterly about the party his father gave for the *prodigal son (his younger brother)*, those who worked all day complained bitterly to the landowner.

Maybe we've lost sight of how we get our lives, our food, and our clothing. Maybe some pseudo-intellectuals consider themselves unworthy of eternal life and persuade us also to give up our hope, our faith, and our common sense. The one-talent person in Jesus' parable of the *Talents* (Matt 25:14-30) teaches the same lesson about work and money. If we lose touch with eternal possibilities and goals, we can lose touch with how we invest our money, our time, and our lives. The five-talent and the two-talent persons both doubled their master's investment in them. They chose the right priorities; they disciplined themselves and worked with the money given to them to be productive. The one-talent person was lazy. Not only that, he believed that his master was hard and unfair. He buried his talent in a napkin because he was shortsighted, lazy, and wicked. The real subject here is not money. It's about the character of our lives. Do we serve God in our relationships, or do we exclude Him and make economic success our top priority?

At the same time Jesus taught another astounding parable, one that is not loved very much by those who stress working for the wrong things and ignoring their relationships. The *story of the sheep and the goats* (Matt 25:31-46) shows that we will be rewarded for working on our relationships, especially if we help needy people. The people who worked hard (*the sheep*) at the highest and best principles didn't even realize that they were doing what pleased God the most. They served Christ unknowingly by helping the poor, sick, imprisoned, and strangers. The people who did nothing (*the goats*) for the needy people around them didn't even realize their negligence in serving Christ.

What Can We Learn to Do Differently?

1. We can learn to see the parallels between what Jesus taught and what excellent organizations practice in the secular world:

◆ These organizations develop good relationships with customers to know their needs and serve them best. Leaders don't coddle and spoil people in their company who resist and complain. They insist on vision, discipline, commitment, and character.

◆ Leaders inspire all their associates by making the work exciting, adventurous, and with high purpose. They create a winning attitude and get everyone working together towards the most valuable possibilities.

◆ These companies use autonomous small groups and teams who volunteer to "sign on." Communications are completely open. They have the authority to get things done, the cooperation of all team members, and the necessary skills included on the team or available to it.

◆ They keep discovering and building on the best and highest values

such as integrity, trust, competence, inspiration, and fair-mindedness. They EXPECT THE BEST!

2. We can learn to see how Jesus' parables, teachings, and actions
have simple and common themes:

◆ Compare the three parables in Matthew 25, the teaching on the
wise and faithful servants in Matthew 24, and the same teaching
in Luke 12. There is a common theme in these. The good people
will be living to do God's will because they love God and want to
serve Him. The bad people will not prepare to meet God because
they hate Him and His will. They don't want to serve Him, and
this shows in all their relationships with others. Notice how they
ignore God's desires and concern themselves with other priorities.
They tend to serve their own selfish agenda. Many in leadership
positions turned out to be corrupt. (See Luke 12:35-48.)

◆ Now take a look at the parable of the Good Samaritan in Luke
10:25-37 and compare it with what we have studied above. The
priest and the Levite were supposed to be good at serving God,
but they walked right by without helping the person in dire need.
They, who considered all Samaritans to be no-good "dogs," had
no compassion, but the Samaritan showed mercy and compassion. He met the needs of the person who had been robbed and
beaten. We see here the same lesson repeated: God wants mercy
and love for others rather than religious hypocrisy. He wants
people to listen to Jesus and be sensitive to the simplicity of what
He teaches and models.

◆ Read Matthew 7 especially verses 1-5 and 15-28. We see the
same pattern in those who judge others and don't examine themselves, the bad tree that can only bear bad fruit, and the foolish
builder who builds his house on the sand. All those mentioned
here by Jesus refused to work at knowing God's will.

Those who cast the log out of their own eyes first, trees that
bear only good fruit, and wise people who build on a rock foundation represent those who listen to Jesus and do what He says.

◆ Finally, read in Matthew 6:19-24 what Jesus said about laying up
treasures in Heaven, having eyes that are good, and serving God
rather than Money as an end in itself. Here we see the same division of people into good and bad, wise and foolish. We must
choose to work for and be guided by Jesus. Could it be any simpler?

There is an astounding parallel between work in secular organizations and work in churches. The major factors include (1) how we

handle people relationships, (2) whether or not we get isolated from the real opportunities, (3) and how well we listen to and use Christ's truth and wisdom. (See 1 Cor 1:26-31; 2:1-16.)

We are confident that churches will keep improving in the way they work for Jesus. They can trust people just as much as the better secular organizations do. They will keep learning new things and keep working and disciplining themselves to grow in the knowledge of God. The Spirit will help them discover "what God's will is — his good, pleasing, and perfect will" (Rom 12:2).

What Can Grassroots Christians Do?

◆ We can learn from our experiences in secular companies that work at putting people first and serving their customers well. With patience and humility we can help other Christians to see new ways to serve God.

◆ We can make discipline a good word by discovering the joy of changing for the better!

◆ Jesus prayed for unity. We need to do the hard work of examining what we believe, making sure we don't exclude those whom God accepts. God wants us to work at bringing people into His family.

◆ God designed and created our eyes and brains. We should work harder in our study of His words. The Holy Spirit helps us, but we can grieve and handicap Him by failing to learn what God wants us to learn. Compare our time spent watching "global gossip" on TV, eating food for our bodies, and eating the Bread of Life. Are we giving Jesus enough time?

◆ God promises to give us joy, if we truly love Christ and His message. Christ gave us God's Word to make our joy complete. We can be filled with incomparable, irresistible joy and hope in Christ but it takes work and discipline. (See 1 Peter 1:3-9,17-25; 2:1-5.)

Jesus often told His trainees to work for the night was coming when no one could work. He disciplined Himself and He didn't see hard work as exploitation. He asks us to live only one life here on this earth, and He expects us to put our hands to the plow and work at knowing and doing God's will. He promises the greatest gift anyone could ever hope for: eternal life in heaven.

◆ Why do we often prefer pleasure for a short time instead of working and disciplining ourselves according to the teachings of Jesus? Why should we choose to remain in the dark? (See John 3:19-21; 8:12; 9:4-5; Eph 5:8-14.)

◆ Let's listen to Jesus and serve the needy and other Christians with dedication.

◆ Jesus, for the joy set before Him endured death by crucifixion. He ignored and thought nothing of the shame connected with such a death (Heb 12:1-2). He had no place to lay His head while He traveled over Palestine doing the work that His Father sent Him to do (Matt 8:18-22). We can say with Him, "I have come to do your will, O God" (Heb 10:7).

◆ Paul is a wonderful example of hard work for a transcendent cause. He worked harder than all the rest, and he looked forward with joy to the crown that Christ had promised to him. (See 1 Cor 15:10; 2 Cor 11:23; 2 Tim 4:8.) He counted everything he had accomplished as a Pharisee as rubbish for the *surpassing worth of knowing Jesus* (Phil 3:7-9). We can follow Paul's famous words telling us to work out our own salvation with fear and respect, for that is how God works in us according to His own pleasure (Phil 2:12-13).

◆ Read the first five books of the New Testament and examine the kind of discipline Jesus followed and taught the Twelve to apply to their lives. Even though faith saves us, God desires for each of us to grow to full maturity in Christ. (See Gal 5:22-26.)

◆ God disciplines us for our own good. We can't pay anything to God for what He gives to us, but we can desire to do His will. Jesus said, "If anyone chooses to do God's will, he will find out whether my teaching comes from God or whether I speak on my own" (John 7:17). God wants us to find out what is pleasing to Him. (See Rom 12:1-2; 2 Cor 5:9; Eph 5:17,20; Col 1:10; 1 John 3:21-23.)

◆ God did not design us to be mere spectators that show up once per week to hear a 30 minute message, inspirational or otherwise. He created us to be in good relationships with Him and with those around us. He wants us to change our hearts and come into a relationship with Him and with each other. It takes work and discipline to achieve what seems so simple to understand. (See Matt 7:6-14.)

A Small Groups Agenda:

We experienced an exciting small group meeting using the following plan:

1. *Icebreaker (30 minutes)*: We had each person tell the group in detail about their first job as a young person. How old were they?

Where did they work? What kind of work was it? What did they learn, etc.?

2. *Read related Bible passages (10 minutes)*: We had each person take turns reading three or four verses until all of Luke 12:13-48 was read through.

3. *Discuss Jesus' teaching (30 minutes)*: We related Jesus' various ideas to our priorities in practical work, how to treat other people, and applying what Jesus taught.

4. *Prayer for needs (10 minutes)*: We invited each person to pray for known needs.

5. *Vision (10 minutes)*: The leaders presented an exciting vision for the future of small groups, how intimacy will be developed and a family climate will become more real.

Conclusions

We can learn a lot from excellent organizations that have successfully inspired their people to work smart, cooperate instead of compete, and achieve great things. They have developed visionary leaders with discipline, integrity, and love for people.

Many churches do the same. We believe that Christ works in all believers. We will continue to work at understanding the needs of God's "customers." The Spirit will motivate us to work at knowing and doing God's will. We will become more like a family as we associate in small groups. Our joy will become complete as we grow in producing the fruit of the Spirit. God will work out His purposes in us as He has promised. We can glorify Christ best in this way.

REFERENCES

1. Doug Sherman and William Hendricks, *Your Work Matters To God*, (Colorado Springs: NavPress, 1987), 269.

2. M. Scott Peck, *The Road Less Traveled*, (New York: Simon & Schuster, 1978), 32, 33, 81, 83.

3. Batten, *Tough-minded Leadership*, 180.

4. Robert Eisenberger, *Blue Monday*, (New York: Paragon House, 1989), 145-149.

5. Ibid., 220-224.

6. Batten, *Tough-minded Leadership*, 23.

7. Kahlil Gibran, *The Prophet*, (New York: Alfred A. Knopf, Inc., 1923 renewal copyright 1951 by Administrators C.T.A. of Kahlil Gibran Estate, and Mary C. Gibran).

8. Waterman, *The Renewal Factor*, 300-337.

9. Ibid., 316-318.

10. Peters, *Liberation Management*, 62-71.

11. Shook, *Honda*, 125-126.

DYNAMICS OF MOTIVATION

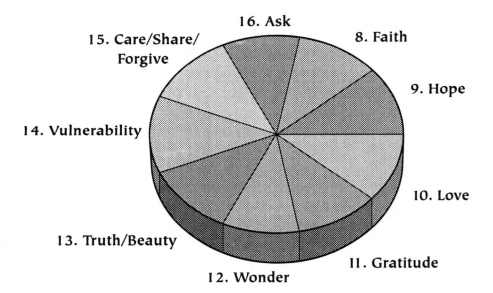

Part Two: The Dynamics of Motivation

In Part Two we cover the dynamics of relationships in Christ. Laws, rules and principles by themselves are not enough. We must also want to serve the one who gives us the laws and principles in the first place.

Jesus challenged the leaders of his own nation because they had misinterpreted and misapplied God's laws. They missed God's intent so badly that God's purpose for them had been nullified. Traditions are good if they are God's traditions, but what actually happened?

Jesus criticized them for making people give their money to "God" (actually to them) rather than supporting their aged parents. Obviously this principle brought more money to the religious leaders, but it voided one of the ten commandments: "Honor your father and your mother, so that you may live long in the land the LORD your God is giving you" (Exod 20:12). He explained to them how they had twisted one of God's fundamental principles:

> Moses said, 'Honor your father and your mother,' and, 'Anyone who curses his father or mother must be put to death.' But you say that if a man says to his father or mother: 'Whatever help you might otherwise have received from me is Corban' (that is, a gift devoted to God), then you no longer let him do anything for his father or mother. Thus you nullify the word of God by your tradition that you have handed down. And you do many things like that" (Mark 7:10-13).

Some years later, Paul explained that the purpose of God's law was to teach us the terrible nature and power of human evil. Laws and principles, even though they are good and important, don't by themselves motivate a person to develop right attitudes. We must have a trust and a motivation that is much higher, more personal, and more effective than simply knowing the right rules. (See Rom 7:7-16.)

How does God overcome the law's ineffectiveness? Christ provides us with the answer! God's children allow the Spirit of God to lead them and we share the glorious life of Christ. In fact, our present sufferings and obstacles are not worth comparing with the tremendous glory that will be revealed to us. In all things God works for the good of those who love him and have been called according to his purpose. (See Rom 8:18-28.) Therefore,

> . . . we are more than conquerors through him who loved us. For I am convinced that neither death nor life, neither angels nor

demons, neither the present nor the future, nor any powers, neither height nor depth, nor anything else in all creation, will be able to separate us from the love of God that is in Christ Jesus our Lord (Rom 8:37-39).

Christ motivates us! We work together with Him, allowing Him to build us up in His love, and allowing Him to motivate us by all the power that He mightily inspires within us. As John stated, "his commands are not burdensome, for everyone born of God has overcome the world. *This is the victory* that has overcome the world, *even our faith*. Who is it that overcomes the world? Only he who believes that Jesus is the Son of God" (1 John 5:3-5).

We must believe that God exists and that He rewards those who seek Him. By faith we anticipate what we hope for and wait patiently for what we do not yet see. We understand that God formed the universe. "[W]hat is seen was not made out of what was visible." (See Heb 11:1-6.)

What happens when we have a dynamic faith in God? *A tremendous hope for the future* in this life and in the life to come motivates us. Christ energizes us by His Holy Spirit and helps us live an abundant life. We look forward to life in heaven, and we work out God's vital and dynamic mission here on this earth.

God motivates us to *love* Him with all our heart, soul, mind, and strength. We can love because He first loved us. He teaches us how to *love* other people as we love ourselves. He gives us the power to see and achieve *an inspired vision* for our lives. *Faith* plus *hope* plus *love* develops in us a true spirit of *gratitude* for every perfect gift that God so generously gives to us. On this foundation comes all of the other attitudes, values and principles that motivate us to glorify God by our lives and our work.

It's vital to keep the *big picture* in focus and to develop leadership skills on that perspective.

To motivate here's what excellent organizations do

1. *Delegate most things to teams.* Allow mistakes, because people must experiment constantly to discover valuable truths and better ways of doing things. People must be vulnerable to mistakes and failures or nothing new and valuable can be learned.

2. *Let teams manage themselves*, because this leads to greater effectiveness than the defensive command and control management style. Freedom motivates, and over-control de-motivates.

3. *Encourage teams to contact customers and suppliers directly.* This opens up valuable opportunities.

4. *Allow peer pressure to provide most of the required control.* This motivates team members effectively and also reveals who needs encouragement or reassignment. Insist on firm character standards, on integrity, positive thinking, and enthusiastic participation.

5. *Reward performance* with bonuses that the team itself decides how to use. Base rewards on *results* and not on *activity*.

6. *Reduce headquarters staff* and give them the option of finding line jobs where they can contribute directly. Make valuable know-how available to all parts of the company by encouraging experts to travel and to communicate by computer.

7. *Allow a free flow of information* with no secrets. This produces faster innovation and problem solving. It encourages valuable participation by those who may have had no previous opportunity to contribute. Openness leaves the organization vulnerable, but this produces far greater advantages and motivation than the *stagnation of stultifying secretiveness*.

8. *Challenge the status quo.* Change upsets, but improvement is impossible without constant innovation. New opportunities come only to those who seek and develop better products, better services, and better solutions.

RECOMMENDED READING

George Barna, *Turning Vision Into Action*, (Gospel Light).

Joe Batten and Mark Victor Hansen, *The Master Motivator*, (Health Communications).

John C. Maxwell, *Developing the Leader Within You*, (Nelson).

Frank Tillapaugh, *Unleashing the Church*, (Regal Books).

Sherwood Eliot Wirt, *Jesus, Man of Joy*, (Here's Life Publishers).

_____, *The Book of Joy*, (McCracken Press).

M. Scott Peck, *The Road Less Traveled*, (Simon & Schuster).

C.S. Lewis, *The Weight of Glory*, (Eerdmans).

Philip Yancey, *The Jesus I Never Knew*, (Zondervan).

Win Arn, Carroll Nyquist and Charles Arn, *Who Cares About Love?*, (Church Growth Press).

Stephen Covey, *The Seven Habits of Highly Successful People*, (Simon & Schuster).

James M. Kouzes and Barry Z. Posner, *The Leadership Challenge*, (Jossey-Bass Publishers).

CHAPTER EIGHT
FAITH

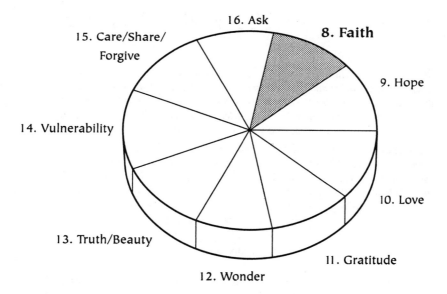

15. Care/Share/ Forgive

16. Ask

8. Faith

9. Hope

14. Vulnerability

10. Love

13. Truth/Beauty

11. Gratitude

12. Wonder

8

FAITH BUILDS ON THE
BEST FOUNDATION

*Trust . . . is the central issue in human relationships both within and outside the
organization. Trust is an essential element of organizational effectiveness as well.
You demonstrate your trust in others through your actions — how much you check
and control their work, how much you delegate and allow people to participate.*
James M. Kouzes and Barry Z. Posner[1]

*Jesus rebuked the demon, and it came out of the boy, and he was healed from that
moment. Then the disciples came to Jesus in private and asked, "Why couldn't we
drive it out?" He replied, "Because you have so little faith. I tell you the truth, if you
have faith as small as a mustard seed, you can say to this mountain, 'Move from
here to there' and it will move. Nothing will be impossible for you."*
Jesus (in Matthew 17:18-21)

Key Points

Highly successful organizations build on faith in people and faith
in the possibilities. Jesus showed that *faith motivates people to expect
the best from God and from themselves.* Leaders can develop more trust
in God's powerful presence and activity. Christians can apply their
faith to produce amazing results; they can inspire the churches to
greater achievement for Christ. Involvement in small groups creates
the most effective relationships and helps believers build their faith
together in community.

✳✳✳✳

How Do Secular Organizations Build on Faith?

◆ How does faith motivate us? Leaders can see and believe in the big picture. We trust in and follow leaders based on their integrity and their trustworthiness. Good leaders honor others and create a climate of trust.

◆ Why is a trust climate best? It gets people on our side and motivates everyone to cooperate. It develops strong and lasting relationships, produces constant innovation, and creates a winning spirit. We accept failures as necessary learning experiences.

◆ Peer pressure in a trust climate keeps individuals more responsible and highly productive than does a command and control environment with low trust.

◆ We respond to the market place in healthy and dynamic ways, because we trust, hear, and treat all people involved with dignity rather than disdain, arrogance, and tunnel vision.

Trust and Faith Motivate

Trust and faith are integral parts of a value system that empowers people and motivates them to maximum levels of happiness, productivity, and actualization.

Faith without passion is like soda water without the sparkle. Without these renewing feelings of trust, faith, hope, and love our behavior on the job, in the home, and in the community will be insecure, defensive, and cynical. We miss the great possibilities.

The sheer practicality of faith is enormous. Faith, trust, and belief are alike. You and I can do virtually anything if our belief in ourselves, our fellow person, and God is strong and growing. We will be in dynamic relationship with others around us and motivated to be the best that we can be.

Joe Batten

Examples of Organizations Stressing Trust and Faith

Jim Burke of Johnson & Johnson: Warren Bennis tells the story of how Jim Burke dealt with the Tylenol crisis that happened a number of years ago. Someone inserted poison into Tylenol capsules, and several people died from using the poisoned medicine. J&J did not know who had committed this crime or how many packages had been poisoned. They could have lost the Tylenol product because of this terrible disaster.

Burke knew that he had to act fast and responsibly. He knew what to do, and he believed that he could do it. He believed in the fairness of the American people and that they would make the right decision in the end. He had a team working on new tamper-proof packaging, and it did in a few days what would normally take several years. Burke had groups with video cameras out with the public recording the consumer's point of view. He and others reviewed these tapes daily to understand people's reactions.

He got advice from everyone because nothing like this had ever happened before. His son commented that this unique crisis really tested Burke's philosophy. Only one other person in the company supported Burke. The head of public relations got angry with him when Burke decided to appear on "60 Minutes." He accused Burke of making an irresponsible decision, the worst in the history of the corporation. Burke believed that he would do OK with Mike Wallace and the viewing audience as long as he told the truth completely.

Jim Burke had faith in himself, in Johnson & Johnson's Credo, in the fairness of the public, and in the process of going public with all the available facts. He said, "We put the public first. We never hid anything from them and were as honest as we knew how to be. It confirmed my belief that if you play it straight, it works." He believed they could save the Tylenol product, and they did.[2]

Three months after the affair, 93% of people polled by Roper said that J&J handled the crisis well. One year after the tragedy, their Nielsen rating was 90% of what it was before the poisonings. Burke exclaimed that the customers "gave us back our business." Tom Peters and Nancy Austin said that Burke's words were exhilarating to them: "'Seeing' a value live . . . is remarkable, yet will always remain impossible for the skeptic and cynic."[3]

As a leader Jim Burke responded in a way that illustrates faith and trust in a number of exemplary ways:
◆ Proceed with trust and openness, and people will usually respond with trust.
◆ Don't compromise with unethical or cowardly behavior.
◆ Have complete integrity, which is the basis of trust.
◆ Take the necessary risks to maintain trust and build a climate of trust.
◆ Know your purpose and have complete faith in it.

Semco S/A: When President Ricardo Semler joined this company started by his father it had 100 employees and was very loosely held together. As it grew to over 1,000 employees he wanted to trust and empower people and not be a bureaucracy. He didn't follow the advice of others that would have produced a traditional organizational structure. He cut management levels from eleven to three, and started autonomous divisions when the number of associates got above 200 to 250. Each division averages about 150 and is led by a partner ("general manager" in traditional companies). Twelve to fourteen people in leadership positions report to each divisional partner, and teams averaging about ten associates report to each leader.

Each person rotates job responsibility every two to three years. They have no nitpicking regulations and no job descriptions. They call workers associates and treat them with dignity. Semco relies on a climate of mutual trust and respect. All associates work on flex time, and the company distributes 23% of after-tax profit to the teams. The teams decide how to spend the money, but most divide it equally. The organization endures, cooperates, and adapts well. Not only do they trust people, they motivate people to use their minds and develop their potential. No corporate manuals exist. Everybody expects to feel responsible for contributing and doing something worthwhile.

Semco asks people who ordinarily might leave to start their own company to stay and start a joint business. They move into a relationship where they have no boss and no subordinates. They set their own salaries, do whatever they want, and are evaluated annually. Seven joint ventures, three companies, and eighteen product lines began this way. Both Semco and the individuals come out much better than if they had parted company.

What does all this illustrate?

◆ We see the advantages that come from a climate of trust and respect for individuals.

◆ Cooperation and innovation result from strong and excellent relationships.

◆ Semco trusts and empowers people to grow and contribute. They get more done.

◆ They honor people for their accomplishments and give them high visibility.

◆ Semco provides a less aggressive and more rewarding climate. This opens up everyone to discover hidden and unexpected opportunities.

◆ They focus on gains and possibilities, not on losses and what can't be done.

◆ They make trust the lubricant of relationships, and many become lifelong and fruitful.[4]

Quad/Graphics: CEO Harry Quadracci and his managers spend a strategic planning day away from the plant every spring. Rather than shut down they let the hourly employees run the presses. They trust people by giving up control and this gives them even better control. The more they delegate to the frontline worker, the better the results and the control.

Quadracci also stressed being in touch with people. He placed the visitors' waiting area between his office and the washroom so he would have to keep in touch with who was visiting. He puts faith in what customers, suppliers, and other visitors have to say.

They operate Quad Camps for customers and employees where the customers spend one full day working through production. He and his associates have them as house guests. This keeps his people and his customers in close communication. They relate directly and don't depend on "the hierarchy to solve problems."[5]

Quadracci trusts employees to work responsibly. He showed it dramatically by giving the truckers the keys to their Peterbilts. The message? We trust you to make the organization successful.[6]

Everyone works on six-member press teams, so you have to take the initiative or else. If you don't want to pull your load, fellow workers give you the boot. "There's no personnel Department at Quad." They hire kids who don't go to college and get them learning on a press team. Everyone works four ten-hour days. On Fridays they go to school at "the firm's Little Red Schoolhouse." Quad is a learning company.

Quad Tech develops new technology constantly, and they sell the technology to others. This keeps the heat on their own R&D efforts. Quadracci trusts his R&D unit, Quad Tech, to keep innovation on the cutting edge. They are always "at work on the next generation of innovation."[7]

Everyone at Quad/Graphics learns to take the initiative. One trucker asked what to back-haul on the return from a west coast trip. Harry said, "How should I know? I don't know anything about driving an 18-wheeler." He turned and walked away — Management by Walking Away. Harry doesn't define responsibility. Nothing is ever "somebody else's responsibility." The person seeing something to do should take the responsibility. Quadracci doesn't tell employees what to do.[8]

At Quad the following prevails:

◆ A climate of trust motivates and empowers all employees.

◆ Autonomous teams replace bureaucracy in this trust climate.

◆ Trust motivates people to learn and innovate for the rest of their lives.

◆ Relationships and cooperation flower in this open, positive climate.

◆ People don't pass the buck because Quad trusts them and expects them to take responsibility and make their own decisions.

Why Faith Was Important to Jesus

◆ He brought *truths* from heaven that were basic to quality life both on earth and in heaven. We need more than anything else to listen to Him and believe in Him (John 6:29).

◆ The *beatitudes* require little or no formal education and start a person on the road to maximum faith in God and then in self. The organizations we've described often educate and motivate their people to achieve excellence in a climate of trust (Matt 5:3-12).

◆ With *faith* we can relate to our Creator and His creation in a way that pleases Him. We believe that He helps us toward this perfect goal, but this requires constant personal innovation and improvement (Matt 5:48).

◆ The *eye* (of faith) is the lamp of the body. If the eye is good, the body will be full of light. Wisdom has a source. Even secular organizations use the principles taught and practiced by Jesus (Matt 6:22-23).

◆ *Trust* and *faith* eliminate anxiety and worry; they motivate people to develop optimum effectiveness. This is the goal of excellent organizations (Matt 6:25-34).

◆ *Asking, seeking,* and *knocking* depend on *faith,* and express the innovative spirit. Many of the excellent companies claim the Golden Rule as their fundamental philosophy, the principle that works the best (Matt 7:7-12). Faith in self and the help that God constantly supplies also leads to maximum achievement in the things that God desires.

◆ With faith we will *build* our lives and everything that we think and do on what God makes possible. Nothing at all is possible without Him. With faith in Christ and in His principles we can face all trials and develop all opportunities. (See Matt 7:24-27; John 15:1-8.)

Not in All Israel

Why did Jesus say of the centurion, "I have not found anyone in Israel with such great faith"? Why was He so amazed? This man had an unusual insight into who Jesus really was. He used his own practical experience as a parable illustrating the spiritual power and authority that Jesus had in the Kingdom of Heaven. Jesus used parables in the majority of His teachings. He made them simple, so simple a child could understand them. They got the point across. They touched people where they were, in their own daily experiences. People remembered them. Once explained, people understood them easily. They also confounded His sophisticated enemies.

The centurion understood that Jesus had the ability and authority to heal his servant. He believed that Jesus had control over nature and over the spiritual realm just as he had control over his soldiers and slaves. So he compared and integrated his own daily experiences with the role that Jesus filled in the invisible spiritual world. It's no wonder that Jesus complimented this man's marvelous faith. Few people use the magnificent world that God has designed and created to figure out what Christ does as the Lord of heaven and earth. This man believed in and treated *the invisible eternal realm* with much more importance than *the little picture of life on earth*. (See Matt 8:5-13.)

The Canaanite Woman's Faith

The woman whose daughter suffered terribly from demon-possession also responded to Jesus with great faith. Jesus drew out her faith by pretending that He could do nothing for her. Her persistence bothered His disciples and they complained to Jesus, "Send her away, for she keeps crying out after us."

She saw that He behaved differently than His disciples did. He used irony to shame the disciples and encourage her to present her dilemma. Jesus told her, "It is not right to take the children's bread and toss it to the dogs."

She came right back with, "Yes, Lord, but the dogs eat the crumbs that fall from their master's table."

What a delicious expression of faith. She completed His parable with one of her own, and Jesus responded with, "You have great faith, woman." God healed her daughter immediately. (See Mark 7:24-30.)

Christ also enables people to succeed when they have faith in their own abilities and in the wonderful potential of the raw materials and natural laws of the physical creation. He gives even greater victories when, like the Canaanite woman, we exercise our faith in Him. "This is love for God: to obey his commands. And his commands are not burdensome, for everyone born of God overcomes the world. This is the victory that has overcome the world, even our faith. Who is it that overcomes the world? Only he who believes that Jesus is the Son of God" (1 John 5:3-5).

What does this work of believing Jesus consist of? Early in His preaching He taught the parable of the wise and foolish builders (Matt 7:24-27). The wise person not only hears His words but puts them into practice. We must put our faith where it matters most, in eternal values and rewards. (See Matt 16:25-26.)

Tough-minded Sayings of Jesus

The day after Jesus fed the 5,000 with five loaves of bread and a few fish, the crowds came back for more. He saw that they thought more about filling their bellies than the significance of His miracle. Jesus told them to work for God, not for the bread that filled their bellies (John 6:27-29). Many of His followers began to leave when He told them, "I am the true bread that came down from heaven. You must eat this bread to have eternal life." They wanted bread alright, but they rebelled when He used bread, flesh, and blood as metaphors for taking His message seriously. They said, "This is a hard teaching. Who can accept it?"

Aware that his disciples were grumbling about this, Jesus said to them, "Does this offend you? What if you see the Son of Man ascend to where he was before! The Spirit gives life; the flesh counts for nothing. The words I have spoken to you are spirit and they are life."

From this time many of his disciples turned back and no longer followed him. "You do not want to leave too, do you?" Jesus asked the Twelve. Simon Peter answered him, "Lord, to whom shall we go? You have the words of eternal life. We believe and know that you are the Holy One of God." (See John 6:43-69.)

Jesus did not let people with critical and negative attitudes stay in their comfort zones. He didn't let people feel proud and conceited in their wrong views and foolish attitudes. He demanded voluntary faith and tough-minded wisdom. He expected the best!

Nicodemus, a Pharisee and Seeking Member of the Highest Council:

Nicodemus, a member of the ruling Jewish council, came to Jesus at night. He knew that Jesus had to come from God because of the wonderful things Jesus did. Jesus astounded him by saying, "You must be born again." Yet people like Nicodemus rejected His testimony even though Jesus told them the truth. Jesus asked, "I have spoken to you of earthly things and you do not believe; how then will you believe if I speak of heavenly things?" He went on to explain that no one had gone up into heaven except the one who came from heaven — Himself. (See John 3:1-15.)

Jesus spoke the most important words ever recorded. Yet today many reject them as false. Many accept Jesus as a great teacher, but they reject Him as the Son of God. People believe some of the things that He said, but not those things that hold us accountable to Him and to God. Some of the most educated and scientific people reject Him with skepticism and cynicism. But Jesus wants us to be *tender-hearted* and *tough-minded*, to seek truth. He wants us to be open to God's reality and not rebellious or cynical. That's why faith in what He said and did is so important. We must avoid reading our own desires back into God's inspired message. We must not create Jesus in our own image. Rather we must accept Him as He really is, and just as the record reads. We must love Him as He reveals Himself. Recorded testimony needs to be given the benefit of the doubt lest we contradict reliable witnesses and read our own theories, desires, and prejudices back into history.

Faith, in truth, leads to great discoveries. Faith motivates us to work towards the most excellent goals and opens our hearts to the greatest possibilities. The great people of faith described in the Bible considered this life on earth to be a training ground for a greater life with God. They knew that God's existence and invisible nature can be plainly seen, and understood from what has been made (Rom 1:18-20). God created our world as a school to train us (and also test us) for eternal life. These believers were not lazy, gullible, and unproductive here on earth. In fact, they believed and loved God. He rewarded them with maturity, perseverance, and strength.

Faith makes us sure of what we hope for and certain of what we do not see. It is based on reasonable evidence, and the plainest evidence of all is the simple record we have of the life of Christ. By faith we also understand that God designed and created the universe. We know by faith that He exists and that He rewards those who earnestly seek Him (Heb 11:1-6).

What All Organizations Need to Consider

The most excellent organizations build a climate of trust. They expect faithful adherence to their vision and goals. They motivate people by having faith in them, but they do insist firmly on ethical standards.

God designed and created nature so that it will respond to those who seek change for the sake of improvement. Christians and churches can learn from these victories that God enables secular organizations to have. We should look at these as parables of what God expects from His people. Instead of being critical and negative we should treat them like Jesus treated the centurion, the Canaanite woman, the tax collectors, the prostitutes, and those despised by self-righteous leaders in their society. We can thank God and glorify Him for making science, technology, and the "modern" world possible. Most of us use these innovations and technological marvels without any qualms. Let's be more positive and thank God for how they demonstrate His impartiality, wisdom, and power. God is not a snob, and He doesn't want His people to give that impression to the world, the world Jesus came to save. Churches can encourage members to be proud of Christ, to study personally how Jesus related to people, and to allow the Spirit to keep their faith growing.

This means constant innovation, change for the better, growth towards perfection in our relationships. We should take our tip from the way Jesus criticized the traditions of the teachers of the Law, the Pharisees, and the Sadducees and not allow our faith to be stifled. We need to work at our faith, going from faith to more faith as we allow God to motivate us as He pleases. (See Mark 2:23-28; 7:1-23; Matt 23:1-39; Gal 5:1; John 8:21-36; Rom 1:16-17; Phil 2:12-13.)

What Can the Grassroots Christian Do?

◆ Jesus expects us to exercise our faith. He criticized His disciples because they had such little faith. They had such a hard time believing that God would do for them the same things He did for Jesus. (See Matt 14:25-33; 17:18-21.) Today we Christians have the benefit of what Jesus did and said, and we also see God working in the world of nature, science, industry, and society.

◆ We can learn to enter in at the narrow gate and walk the narrow road, the Christ Way to highly effective ministries. Like the disciples with their little faith, we often spend most of our time on unimportant things. Tom Peters tells us that poorly designed organizations "soak up time like a sponge." God has given each of us a lot of time, and we can choose to use much more of it for Jesus.[9]

◆ Grassroots Christians can bring additional life to dynamic, living churches. The grassroots movement that Jesus started with His twelve disciples and Paul lives today. His kingdom continues to grow silently and powerfully like the Growing Seed and Mustard Seed Parables teach (Mark 4:26-32).

◆ Facing adversity produces character and teaches us to be highly effective in our church ministries. We have focused on experiences in excellent companies. Many of us have learned the same lessons the hard way in companies that have failed to innovate effectively and failed to trust and serve customers, employees, and suppliers well. Developing excellent methods and values in an unsupportive climate parallels what Jesus faced.

◆ We can help others to be motivated by their priceless faith in Jesus. We can inspire others. We do need patience with those who have been long accustomed to comfortable traditions and specta- tor roles. Jesus and His disciples exercised patience daily. Remember what Jesus said in His hometown synagogue: "Only in his hometown and in his own house is a prophet without honor." By exercising faith and hard work many people have learned the value of Jesus' principles (Matt 13:57; Luke 4:24).

An Agenda on Faith and Trust for a Small Group:

1. *Icebreaker (20 minutes)*: Have each person present tell the others how specific people taught you as a young person to trust and have faith. Tell how you trusted them because they were trustworthy and faithful.

2. *Read related Bible passages (10 minutes)*: Have each person read five or six verses until the following references have been covered: the eleventh chapter of Hebrews and the story of the Roman centu- rion in Matthew 8:5-13.

3. *Discuss Jesus' teaching (30 minutes)*: All discuss how the above Bible accounts can apply to everyday life in a practical way. Have people tie in the discussion with the icebreaker stories.

4. *Prayer for needs (20 minutes)*: Invite each person to express personal needs and then pray.

5. *Vision (10 minutes)*: The leader summarizes and gives his vision for the future growth in the group's faith. Also include the future goals and vision of the congregation.

Conclusions

◆ God predicted through Isaiah that His word would not return to Him empty but would achieve the purpose for which He sent it. As the heavens are higher than the earth, so His ways are higher than our ways (Isa 55:8-13). Jesus taught most things in parables taken from a secular setting. This is why we can use expressions of trust in secular organizations as parables. To avoid being ineffective, hypocritical, and snobbish, churches should learn from the excellent examples of faithfulness we observe in today's society.

◆ Based on how Jesus praised outsiders with great faith, we believe He wants us to do the same. Jesus is not a snob. He never shows either partiality or favoritism. He exalts the humble and humbles the proud. We should put faith in His leadership principles.

◆ God uses faith, hope, and love to inspire and motivate us. The way He continues to do this today in our own age excites us.

REFERENCES

1. Kouzes and Posner, *The Leadership Challenge*, 146.

2. Warren Bennis, *On Becoming a Leader*, (New York: Addison Wesley, 1989, 1994), 152-154.

3. Peters and Austin, *A Passion for Excellence*, 390-391.

4. Garfield, *Second to None*, 6-8, 39, 100, 132, 157-165.

5. Waterman, *The Renewal Factor*, 154, 175-176.

6. Kouzes and Posner, *The Leadership Challenge*, 203-209.

7. Peters, *Liberation Management*, 146, 221, 405-406, 524-505.

8. Peters and Austin, *A Passion for Excellence*, 256.

9. Peters, *Liberation Management*, 80.

CHAPTER NINE
HOPE

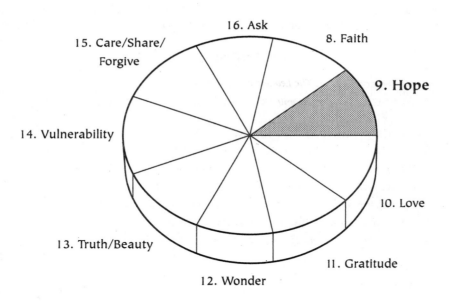

16. Ask

15. Care/Share/
Forgive

8. Faith

9. Hope

14. Vulnerability

10. Love

13. Truth/Beauty

11. Gratitude

12. Wonder

9

LIFE IS FULL OF HOPE, SO WHY BE CYNICAL?

God has chosen to make known among the Gentiles the glorious riches of this
mystery, which is Christ in you, the hope of glory. . . . My purpose is that they may
be encouraged in heart and united in love, so that they may have the full riches of
complete understanding, in order that they may know the mystery of God, namely,
Christ, in whom are hidden all the treasures of wisdom and knowledge.
Paul (in Colossians 1:27-2:3)

The Bible calls us to see beyond the grim reality of history to the view of all eternity,
when God's reign will fill the earth with light and truth. . . . All the beauty and joy
we meet on earth represent "only the scent of a flower we have not found, the echo
of a tune we have not heard, news from a country we have never yet visited."
The prophets proclaim that such sensations are not illusions nor mere dreams, but
advance echoes of what will come true. We are given few details about that future
world, only a promise that God will prove himself trustworthy. When we awake in
the new heaven and new earth, we will possess at last whatever we longed for.
Philip Yancey[1]

Key Points

Each person has the choice of "living for the moment" or "living
for a better tomorrow," and we all make that choice every day. To
live by hope means to go beyond thinking about what has been tra-
ditionally believed possible and to believe that with Christ *all things*
are possible. We have a wonderful hope as believers in God. With

God's help nothing can prevent us from reaching our goal — nothing but our own lack of hope.

Secular companies have discovered the power of hope for motivating their associates. Jesus reveals to us that God never fails us in anything we do according to His will. The churches can also discover the great things that God makes possible for those who hope in Him. Many Christians have experienced in their daily work the power of hope in bringing about great solutions and victories. Small groups cultivate a hopeful climate that motivates us to maximum service and effectiveness.

✷✷✷✷

Desire and Hope

Hope is the universal nourishment of the human being. Desire and expectation are inseparable from hope. Without hope there would be no reason to do anything at all. Hope motivates us and brings dreams, goals, action plans, priorities, and standards into the dynamic path of achievement.

Joe Batten

To Rekindle Hope

We don't need leaders to tell us what to do. . . . We need them to symbolize and voice and confirm the most deeply rooted values in our society. . . . And we need them to rekindle hope. So many of us are defeated people — whatever our level of affluence or status — defeated sometimes by life's blows, more often by our own laziness or cynicism or self-indulgence. The first and last task of a leader is to keep our hope alive — the hope that we can finally find our way through to a better world . . . .

John Gardner[2]

Faith is being sure of what we hope for. When we hope, we expect, anticipate, and desire what we believe will happen in the future. Faith, hope, and desire inspire and motivate the people in organizations to make things happen. Possibilities become realities.

Excellent leaders make their vision of the future exciting. They move forward with enthusiasm, and they paint the adventure into the future with excitement, passion, and hope. They impart to their people the desire to achieve whatever is necessary to reach the goal.

Visionary leaders look at the possibilities, not the probabilities. Faith and hope in the future go together. You can't have one without the other. Combine these with love (see our next chapter) and nothing will be impossible for you.

How Do Secular Organizations Build with Hope?

Apple Computer: When the Home Brew Computer Club started in Menlo Park in 1975 no one believed that personal computers would become a major world market. To members of this club Steve Wozniak revealed the circuit designs for his Apple Computer. People meeting in this club later founded many leading Silicon Valley companies.[3]

Steve Jobs, Steve Wozniak, and Mike Markkula started Apple Computer. Jobs wanted to have a company that would change the world. He got little support for his new computer ideas at Atari. Hewlett-Packard didn't readily accept Wozniak's idea's. Mike had retired from Intel and became Apple's source of venture capital and mature leadership values. From the beginning the three founders created a climate of excitement, hope and adventure. Wozniak's ingenious Apple II design started the home computer revolution and became their bread and butter product.[4]

In 1984, only seven years from their beginning, Apple created the Macintosh, another smashing success, a very user-friendly computer with top quality graphics. After struggling to follow manuals on the Atari, Commodore, and IBM compatible computers, users loved the simplicity of the icons and the mouse. However, one professional computer engineer told us, "I hate the Macintosh. It makes my job unnecessary." The professionals may have hated the Mac, but the computer "illiterates" loved it.

Frank Rose tells of Apple's transition from a fast growth company to a more stable market-led company. The visionary co-founder Steve Jobs was energetic, charismatic, and a fantastic innovator, but according to John Sculley he was erratic, driving, and manipulative as a leader. In early 1983 Jobs brought in Sculley, former president of PepsiCo, to be president of Apple. Sculley worked patiently with Jobs for more than two years. As Executive Vice President of the Macintosh division, Jobs spark-plugged the development, production, and marketing of the Macintosh. He also held the position of Chairman of Apple. He envisioned the Mac like Henry Ford did the Model T. It would be the people's computer, the inexpensive "appliance" with closed configuration. The Mac's sales goal was 85,000 units per month.

Actually, the Apple II accounted for 70 percent of sales in the Christmas season of 1984. Sales of the Macintosh, which started the year with a bang, dropped to almost 20,000 units per month. Apple had built one billion dollars of inventory and sold only $700,000. They were in real financial trouble even though they had the best quarter in the company's history.

When Apple began to lose money in 1985, Sculley and the board asked Steve Jobs to step down as manager of the Macintosh division. Sculley says that Jobs focused too much on technology and didn't listen closely enough to the business market. Jobs decided to leave Apple and start a company to develop a new computer with artificial intelligence.

Sculley had been an expert in marketing at PepsiCo. Now in full leadership at Apple, he turned it into a customer-sensitive company. He gave the workers at Apple greater hope and confidence and responded to the needs and desires of workers, suppliers, and customers.[5]

Debi Coleman had held several different controller positions in the Macintosh group. She experienced "boundless opportunity" at Apple, became vice-president of worldwide manufacturing, and finally Chief Financial Officer. As factory manager at the Macintosh plant in Fremont, she desired to be "the best leader in the world." She spent five hours each day on the production floor and dramatically increased productivity, quality, and morale. Kouzes and Posner called her type of leadership "VIP — vision-involvement-persistence." Leaders they interviewed of this type "had *visions* and dreams of what could be. They had absolute and total personal belief, and they were confident in their abilities to make extraordinary things happen." In other words, they had confidence, desire, and hope; they motivated their people to great achievements by their inspirational leadership.[6]

Sculley encouraged Alan Kay to "invent the future." Kay's and Sculley's hope focused on networking and cooperation. Everyone would be linked together by computer networking. Bank transactions would be done from your home computer. Everyone would have immediate worldwide access to all information — virtual reality. The computer would have internal programs that continuously searched databases, analyzed and presented information in the optimum format.[7]

Instead of keeping everything in house, Apple now farms out all it can to companies that do the most excellent job. In other words it networks with the most effective and excellent sources of needed technology and service. Apple keeps in house what it considers essential: design and marketing. As a result it brings in about twice the revenue in dollars per employee than does IBM, and about four times that of Digital. With less middle management, frontline employees experience much more freedom and responsibility.[8]

Sculley tells new employees that Apple can't guarantee a lifelong job, but "what Apple can — and does — promise is that, whether you're aboard for three months, six years, or, unlikely as it may be, 16 years, you will be constantly learning, constantly challenged. At the end, you will be demonstrably better positioned in the local or global market than you would have been had you not spent the time with us."

Tom Peters says, "I think that's a good deal. It puts the bouncing ball in my court. . . . My true security and superior stipend depend on my own initiative and my own thirst for learning. It's my job (and my life), and I take responsibility for it."[9]

Steve Jobs illustrates more the entrepreneur who starts a company with personal charisma and makes most of the key decisions himself. John Sculley leads primarily by example and integrity. He constantly inspires everyone with his exciting hope and vision of what can be. He led Apple back into profitability, focusing production, marketing, and technology on what the business customers really needed and wanted.

◆ In 1983 and 1984 he shared Jobs' dream that the Macintosh would be an inexpensive "appliance" or "commodity" like the Model T Ford was.[10]

◆ In late 1984 the Mac had saturated the market and the sales rate had dropped to a very low figure. He realized that the strategy had to be changed or Apple would go bankrupt. They had their first quarterly loss in 1985, and stock prices dropped from as high as $70 to $15 per share. The real market was business users, and the Mac wasn't either powerful or adaptable enough to compete with the IBM PC in this market.[11]

◆ Sculley was given a full vote of confidence by the board, and Steve Jobs was asked to step down as the Executive VP of the Macintosh division. He was asked to stay on as Chairman of Apple's Board, but he left to start NEXT.[12]

◆ Sculley restructured the organization to eliminate bitter competition between the Mac and Apple II divisions. He chose his team, shut down several manufacturing plants, and reduced personnel by 20 percent. This brought unity and hope to the whole organization.[13]

◆ He modified the Macintosh to give it increased RAM memory, built-in hard disk storage space, and open configuration for add-on circuit boards to make it adaptable for a variety of uses. Apple proceeded to develop many new business-oriented products for the future.[14]

◆ Sculley hired a new advertising firm and adopted the campaign theme of "the Power to be Your Best."[15]

◆ By the spring of 1987 Apple was selling more than 50,000 Macs per month. The stock price was above $50 per share and on its way up to $70 per share.[16]

◆ Thomas Watson's daughter invited Sculley and his wife Leezy to their home in Maine for a weekend in the summer of 1985. Watson, retired Chairman of IBM, told him, "As long as Apple can continue to innovate and hold together the things it believes in, it will pull through. . . . It's going to take a lot of hard work, but what you can't lose is the innovation. You're doing the right things." This was a tremendous encouragement to Sculley coming from "the living symbol of Apple's toughest competitor."[17]

What Did Jesus Teach about Hope?

Jesus brought a new "wine," and he chose new "wineskins" to put it in. He taught people to turn from a one-nation religion and spread God's Kingdom throughout the whole world. Instead of selecting religious experts, He chose common people as His ambassadors — fishermen, a tax collector, a revolutionary. He fulfilled Isaiah's prophecy in Isaiah 42:1-4, ". . . he will proclaim justice to the nations. . . . In his name the nations will put their hope" (Matt 12:18-21).

In His most famous prayer, Jesus asked for God's Kingdom to come and His will to be done on earth as it is in heaven. Then He told His followers to desire and seek God's kingdom and righteousness above all else. We can stop worrying about food, drink, and clothing because God knows that we need them. If we give top priority to what really matters, then God will provide everything else that we need as a matter of course. We must listen to Jesus and put our hope in Him. He has the words of life (Matt 6:25-34; John 6:68).

As human beings we fear death more than anything else.

Naturally we hope to live forever. People asked Jesus, "What must I do to inherit eternal life?" Jesus told one man to give up all his riches in order to have treasure in heaven, and then follow Him. He asked another man, "What is written in the law? How do you read it?" This man knew the right answer: "Love the Lord your God with all your heart and with all your soul and with all your strength and with all your mind" and "Love your neighbor as yourself." Jesus gives us the true meaning of our lives and the only hope that fulfills our deepest longing and desire (Luke 10:25-28).

He also tells us to bring this wonderful hope of eternal life to all people on the earth. God doesn't want a single little one to be lost (Matt 18:14). He is not willing that any should perish (2 Peter 3:9-10). That is why He told His disciples just before He left them and ascended back into heaven, "go and make disciples of all nations, baptizing them in the name of the Father and of the Son and of the Holy Spirit, and teaching them to obey everything I have commanded you. And surely I am with you always, to the very end of the age" (Matt 28:19-20).

The hope that Jesus brought into the world gives meaning to all life and all nature. Paul meant the same when he wrote,

> In fact, all creation is eagerly waiting for God to show who his children are. Meanwhile, creation is confused, but not because it wants to be confused. God made it this way in the hope that creation would be set free from decay and would share in the glorious freedom of his children. We know that all creation is still groaning and is in pain, like a woman about to give birth.
>
> The Spirit makes us sure about what we will be in the future. But now we groan silently, while we wait for God to show that we are his children. This means that our bodies will also be set free. And this hope is what saves us. But if we already have what we hope for, there is no need to keep on hoping. However, we hope for something we have not yet seen, and we patiently wait for it (Rom 8:19-25, CEV).

In order to give hope to all without prejudice we must be sensitive to where people are coming from. That's why Jesus went to the sick, sinful, and poor rather than to those who considered themselves righteous and healthy. (See Matt 9:10-13.) We should not exalt ourselves above those "little ones" that God wants to bring into His Kingdom. When Paul said, "I am all things to all men that I might by all means help to save some" (1 Cor 9:19-23), he did not mean,

"When in Rome I do as the Romans do." He was not telling us the end justifies the means. He was doing the same as Jesus. He was walking in other people's moccasins and making himself vulnerable to those he met so that he could impart to them the hope of the good news, Jesus in us, the hope of glory (Col 1:25-27).

What are the parallels between Jesus' teaching and what happens at secular organizations like Apple Computer? Jesus helps us to see a bigger picture than the worries and concerns of our short lives on earth. (See Matt 6:25-34.) He enables us to face trials and troubles. With Him we can have hope for great things beyond the present crises. Sculley helped the people at Apple to bounce back from a real crisis and look to the future with hope.

Jesus treated people as important to God. *No one is beyond God's love* (John 3:16). That's why Jesus came, to tell us this good news and to get us to change our hearts and minds. He predicted trouble and persecution for His followers, but He also told them that God would give us ultimate victory over the problems of life. Sculley helped the people at Apple to change their viewpoint and to see the great possibilities ahead. He knew that it would be hard work, but he set the example and put Apple on an exciting course.

What the Churches Need to Consider

◆ People can do much more than many leaders believe, but leaders must lead by example, trust in people, and provide a climate of hope. God gives His family endless opportunities and He is able to do far more than we can ever think or imagine (Eph 3:20).

◆ The tremendous technical progress we see in secular society comes from God's wonderful capabilities designed into Creation. Churches ought to have hope in the steady growth of God's kingdom based on what God allows mankind to accomplish in the realms of science, technology, and commerce. He causes His kingdom to advance like the growth of a tree from a very small seed. We can exercise great hope in God's eternal care based on His blessings in the physical world. (See Mark 4:30-32; Rom 8:28.)

◆ Jesus did not focus on protecting human traditions. He stressed growth in truth, growth in love for all people including our enemies. God can handle anything, and He will bring everything in heaven and on earth into conformity with His will. (See Matt 5:43-48; Eph 1:15-23.)

The Development of Vision and Hope

Our tough-minded view places great importance on the strength of the self-image. Self-image has a future dimension, it doesn't only exist "right now." We see people as growing, developing, stretching, and seeking. Part of the future aspect of the self-image is simply a growing awareness:

◆ that there is a future;
◆ that we can imagine ourselves in that future;
◆ that planning for the future is exciting and important; and
◆ that it is desirable to dream.

This awareness of the future is essential to human life and a vital ingredient of our value system as well. Each person has the choice of "living for the moment" or "living for a better tomorrow," and to one extent or another we all make that choice every day.

. . . Future awareness is the view of the possible.

. . . Vision is the transcendent view of the possible.

To transcend means to go beyond thinking about what has always been believed possible and to believe that there is nothing that is impossible.

[This is] . . . not merely a practical view, . . . but a truly transcendent view of those possibilities — fueled by hope.

Joe Batten[18]

What Can the Grassroots Christian Do?

◆ We should cultivate great hope and confidence. Every good gift comes down from Him (James 1:17). Christians working in secular jobs can take hope from their experience of God's tremendous providence. We sometimes turn His gifts to evil uses and accept them without gratitude. But this should take nothing away from God's power and wisdom.
◆ We should not be discouraged. God is not slow or powerless. He knows what He is doing. Let's take heart and hope like Abraham did: when everything seemed hopeless,

Abraham in hope believed and so became the father of many nations, just as it had been said to him, 'So shall your offspring be.' Abraham's faith never became weak, not even when he was nearly a hundred years old. He knew that he was almost dead and that his wife Sarah could not have children. But Abraham never doubted or questioned God's promise. His faith made him strong, and he gave all the credit to God.

Abraham was certain that God could do what he had promised. So God accepted him. Just as we read in the Scriptures. But these words were not written only for Abraham. They were written for us, since we will also be accepted because of our faith in God, who raised our Lord Jesus to life. God gave Jesus to die for our sins, and he raised him to life, so that we would be made acceptable to God (Rom 4:18, NIV; 19-24, CEV).

◆ The Apple story illustrates how companies succeed by putting their hope in the possibilities, but Apple became a success quicker than most companies do. It grew to be a Fortune 500 company in only seven years from its founding, faster than any previous company. The Apple story makes a good parable for what God will do for his people when we put our hope in Him.

◆ Led by John Sculley, Apple rebounded in less than one year from its first major crisis. If hope can inspire companies like Apple, hope can surely inspire us to rebound from crises. With God's help nothing can defeat us even in the face of great adversity.

◆ Our hope in God will help us grow spiritually mature. Not only is our hope of eternal glory based on Christ living in us (Col 1:27), but also "we know that in all things God works for the good of those who love him, who have been called according to his purpose" (Rom 8:28).

◆ By serving Jesus in our daily work we learn His view of life. The people in our churches need to hear modern parables. These show dramatically and practically how we learn to hope in Christ.

An Agenda on Hope and Desire for a Small Group:

1. *Icebreaker (20 minutes)*: Ask each person in the group to tell a story from earlier in their life when they really hoped for something and what actually resulted from their hope.

2. *Read related Bible passages (10 minutes)*: Have each person participate in reading the following references: Hebrews 11:1-2; Romans 4:16-25; Luke 18:35-43 and 19:1-10.

3. *Discuss Jesus' teaching (30 minutes)*: Have all discuss how the people in the above Scriptures dealt with their hopes. Relate this to how hope plays an important role in our own lives today.

4. *Prayer for needs (20 minutes)*: Invite each person to express personal needs and then pray.

5. *Vision (10 minutes)*: The leader summarizes and gives his vision for the future in understanding the group's hopes and desires. Also include the future goals and vision of the congregation.

Conclusion

We can have great hope by reaching toward the greatest possibilities. We can center our priorities on the word of God. God works in this world in marvelous ways pouring out His blessings on all people. If we center our hearts and minds on His promises and His presence, our hope will never let us down. We can learn from adversity and from incidental failures. We can treat all the events around us as sources of parables like Jesus did. God works constantly in His world to give us hope for the future.

REFERENCES

1. Philip Yancey, *Disappointment With God*, (New York: HarperPaperbacks, 1991), 298-299. Yancey quotes C. S. Lewis, *The Weight of Glory*, (Grand Rapids: Eerdmans, 1972), 5.

2. John Gardner, *No Easy Victories*, (New York: Harper & Row, Publishers, 1969), 134.

3. Peters and Austin, *A Passion for Excellence*, 219-220.

4. Ibid., 41, 148.

5. Frank Rose, *West of Eden*, (New York: Viking, 1989), 314-337. Also see Michael Moritz, *The Little Kingdom*, (New York: William Morrow and Co., 1984).

6. Kouzes and Posner, *The Leadership Challenge*, 5-7.

7. Ibid., 87.

8. Peters, *The Tom Peters Seminar*, 128. Peters, *Liberation Management*, 152, 157.

9. Peters, *The Tom Peters Seminar*, 112.

10. John Sculley, *Odyssey*, (New York: Harper & Row, Publishers, 1987), 162-163.

11. Ibid., 255, 270.

12. Ibid., 242, 284-287, 314.

13. Ibid., 287-291.

14. Ibid., 379, 385-386.

15. Ibid., 380-383.

16. Ibid., 387.

17. Ibid., 307-308.

18. Batten, Havemann, Pearce, and Pedersen, *Tough-Minded Parenting*, 101.

CHAPTER TEN
LOVE

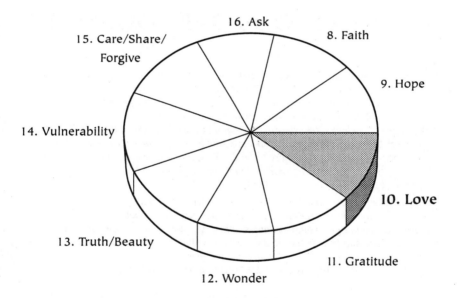

16. Ask

15. Care/Share/
Forgive

8. Faith

9. Hope

14. Vulnerability

10. Love

13. Truth/Beauty

11. Gratitude

12. Wonder

10

LOVE YOUR NEIGHBOR
AS YOU LOVE YOURSELF

Examine what lies in back of discipline — what provides the motive,
the energy for discipline. This force I believe to be love. . . .
I define love thus: The will to extend one's self for the purpose
of nurturing one's own or another's spiritual growth. . . .
When I genuinely love I am extending myself, and when I am extending myself I am
growing. The more I love, the longer I love, the larger I become. Genuine love is
self-replenishing. The more I nurture the spiritual growth of others,
the more my own spiritual growth is nurtured.
Scott Peck[1]

Love the Lord your God with all your heart and with all your soul
and with all your mind. . . . Love your neighbor as yourself.
A new command I give you: Love one another. As I have loved you, so you must
love one another. By this all men will know that you are my disciples,
if you love one another.
Jesus (in Matthew 22:37-40 and John 13:34-35)

Key Points

We can learn to respect and admire others only as we become aware of our own value in the eyes of Jesus. In this chapter *we stress love as the finest motivator of the human mind*. We enrich the human condition best by spreading the realization that love is the most *practical* power in the world. This is what the Law and Prophets were meant to reveal. We achieve great goals because the love of Christ motivates us.

Excellent organizations find genuine love to be a highly effective motivator. Jesus saw love as the fundamental attitude enabling His followers to develop great spiritual power. Churches sometimes underestimate the power of love to motivate. They can learn from members who experience love in action on their jobs. Christians experience love in relationships with "outsiders" just as Jesus did. He constantly commended people who self-righteous people looked down on. The fruits of the Spirit develop from love, and small groups provide the community for best experiencing love.

✳✳✳✳

God Loves Us Much More . . .

It should be perfectly clear to readers who have come this far that we can learn to respect and admire others only as we become aware of our own potential and how much God loves us. We perceive, relate to, and help unleash the strengths and spiritual gifts of others only as we discover our own.

◆ Can we respect others if we do not respect ourselves?
◆ Can we identify others' strengths and gifts if we don't allow God to help us know ours?
◆ Can we help build the other person if we don't know our own character-building materials?
◆ Can we love and admire the other person if we do not have a proper sense of our personal worth?
◆ Can we love ourselves and others if we don't know and love God through Christ?

Surely no rational person will question the need for a vast improvement in our various efforts to create a better world, a better society, better communities, better organizations, companies, and homes. We enrich many lives when we interact with each other with love, friendship, and good will. God loves us as He creates us in His image and prepares us to live in Heaven with Him. How do we come to love ourselves? By learning to know God as Father and realizing how much He loves us. His message in the Bible and His Spirit give us life. We grow in our knowledge of Christ and make the decision daily to follow Him, love Him, love others, and love ourselves. (See John 1:18; 3:16; 13:34-35; 14:23; Rom 8:12-17; 1 Peter 1:22-25.)

God's Spirit lives in us and teaches us with spiritual words and ideas. God sees into our hearts at all times, because He loves us. (See 1 Cor 2:9-16; Ps 33:12-18.) Willard Tate tells us the story of

Isaac Watts, the great hymn writer. He kept admiring the plaque on the wall of the elderly lady who lived next door. "'Isaac,' she said, 'I want to give you that plaque. I've watched you look at it, and I want you to have it.'

"The plaque read, 'Thou God seest me,' from Genesis 16:13.

"The lady went on, 'Now, Isaac, people are going to tell you that verse means God is looking over your shoulder, trying to catch you doing something wrong. But don't you believe them. Isaac, what it means is that God loves you so much, He can't keep His eyes off you.'"

Tate comments: "I'm just now beginning to understand it because I've just been experiencing the love of grandchildren for a few years. . . .

"I see them almost every day, and I can happily watch them for hours. Do I do that so I can catch them doing something wrong? Oh, no! I watch them because I love them so much I can't keep my eyes off them. And God loves me more than I love my grandchildren."[2]

We experience the very same thing with our children and grandchildren. God doesn't look for our weaknesses in order to punish us any more than we do with our grandchildren. Joe describes his wonderful experience with Steven:

My grandson Steven's life began very tenuously. Born two months premature, he spent the first two months of his life in ICU at the hospital. His mother and father stayed with him constantly. His survival was questionable, and his mother and father almost incessantly leaned over the incubator and told him,

"Steven, we love you, you're full of love."

"Steven, God loves you, you're full of God."

Needless to say, Steven survived and, after heart surgery, blossomed into a healthy and husky boy.

When he was two and a half, I returned from out of town on a Friday afternoon and immediately headed for his house. I planned to take him for a ride, watch airplanes land, and do other things we often did.

I fastened him with the seat belt as he perched on the armrest, and we started down the street. After two blocks Steven said, "Grandpa, pull over and stop."

I did so and then he leaned over, looked in my eyes and said, "Grandpa, I just want you to know that I love you and Grandma, and I love Mommy and Daddy, and I love Aunt Gail and Kyle. (Shawne wasn't born yet.) Then he said, "All right, Grandpa, drive on."

As I drove down the street my eyes were blurred with the emotion and gratitude for this splendid young boy.

Then, a few blocks later he again said, "Grandpa, pull over and stop." I did so. Then he said, "Grandpa, unfasten this belt so I can sit on your lap and see into your eyes." When I had done so, he looked deeply into my eyes and said, "I just want you to know that I love everybody in my world. . . . O.K. Grandpa, now drive on."

As I drove on, I was filled with gratitude and the sure feeling that this boy would have a *great* life. Now twelve years later, he is a healthy and happy guy.

What would happen to the "problems" between people and groups if hate and fear could be supplanted by *love* and *courage*? What are the implications for our jobs? Our homes? Our lives? Dr. Karl Menninger, the great psychologist, said, "love cures people — both the ones who give it and the ones who receive it."

John tells us, "God is love. Whoever lives in love lives in God, and God in him. . . . There is no fear in love" (1 John 4:16-18).

How Do Secular Organizations Teach Love?

Love is not necessarily sentimental. It can be both tough-minded and tender-hearted. Vince Lombardi, the coach of the champion Green Bay Packers, was tough and he was excitable, but he loved his players. When asked how he pulled together such a makeshift group of players to win the Super Bowl, he said, "These guys love each other."

He really believed in love and told the following to the American Management Association: "Mental toughness is humility, simplicity, Spartanism. And one other, love. I don't necessarily have to like my associates, but as a person I must love them. Love is loyalty. Love is teamwork. Love respects the dignity of the individual. Heartpower is the strength of your corporation." After quoting Lombardi, Kouzes and Posner said, "possibly the best-kept secret of successful leaders is love: being in love with leading, with the people who do the work, with what their organizations produce, and with those who honor the organization by using its work. Leadership is an affair of the heart, not of the head."[3]

Those who lead excellent organizations hold people accountable, but they also treat them like family. They expect people to cooperate, work hard, produce outstanding results, and love who they work with and what they are doing. Love brings out the best in people, and love makes life more rewarding and more productive. When we expect the best of people, we show them our love, the best of all possible gifts. (Please read this sentence again and again.)

How Love Challenged Big Ed

The greatest single breakthrough in human empowerment comes when leaders discover that love is the most practical thing in the world. Faith, hope, and love last forever and work miracles together.

We are now in the Age of the Mind and all we do that is practical is a product of minds. The finest teacher for the mind is love. Socrates said, "Human nature will not easily find a helper better than love."

In a seminar on Tough-Minded Leadership, Big Ed discovered love: "When I heard you suggest that we tell those closest to us that we really loved them, I thought it was a bunch of sentimental garbage. I wondered what in the world that had to do with being tough. . . .

"That night as I sat across the living room from my wife, your words were still bugging me. What kind of courage would it take to tell my wife I loved her? . . . Suddenly, I got up, walked across the room, nervously pushed her newspaper aside and said, 'Alice, I love you.' for a minute she looked startled. Then tears came to her eyes and she said swiftly, 'Ed, I love you, but this is the first time in twenty-five years you've said it like that.'

". . . I began to read books on the subject. Sure enough, Joe, a lot of great people had a lot to say and I began to realize the enormous practicality of applied love in my life, both at home and at work.

"As some of you guys know, I really changed the way I worked with people. I began to listen more and to really hear. I learned what it was like to try to get to know people's strengths, rather than dwelling on their weaknesses. I began to discover the real pleasure of helping people build their confidence. Maybe the most important thing of all was that I really began to understand that an excellent way to show love and respect for people was to expect them to use their strengths to meet objectives we'd worked out together."

Joe Batten[4]

The Golden Rule in Excellent Organizations

Jesus equated loving others and loving God with all your heart, soul, strength, and mind with *doing to others as you would have them to do to you* (The Golden Rule, Matt 7:12). For the two great commandments He said, "All the Law and the Prophets hang on these two commandments" (Matt 22:40). For the Golden Rule He said, "this sums up the Law and the Prophets."

Paul said essentially the same thing: "Let no debt remain outstanding, except the continuing debt to love one another, for he who loves his fellowman has fulfilled the law. . . . Love does no harm to its neighbor. Therefore love is the fulfillment of the law" (Rom 13:8,9).

Tom Peters and Nancy Austin quote many excellent and successful leaders who mention the Golden Rule:

◆ John McConnell runs Worthington Industries with "a one paragraph statement of philosophy, a Golden Rule: Take care of your customers and take care of your people, and the market will take care of you."

◆ Bob Swiggett of Kollmorgen says, "It's all about trust and the Golden Rule. . . . The leader's role is to create vision. . . . It's coming out with an atmosphere of understanding and trust — and love. . . . Tyranny is not tolerated here. . . . We preach trust and the golden rule."

◆ Tom Monaghan, of Domino's Pizza says, "Pay attention to the Golden Rule, and the world is yours."

◆ "Mo Siegel of Celestial Seasonings and, yes, old Tom Watson, Sr., of IBM also hold to the Golden Rule. Steel. Electro-optics. Pizza. Computers. And all of the best top leaders say it's 'just' the Golden Rule."[5]

◆ A marketing director of Milliken wrote, "I guess if we will just follow the Golden Rule — 'Do unto others as you would have them do unto you' — we will become more efficient in our dealings with all people, including our customers!"[6]

Warren Bennis quotes Don Ritchey, the former CEO of Lucky Stores: "I start with the presumption that most people want to be ethical: It's sort of a Golden Rule philosophy."[7]

Jan Carlzon of Scandanavian Airlines Systems says, "If I had only one management rule to give to everyone it would be the golden rule. . . . In my experience, there are two great motivators in life. One is fear. The other is love. . . . A person who is afraid doesn't dare perform to the limits of his or her capabilities."[8]

Mary Kay Ash starts off her bestselling book on people management with the first chapter entitled "Golden Rule Management." The last chapter of her book is "Live by the Golden Rule on and off the Job." She says:

> Beginning my own business . . . I vowed that my company would never repeat the wrongs that I had witnessed. People would be treated fairly; I would always think, "If I were this person, how would I want to be treated?" To this day, when I am searching for a solution to a people problem, I ask myself this question. And when I do, even the most difficult problem soon becomes unraveled.
>
> While many people think there's no place for the Golden Rule in the business world, at Mary Kay Cosmetics it's part of our business foundation. Furthermore, I don't think effective people management can be achieved in any other way.[9]

How Does Motivation by Love Actually Work Out?

1. *It treats people with dignity*: This means giving people the opportunity and coaching them to develop to the maximum effectiveness. People need to accept maximum responsibility and to grow to be the best they can be. Most people flourish when challenged in a loving and supportive climate.

2. *It makes relationships important and productive*: We treat people as partners and associates, not just employees. Loving relationships are long-lasting. We are in this for life and beyond. Cooperation, love, and friendship bring greater growth and rewards than competition. Suppliers, employees, and customers work as a team. They work to make society a better place for all, because God wants His will to be done on earth like it is in heaven.

3. *It produces an opportunity climate*: In this climate people keep improving and innovating better ways to meet their own needs and the needs of others. We develop the resources that God has designed and created into the world. This glorifies Him and trains us for the greatest climate of all, heaven. It helps us accept hardship because we cooperate with and encourage each other.

4. *We make fairness a top priority*: We base rewards on actual performance. We learn to be servants to others and that more blessings come from giving than from receiving.

5. *It gives freedom and promotes good judgment*: People make exciting and unanticipated discoveries when they think creatively and independently. Today's knowledge culture requires great teamwork. Love teaches people to think. When rules become more important

than people, following rules dogmatically eliminates all traces of wisdom and judgment.[10]

Because Someone is Different Must We Fear Them?

Stephen Covey gives us two examples that illustrate how genuine love can take the place of fear and reaction:

◆ In the first illustration, one associate shared this experience:

> [A] junior in the organization who'd only been with us a couple of years walked up to me and said, "This thing is never going to work. I don't think we should do it at all."
>
> I felt like saying, "That's the dumbest thing I've ever heard!" But I just gritted my teeth and said, "I value differences. Why don't you come in and we'll talk about it?"
>
> In fifteen minutes, that individual outlined all of the major potholes in my plan and created a whole new paradigm for me. It was such a powerful learning experience, I started a process of polling, talking to, listening to all of the stakeholders I could find. . . . I still have stacks of notes I draw out of from time to time to allow me to get around the potholes.

◆ In the second illustration on becoming a Leader/Servant, Covey writes:

> I remember my first experience working with a truly empowering leader. . . .
>
> This man said, "Stephen, I see my role as one of being a source of help to you. . . . I really mean it, Stephen, I'd like to come and visit with you, but perhaps this is not an appropriate time. . . .
>
> When I did ask him to visit a few weeks later, he took the same attitude. I met him at the airport and asked what he wanted to look into. But he said, "I'm here to help. We'll do whatever you would like." So I took him to a meeting, and I said, "It would help if you were to reinforce this point that I'm trying to get across." So, he did it. Then I made another request and he fulfilled it."
>
> Well, I started feeling, "I'm the one that's responsible. He's here to help me." And I started being very open to him. . . . But he never told me what to do. He always said, "You might consider this option" or "Had you thought about this possibility?"
>
> . . . Shortly after that I went to work with another supervisor who was a very fine person as well, but very controlling. And I eventually found how easy it was to just do what he told me to do.

But there was no creative opportunity. I felt totally disempowered. So I found most of my satisfactions off the job, not on the job. And all the people around this person did this same thing. They accommodated his style.

It's these kinds of experiences that help me contrast empowerment and control.[11]

Do you suppose that Jesus intended the above when He said "Love your neighbor as yourself"?

Covey's experiences certainly agree with similar experiences of the authors. Warren Howard's supervisor on his first job, (at UniRoyal in Providence, R.I.), would not make decisions for him, but always asked him, "What additional information do you need to make a decision? Get all the facts that you need, and then come to me with your decision."

When you read the New Testament, check out what Jesus said, and you'll see that he usually answered questions by asking a question in return. He expected both his disciples and his enemies to think for themselves. He expected people to take Him seriously and to love others as He loved.

What Did Jesus Teach about Love?

God sent Jesus into the world as His ultimate message of love. The law came through Moses, but God's love and truth came through Christ. Faith and hope surely do motivate us, but what motivates us more dramatically and quickly than anything we know of? Love does! Because Christ loved us, we love Him and the people around us. He came to His own people and His own world, but they didn't receive Him. However, He gives power to those who do receive Him, the power to be children of God. He came to make God known to us, so we would love Him as our Father. (See John 1:1-18.)

◆ *God Expects Our Best*: God sent Jesus into the world to save the people of the world and not to condemn them. He loved us so much that He sent His only Son into our world so that whoever believed on Him might have eternal life. We need to expect the best from God because that is what He gives us. Jesus came that we might have abundant life, eternal life (John 10:10). *He expects the best from us because that's what is good for us*. We gain nothing by being lazy in our love for God, and we are not wise to remain as little children tossed around by every wind of doctrine. God knows what we need the most. He wants us to be as productive as we can be in His kingdom and in His love.

◆ *It's Not Good to be a Mere Spectator and Critic*: Jesus said, "From everyone who has been entrusted with much, much more will be asked" (Luke 12:48) and "to everyone who has, more will be given" (Luke 19:26). Jesus never taught His followers to be stagnant and unproductive. When He told them to "work for the night is coming," He did not encourage them to be spectator Christians, yet we know many who feel and act like their job is to sit, soak, and criticize for Jesus. He expects all of us to be our best and do our best. This is for our own good, for our own benefit, but we also benefit God when we are productive. We glorify Him by our productivity. We help bring others into His kingdom. (See John 15:7-17; 2 Peter 1:3-11.) He expects involvement, commitment, and conviction.

◆ *He Loved His Enemies*: When the teachers of the Law and the Pharisees opposed and persecuted Jesus they hurt themselves most of all. They gained nothing by their opposition to God. Jesus loved them by telling them what they needed to know. He also prayed on the cross, "Father, forgive them, for they do not know what they are doing" (Luke 23:34).

◆ *He Didn't Want Them to Reject God's Spirit*: Jesus grieved over the failure of His people to recognize that God had sent Him. We can see that He really wanted the best for them when He said, "O Jerusalem, Jerusalem, you who kill the prophets and stone those sent to you, how often I have longed to gather your children together, as a hen gathers her chicks under her wings, but you were not willing. Look, your house is left to you desolate. For I tell you, you will not see me again until you say, 'Blessed is he who comes in the name of the Lord'" (Matt 23:37-39).

He called people snakes and vipers when they spoke out against the Holy Spirit. He didn't want them to be beyond God's forgiveness, but He had to warn them of that possibility in no uncertain terms. He loves us and He loved His enemies. He lost His life by speaking the truths they needed to know the most. We need to learn that people "will have to give account on the day of judgment for every careless word they have spoken. For by your words you will be acquitted, and by your words you will be condemned" (Matt 12:36-37).

◆ *God and Money*: We can't love God and Money at the same time, because we will serve one and hate the other (Matt 6:19-24). We can't hold simultaneously to God's traditions and to mere human traditions that oppose and nullify God's word (Mark 7:1-13). We must give up everything that stands in the way of the abundant life that God wants to give us. Christ reveals all the richest treasures of wisdom and knowledge, and we must give top priority to knowing Him and doing His will. (See John 7:17; Col 2:2-3.) If we don't want to know what is pleasing to God and obey Him with all our hearts, minds, and strength, then Christ has to open our eyes in whatever way it takes. He may be forced to shock us and even punish us. That's because He loves us and not because He hates us.

◆ *Opposition from Those Closest to Us*: What can we do when those closest to us react violently and abusively to our love for Christ? Jesus warns us again that our enemies will be the people in our own household, our loved ones. (See Matt 10:35-36.) Do we realize that we have no alternative but to love Jesus more than we love those closest to us? We don't really hate them, but it looks like hate to them. That's why Jesus shocks us with this statement: "If anyone comes to me and does not hate his father and mother, his wife and children, his brothers and sisters — yes, even his own life — he cannot be my disciple. And anyone who does not carry his cross and follow me cannot be my disciple. . . . In the same way, any of you who does not give up everything he has cannot be my disciple" (Luke 14:26-27, 33).

◆ *Love Will Be Victorious in the Long Run*: Jesus prayed that we who believe would all be one as He and God are one. He told Nicodemus that "Just as Moses lifted up the snake in the desert, so the Son of Man must be lifted up" (John 3:14), and He told the religious leaders, "When you have lifted up the Son of Man, you will know who I am. You will also know that I don't do anything on my own. I say only what my Father taught me" (John 8:28, CEV). God works in everything for the good of those who love Him (Rom 8:28). Jesus wanted these religious experts and leaders to come to their senses, to change their hearts, and accept Him as God's Son. It's true that the priests and leaders mocked, beat, and murdered Him. It's also true that later "a large number of priests became obedient to the faith" (Acts 6:7). We never know how God will turn a seeming loss into a victory. Christ showed tremendous love to Paul. Even though Paul originally persecuted Christians, Jesus knew that Paul would respond to His love. When Jesus showed him where he was wrong, he changed his heart and became the greatest worker for Jesus that the world has ever known. (See 1 Tim 1:12-17.)

◆ *God's Love Never Fails*: God makes many promises of prosperity and victory to us who seek to love Him and others (Ps 37:4). All the wonders of science and Nature prove that God designed and created great potential into the universe and into our lives. God wants us to work hard, practice integrity, take risks, give up traditions and habits that limit us, cooperate together with love, believe and hope in His great possibilities. He enables us to discover and develop what Jesus came to bring us, abundant and complete life (John 10:10). Life in heaven will certainly be more wonderful and abundant than life on earth. Life in this world can be great also, because God makes it great. Even in hardship and suffering we can look forward to the future with joy and confidence. Paul expressed it so wonderfully: "In everything we have won more than a victory because of Christ who loves us. I am sure that nothing can separate us from God's love — not life or death, not angels or spirits, not the present or the future, and not powers above or powers below. Nothing in all creation can separate us from God's love for us in Christ Jesus our Lord" (Rom 8:37-39, CEV).

Why does Christ do all this for people? We lived in darkness because of our addiction to evil. We loved the darkness. God sent the light of truth into our world. We didn't want His light because that exposed our wickedness. But those who love the truth and live by it come into God's light. We want people to know that God helps us do whatever we do. God motivates us to love truth and live by truth. (See John 3:19-21.)

The Least Can Have Great Love: Simon the Pharisee invited Jesus to dinner. A sinful woman discovered that Jesus was there. She came up to Jesus and wet His feet with her many tears. She wiped his feet with her hair, and with a jar of perfume she anointed His feet. This offended the Pharisee. He said to himself, "If this man were a prophet, he would know who was touching him and what kind of woman she is — that she is a sinner."

Jesus told Simon, "Two men owed money to a certain money lender. One owed him five hundred denarii, and the other fifty. Neither of them had the money to pay him back, so he canceled the debts of both. Now which of them will love him more?"

Simon replied, "I suppose the one who had the bigger debt canceled."

"You have judged correctly," Jesus said.

Then he confronted Simon with his need to know his lack of love: "Do you see this woman? I came into your house. You did not give me any water for my feet, but she wet my feet with her tears and wiped them with her hair. You did not give me a kiss, but this woman, from the time I entered, has not stopped kissing my feet. You did not put oil on my head, but she has poured perfume on my feet. Therefore, I tell you, her many sins have been forgiven — for she loved much. But he who has been forgiven little loves little" (Luke 7:36-48).

No Greater Love Than This: Just as Jesus confronted Simon with his need for greater love, on the night before He was crucified, Jesus told His disciples, "By this all men will know that you are my disciples, if you love one another. . . . My command is this: Love each other as I have loved you. Greater love has no one than this, that he lay down his life for his friends." (See John 13:35; 15:9-17.)

Paul's Famous Description of Love: Paul put top priority on love just as Jesus did: "If I speak in the tongues of men and of angels, but have not love, I am only a resounding gong or a clanging cymbal. If I have the gift of prophecy and can fathom all mysteries and all knowledge, and if I have a faith that can move mountains, but have not love, I am nothing. If I give all I possess to the poor and surrender my body to the flames, but have not love, I gain nothing.

"Love is kind and patient, never jealous, boastful, proud, or rude. Love isn't selfish or quick tempered. It doesn't keep a record of wrongs that others do. Love rejoices in the truth, but not in evil. Love is always supportive, loyal, hopeful, and trusting. Love never fails . . . For now there are faith, hope, and love. But of these three, the greatest is love" (1 Cor 13:1-3, NIV; 4-13, CEV).

What Do Churches Need to Discover?

Love Others as God Loves Us: Can we learn to love ourselves and appreciate our own strengths and potential? Can we love others, even those who might be our enemies? It takes a tough-minded love to work through differences with a person that hates us.

Can we love as God and Christ love us? Two thousand years ago, Jesus said to his close followers, "Love one another." We have the potential to love as God loves us. He makes us in His image, and He leads us toward perfect love, love without fear, suspicion and hatred. God makes science and industry possible, but their full value can't be recognized and developed in a climate of bitter competition, antagonism, and cynicism. Cooperation, love, and productive work have to come through the leaven of loving one another.

Love Even Our Enemies? Why do we need to love our enemies?

What does God accomplish by loving both the good and the bad, by sending His rain and His sunshine on the wicked as well as on those who please Him? How did Jesus treat His enemies, and why did He do what He did? Paul tells us not to overcome evil with evil, but to overcome evil with good. Peter tells us to always be ready to give a good reason for the hope within us, and to do it with gentleness (1 Peter 3:13-16). Why? Because God may grant that those we deal with may be influenced by our loving behavior and decide to change their hearts and their ways. We simply don't always know whom we influence for good nor how God uses us to reach those He loves. Paul told Timothy the same thing (2 Tim 2:23-26). God gives us the strengths and the gifts that we have so we can use them to help others see their possibilities.

Can We Learn from Outsiders? Churches can learn much from organizations that successfully harness God's natural resources and laws. We can also learn much from Christ and His parables. We believe that church leaders will become more open to these hard earned and dynamic truths. God keeps pouring out His blessings on people throughout His world, *especially on those who continuously seek wisdom and knowledge.* We who know God can take heart from the changes He brings. He sustains all good things. Let's not lose our opportunities to love people, especially those who have been the victims of dogmatic and legalistic religion. Christ will use us to bring His love and His good news to the ends of the earth.

What Can the Grassroots Christian Do?

◆ Stress cooperation and healthy relationships. Create a climate of growing intimacy with others. Work together effectively and glorify Christ before our neighbors. Honor people like Jesus did and give them evidence that God loves them. Sympathize with where others are coming from like Paul did. (See Rom 14:1-15:7; 1 Cor 9:19-23.)

◆ Develop a love for Christ that will allow His Spirit to lead us. We don't have to be rebels to examine our traditions and exalt the priorities of Christ. By centering our hearts and minds in Him we can question human priorities in a way that builds on strengths and faces up to weaknesses. The wisest people recognize that they haven't arrived. (See 1 Cor 1:18-2:16; Matt 23:1-39.)

◆ Be concerned with our own tendency to be mere spectators. We need more creative innovation for discovering what really pleases God. We can be sure of one thing: God is not through with us and

He wants us to have fully developed characters. (See 1 Cor 13:1-13; Gal 5:22-26; 6:7-10; Heb 2:1-4; 10:24-25.)

◆ Avoid overintellectualizing. If we see our biggest opportunities as those of the heart then our minds will follow. Let us center our lives on the love of Christ and His priorities, and avoid the gray areas that create pride, dissension, and divisiveness. (See Rom 16:17-19; 1 Cor 1:10; 2 Cor 13:5-9; 2 Tim 3:10-17; Titus 3:9-11.)

◆ Work to eliminate layers of hierarchy. Everywhere organizations are discovering that people can be more productive with love, trust, and light supervision. Jesus and His disciples stressed *relationships, not authority.* An opportunity climate comes with maximum decentralization and delegation. We need to avoid arrogant and dogmatic leadership styles that aren't effective or Christlike. (See Matt 20:20-28; Phil 2:1-11.)

◆ Grasp a great opportunity by claiming God's science and God's technology. God supplies all the wonders that humankind develops through science. These declare God's glory and wisdom no matter what philosophers say: "There is no speech or language where their voice is not heard. Their voice goes out into all the earth, their words to the ends of the world" (Ps 19:3-4). Paul knew what he was talking about when he described the foolishness of people who deny God's existence. Our own existence and the fantastic wonders of the universe clearly prove God's existence. (See Rom 1:18-20; Col 1:15-20; 2:1-8.)

  1. Show gratitude for His blessings and wonders by understanding the connection between miracles, Nature, and science.

  2. Glorify Him by productively using His world and the physical wonders in it.

◆ Examine our traditions to make sure they aren't barriers to those Christ wants to reach. Let's not spoil ourselves and indulge in our own comfort by sentimentally exalting things that aren't really what God desires. Relationships and love are more important than having our way. Whatever we do let's use common sense and focus on right attitudes. Attitude is everything!

◆ Glorify Him seven days a week, not just on Sundays:

  1. Let Him help us on our job; He designed everything and everyone that we work with.

  2. Be aware of God's wonders all around us. He creates things too wonderful to be false. He overwhelms us with evidence.

  3. Don't inadvertently give Satan the glory by attributing to him God's science.

  4. Penetrate all secular organizations with God's love. Pray for them.

5. Be a source of Christ's love in our circles of influence, in our natural network of friends and relatives.

6. Trust Christ to keep on loving us no matter how great the obstacles or how hard the circumstances. God will help us handle them.

◆ Let us center our hearts, minds, and lives on Jesus' inexpressible love for us:

1. Join Paul in saying, "I have been crucified with Christ and I no longer live, but Christ lives in me" (Gal 2:20). Paul stimulates our love with, "Christ died for us at a time when we were helpless and sinful. No one is really willing to die for an honest person, though someone might be willing to die for a truly good person. But God showed how much he loves us by having Christ die for us, even though we were sinful" (Rom 5:6-8, CEV).

2. Jesus gave His greatest secret to His disciples: "As the Father has loved me, so have I loved you. Now remain in my love. If you obey my commands, you will remain in my love, just as I have obeyed my Father's commands and remain in his love. I have told you this so that my joy may be in you and that your joy may be complete. My command is this: Love each other as I have loved you. Greater love has no one than this, that he lay down his life for his friends. You are my friends if you do what I command" (John 15:9-14).

Love Is the Toughest-Minded Emotion in the World

This is a strong statement! Please note the nine ingredients of love as described by the apostle Paul:

Patience	Love is patient
Kindness	Is kind
Generosity	It does not envy
Humility	It is not proud, it does not boast
Courtesy	It is not rude
Unselfishness	It is not self-seeking
Gentleness	It is not easily angered
Mercy	It keeps no record of wrongs
Sincerity	Love does not delight in evil but rejoices with the truth

Material things cannot be great. *The only greatness is unselfish love.* What we *are* stretches past what we *do.* One of the greatest abiding statements of love by Christ is, "Whoever welcomes a little child like this in my name welcomes me" (Matt 18:5).

Joe Batten[12]

Experiment with Your Own Small Group

Invite several friends, including relatives, to your home for a meal or snacks. Discuss why love is the greatest motivator in the world using the following plan:

Icebreaker: Start by asking each person to tell a story from their youth about someone they remember for their love and kindness.

Reading: Read aloud the parable of the Prodigal Son in Luke 15:11-31 and ask another person to read what Jesus said in John 15:9-17.

Discussion: Ask the people present to make comments on how the stories from their own youth relate to these two readings. You will want to prepare ahead of time a list of questions like the following to stimulate the discussion:

◆ How do we respond when we see a person having problems?
◆ How did our parents show us love like the prodigal's father did?
◆ How do we avoid behaving like the older brother?
◆ What does the love of Jesus mean to us personally?

Prayer: Invite those who feel comfortable with praying to participate as each person in the group prays for their own needs and the needs of others.

Vision: Thank people for coming and indicate how this kind of intimacy and friendship can help us to grow in our love for each other. Consider meeting again.

You Can Do It!

Conclusions

Love produces great results! Love motivates us to be both tender-hearted and tough-minded, whatever the circumstances require. *We love the most when we expect our best and when we expect the best from others.* Society needs a revolution of love — a revolution of the heart. Christ trains us Christians for this revolution produced by the Spirit. It happens when we walk the Christ-road with Him to a highly effective life. We follow this road when we say with Paul, "The life I live in the body, I live by faith in the Son of God, who loved me and gave himself for me" (Gal 2:20).

REFERENCES

1. Peck, *The Road Less Traveled*, 82, 160.

2. Willard Tate, *Habits of the Loving Heart*, (Nashville: Christian Communications, 1992), 139-140.

3. Kouzes and Posner, *The Leadership Challenge*, 271.

4. Adapted from Batten, *Tough-minded Leadership*, 181 and 148.

5. Peters and Austin, *Passion for Excellence*, 238.

6. Ibid., 19-20.

7. Bennis, *On Becoming a Leader*, 165.

8. Merrill J. Oster, *Vision-Driven Leadership*, (San Bernardino: Here's Life Publishers, 1991), 122-123.

9. Ash, *Mary Kay on People Management*, 2, 10.

10. Oster, *Vision-Driven Leadership*, 84-91, 113-139.

11. Covey et al., *First Things First*, 249-253.

12. Batten et al., *Tough-Minded Parenting*, adapted from 139-140.

CHAPTER ELEVEN
GRATITUDE

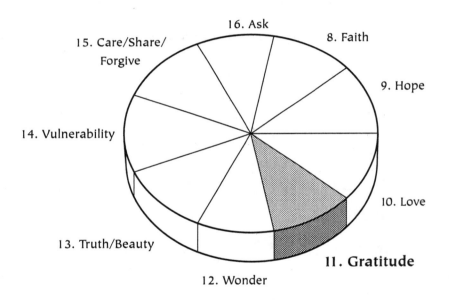

16. Ask

15. Care/Share/
Forgive

8. Faith

9. Hope

14. Vulnerability

10. Love

13. Truth/Beauty

11. Gratitude

12. Wonder

11

GRATITUDE — OUR RESPONSE TO LOVE AND WONDER

*A loving heart is a thankful heart — thankful for life, for God's grace, for friends
and family, for the beauty of the world, for freedom and for a lot of other things.
It's filled with gratitude to God for all His blessings
rather than with resentment for what it doesn't have.
. . . Even people going through tough times have a lot of things for which they can
be thankful if they choose to be. . . . We fail to think we're blessed most of the time
. . . but it's not because we haven't been blessed.
Instead, it's because we take so many of our blessings for granted.
. . . James tells us we should even consider it joy when we encounter trials, knowing
they help us to grow in Christlikeness (James 1:2-4).
Hebrews 12:1-13 gives us the same message. Gratitude produces happiness;
ingratitude produces unhappiness. It couldn't be simpler.*
Willard Tate[1]

Key Points

We can never have too much gratitude for the wonderful things
we receive in our lives. We experience plenty of evil and hardship in
this world, but *attitudes of wonder and gratitude can give us victory over
depression and cynicism.* Many secular organizations recognize that
possibilities and opportunities open up when they give and encourage gratitude. Jesus teaches us to be thankful. Our greatest joys
come through gratitude to God for His perfect and wonderful gifts.
Churches can improve greatly in recognizing and being grateful for

197

the presence and guidance of the Spirit of Christ. Many Christians in secular jobs have experienced both the physical and spiritual blessings of Christ. The churches need to learn from these experiences, and intimate small groups provide the ideal medium for building body life through thankfulness to God.

****

Leaders in Excellent Secular Organizations Show Gratitude

Leaders in organizations like Apple, America West, Honda, HP, IBM, Johnsonville Foods, Kollmorgen, Mary Kay Cosmetics, Milliken, Scandinavian Airlines Systems, and Stew Leonard's, Inc. cultivate gratitude for their suppliers, employees, associates, and customers. And these people reciprocate with gratitude and excellence in relationships. Organizations and people in general responded with a great display of worldwide gratitude and concern at the time of the Apollo 13 rescue.

Apollo 13: Jim Lovell, Jack Swigert, and Fred Haise rode out one of the most exciting adventures in the history of space travel. Just 48 hours before liftoff Ken Mattingly had been replaced by Swigert. All of them had been exposed to measles, but Mattingly had not been immunized. The flight surgeon "thumbed Mattingly out of the lineup."[2]

1.   *1:13 p.m. CST on Saturday, April 11, 1970*: The Saturn 5 Rocket lifted them off and two and a half hours later (3:48 p.m.) the Saturn third stage rocket blasted them out of earth orbit to head toward the moon, "three men in a can zipping along at 25,000 miles an hour."[3] At 5:14 p.m. the Odyssey command module, now separated from the Saturn, docked with the Aquarius lunar excursion module (LEM) and extracted it from the third stage.[4]

2.   *7:53 p.m. on Sunday, April 12th*, about 31 hours after liftoff, mission commander Lovell fired Odyssey's engine to put Apollo 13 into the planned trajectory for orbiting the moon. Later when they would be orbiting the moon, Lovell and lunar module pilot Haise planned to descend to the moon's surface in the lunar excursion module (LEM) and later return and redock with Odyssey.[5]

3.   *9:07 p.m. on Monday, April 13th*, about 56 hours after liftoff: Mission Control asked the crew on the Odyssey, now 200,000 miles out from the earth, to stir the cryo tanks. Command module pilot Swigert "threw the switch to stir all four cryo

tanks." About 16 seconds later, "a bang-thump-shudder shook the ship. . . . Swigert . . . felt the spacecraft quake beneath him. Lovell . . . felt a thunderclap rumble through him; Haise, still in the tunnel [between Odyssey and Aquarius], actually saw its wall shift around him." *The alarm sounded and a warning light went on:*[6]

◆ Pressure in oxygen tank number two, with half the ship's oxygen, fell to zero. It was "dry as a bone."[7]

◆ Main bus B showed low voltage. Two out of the three fuel cells showed no pressure.[8] Bus A began to show low voltage.

◆ Ten minutes after the bang the "spacecraft was still swaying and wobbling." Lovell saw a cloud of gas outside his window. He looked over at the gage for O_2 tank number one. This tank would have held enough oxygen for the trip, but "the needle for tank one was well below full and visibly falling." Tank two was empty, and when tank one dropped to empty the crew would not have enough oxygen.[9]

4. *This left them only one option:* They must power down the Odyssey command module and use the Aquarius LEM as a "lifeboat." Fred Haise, the lunar module pilot, and the people in Mission Control, would have to learn how to stretch its very limited resources. The Odyssey command module must still be powered back up at the end of the trip. Only it could survive reentry into the earth's atmosphere. The astronauts started to shut down Odyssey to conserve power and oxygen for reentry. At the same time they powered up Aquarius to be their "lifeboat."[10]

◆ Lovell and Haise entered the guidance coordinates into the Aquarius' computer, powered up Aquarius while Swigert powered down the Odyssey command module.[11]

◆ They had about *90 hours before reentry.* Aquarius had only enough electricity and water for *45 hours,* and CO_2 scrubbing for about *36 hours.* They had planned just enough for two people to make a day-and-one-half exploration on the moon's surface and return to Odyssey. Now three people would have to survive more than three days in the Aquarius LEM, something they had never planned for.[12]

5. *2:43 a.m. on Tuesday, April 14:* At 61 hours and 30 minutes from liftoff, immediately after the crew switched to Aquarius LEM, they ignited the thruster engines for a quick burn. This would get them about 130 miles above the moon's surface and in the right trajectory for a slingshot free-return around the back of the moon and toward home. The maneuver came out perfectly.[13]

- ◆ Grumman, the manufacturer of the LEM, called in its people to help with the emergency. One thing was sure: Mission Control needed all the expertise they could get to help save the spacecraft and its crew.[14]
- ◆ The next procedure or PC + 2 burn was scheduled for "two hours after persynthion — or closest approach to the back side of the moon." The "spacecraft would fire its engine, changing its course just enough to aim it precisely toward Earth" and make splashdown at noon on Friday, April 17th. They would have to come up with a solution to the carbon dioxide problem long before then.[15]

6. *8:40 p.m. on Tuesday, April 14th*, 79 hours and 27 minutes from liftoff: After swinging around the back of the moon Lovell ignited the thrusters for the PC + 2 burn. He put the spaceship on a perfect trajectory for the Friday noon reentry.[16]

- ◆ Aquarius required 55 amps of electrical current for normal operation. They shut down all but the very minimum of equipment to get the electrical usage down to 12 amps. They reduced water usage from the normal 6.3 pounds per hour to 3.5. But how would they solve the carbon dioxide problem?[17]
- ◆ Carbon dioxide (CO_2) pressure normally ran between 2 and 3 millimeters of mercury. This would rise quickly when the lithium hydroxide (LiOH) cartridges got saturated. In less than 36 hours, when the CO_2 pressure reached 15 millimeters, the astronauts would start to be asphyxiated. Engineers on the ground would have to figure out how to fit the *square lithium hydroxide cartridges* from the Odyssey command module into the *round receptacles* on the LEM. They never seriously considered this possibility before.[18]
- ◆ The engineers in Houston experimented with the square cartridges for a day and one-half in their lab. By early Wednesday morning, April 15th, they came up with a "cut-and-paste modification" that worked.[19]
- ◆ The carbon dioxide pressure in Aquarius had by now risen to 13 millimeters of mercury. The modification had been worked out just before CO_2 poisoning was beginning. Starting at 2:23 p.m. on Wednesday Swigert took an hour to build the first canister. From the Odyssey he used a roll of duct tape, a pair of scissors, and one of the square lithium hydroxide canisters. He also used heavy cardboard from his book of LEM procedures and plastic wrapping from their thermal undergarments used for walking on the moon. He attached the queer-looking

contraption to the tubing of one of the pressure-suit hoses. He listened for the sound of air being pulled through the canister. "Softly, but unmistakably, he could hear air being drawn through the vent slats and, presumably, across the pristine lithium hydroxide crystals."[20]

◆ The controllers in Houston watched the carbon dioxide read-out. Lovell, Swigert, and Haise stared at their instrument panel. The needle "began to fall, first to 12, then to 11.5, then to 11 and below." Six hours later, "the cockpit CO_2 had dropped to a scant 0.2 percent of the overall air mass."[21]

7. *2:23 p.m. on Wednesday, April 15th* right after the CO_2 problem was solved:

◆ "The trajectory was becoming mysteriously shallower. It was falling to 6.3 degrees and below." For a safe reentry the target angle was 6.5 degrees. It could be no less than 5.3 degrees. It was falling too fast, and now they would have to make another burn.

◆ At 10:31 p.m. (105 hours and 18 minutes after liftoff) Lovell made another burn of Aquarius' engine to put the spaceship back into the center of its reentry corridor. They couldn't understand what was causing the ship's trajectory to keep falling.[22]

8. *8:00 a.m. on Thursday, April 16th:* They were now 130,000 miles out from earth, almost half way home, and the final steps were being planned:

◆ Even after Wednesday's correction the trajectory was "just a fraction above 6.0 degrees and continuing to fall." To correct this Lovell planned to power up the LEM for "another mid-course maneuver at about five hours before reentry."[23]

◆ They also had to adjust the ballast weight on the command module since they had no moon rocks and soil samples on board as had been originally planned.[24]

◆ From 7:30 to 9:15 p.m. on Thursday, Houston read up stacks of check lists to the spaceship. Mission Control told Swigert, "We did run simulations on all of this, so we do think we got all the little surprises ironed out." Since Odyssey was very cold from being down three days, they risked power-up-failure from electrical shorts caused by condensation.[25]

9. *6:52 a.m. on Friday, April 17th,* about five hours before reentry the following maneuvers were started:

◆ Lovell again put the spaceship into the correct trajectory. At the same time, the powerup of the command module was being completed. Miraculously, there were no electrical shorts or instrument failures![26]

◆ At 7:14 a.m. Swigert jettisoned the service module. What the astronauts saw shocked them. "Panel four . . . made up about a sixth of the ship's external skin. . . . Now, it appeared, the entire door was gone, ripped free and blasted away from the ship. . . . Where oxygen tank number two was supposed to be, Lovell saw, to his astonishment, a large charred space and absolutely nothing else. . . . 'And there's one whole side of that spacecraft missing!' Lovell radioed to Houston."[27]

◆ At 10:43 a.m., 141 hours and 30 minutes after liftoff, Swigert jettisoned Aquarius and it somersaulted away. They had only one hour and 15 minutes until splashdown.[28]

10. *11:53 a.m. on Friday, April 17th*: Reentry began 14 minutes before splashdown. Their 25,000 mile per hour plunge was slowed to 300 miles per hour when they entered the earth's atmosphere.

◆ Two good drogue chutes "billowed open" slowing the ship to 175 miles per hour.

◆ The drogues jettisoned themselves and the three main chutes flew open. They were now descending at a little more than 20 miles per hour.[29]

11. *12:07 p.m. on Friday, April 17th*: 142 hours and 55 minutes after liftoff, they splashed down in the Pacific Ocean.

◆ Those on the USS Iwo Jima saw three mammoth clouds of cloth fabric a few hundred yards away. They all cheered with gratitude!

◆ In Odyssey Jim Lovell said, "Fellows, we're home."

◆ In Houston, Marilyn Lovell through "a film of tears and a swarm of people . . . watched the television in her family room as Odyssey struck the water and the three parachutes . . . flattened themselves on the ocean." Her friend Betty answered the phone in the master bedroom and called out, "Marilyn, it's the White House again."

She picked up the receiver and "heard the deep, familiar voice. 'Marilyn, this is the president. I wanted to know if you'd care to accompany me to Hawaii to pick up your husband.'"

"'Mr. President,' she said at last, 'I'd love to.'"[30]

A Tremendous Response of Gratitude

The whole world watched as the best of science and engineering, teamwork and leadership struggled to save the Apollo 13 crew out of almost sure tragedy. More than any others the families of the astronauts were full of relief and gratitude. This fantastic rescue amazed and thrilled the whole world. Gratitude poured out to an extent hardly ever seen.

◆ With less than three hours of sleep per day the three astronauts maintained a calm and cool courage to bring the spaceship home.

◆ The people in Mission Control developed and tested totally new procedures. They discovered how to use the Aquarius LEM and the Odyssey command module in ways never done before. No one had ever expected to operate without the damaged and destroyed equipment in the service module. Gene Kranz, lead flight director, strongly cut off any cynicism that might discourage the attempt to bring the astronauts back home safely.

◆ The two engineers who modified the Odyssey lithium hydroxide canisters for use in the Aquarius came up with a major life-saver.

◆ Ken Mattingly played a key role in the simulator. He eventually got to the moon as command module pilot on Apollo 16, a 21-day mission to the moon starting on April 6 and ending on April 27, 1972.

Just as Apollo 13 carried men traveling between the earth and moon, Earth carries human travelers as a spaceship orbiting the sun. We need gratitude and respect for our Designer, Creator, and Source of life just as Lovell, Swigert, and Haise listened to and cooperated with Mission Control in Houston.

Notice the limitations of Apollo 13 when it came to oxygen, water, electricity, and a means of getting rid of poisonous carbon dioxide. God has designed and created spaceship Earth with no such problems or limitations. We have plenty of oxygen, water, and electricity. God's vegetation is designed to constantly convert CO_2 into oxygen and water.

Jesus expected people to show gratitude for what God does in their lives. He praised those who showed such gratitude and love. But He also knew that many would not listen even to Him, the only One who ever came down from Heaven. Adam and Eve didn't choose wisely between the voices of God and the devil. We need to learn from their mistake. We need to learn from this parable of Apollo 13 and have the same overwhelming kind of gratitude to God that people had when the astronauts splashed down in the Pacific Ocean. God does everything for our care and in our best interest.

The Challenge of Gratitude

Do you have an "attitude of gratitude"? Or do you have "hardening of the attitudes"? You can't have a full measure of both. They cannot coexist.

Hardening of the attitudes may very likely be the most insidious and pervasive disease of humankind since the beginning of civilization. Such rigidity has been the root cause of socially and psychologically disintegrating behavior, manifested in a broad spectrum of illnesses, war, crime, and the trillions of petty thoughts and actions that have stultified people and taken the rich bloom from life's possibilities.

I'm not talking about gratitude as an occasional action. I'm talking about a continuous, ongoing process of being or experiencing. At the very least, the "act" of gratitude requires that we summon up an awareness of positive, of good realities, sensed as well as seen. As we gain skill in being and staying aware of these good feelings and experiences, the finest kind of mental nourishment can evolve.

The converse, of course is true. When our minds are not fed a diet of gratitude, they become breeding places for the darker side of ourselves.

Please examine the following exercise thoughtfully and complete each portion. . . . Replace [each] negative feeling with a positive . . . something you feel grateful for. I realize this is not easy. It requires most of us to reverse the conditioning of a lifetime . . . real growth can begin.

Negative Feeling	Positives Perceived
Alienation from loved ones	_____
Despair	_____
Valuelessness	_____
Boredom	_____
Meaninglessness	_____
Hopelessness, defeat	_____
Dryness, staleness	_____

Joe Batten[3]

What Did Jesus Teach about Gratitude?

◆ Jesus expected the ten lepers to be thankful for their healing, but only the Samaritan thanked Him. He was amazed and asked, "Were not all ten cleansed? Where are the other nine?" Jesus understood our human tendency to take God's presence and care for granted. Often those who live with the greatest problems still find time to be grateful to God (Luke 17:12-19).

◆ Mary anointed the feet of Jesus with expensive perfume. She sat at His feet listening to Him. The disciples criticized Mary for her waste, but Jesus praised her for her love and gratitude. He told His disciples, "She has done a beautiful thing to me. . . . When she poured this perfume on my body, she did it to prepare me for burial. I tell you the truth, wherever this gospel is preached throughout the world, what she has done will also be told, in memory of her" (Matt 26:10-13).

◆ Those invited in the parable of the wedding feast were not thankful and they gave excuses. This parable portrays our human condition. We find ourselves living in a very temporary world, like the astronauts experienced on their trip to the moon. Somehow we find it very hard to be grateful to our Creator. Jesus ended this parable with how God looks at those who despised Him and were not grateful: "I tell you, not one of those men who were invited will get a taste of my banquet." (See Luke 14:16-24.)

◆ Jesus expected childlike gratitude and acceptance. Much more would be given to one who expressed gratitude for what he already had. He often used children as examples of the attitude of gratitude and sincerity that pleased God. Jesus pointed out that the Kingdom of God belonged to those who behaved like little children: "I tell you the truth, unless you change and become like little children, you will never enter the kingdom of heaven" (Matt 18:2; 19:14).

◆ The man born blind was thankful, but the Pharisees scorned him by saying, "You were steeped in sin at birth; how dare you lecture us!" They threw him out. Shortly after that Jesus told the Pharisees, "If you were blind, you would not be guilty of sin; but now that you claim you can see, your guilt remains" (John 9:34, 39-41).

◆ We can anticipate a wonderful experience of gratitude when we eventually stand in the presence of Christ to give our accounting to Him. With Paul we can exercise our faith and common sense to believe: "What may be known about God is plain . . . . For since the creation of the world, God's invisible qualities — his eternal power and divine nature — have been clearly seen, being understood from what has been made. . .") (Rom 1:19-20).

◆ David tells us, "The heavens declare the glory of God; the skies proclaim the work of his hands. Day after day they pour forth speech; night after night they display knowledge. . . . Their voice goes out into all the earth, their words to the ends of the world" (Ps 19:1-4).

◆ Later he wrote, "How many are your works, O LORD! In wisdom you made them all; the earth is full of your creatures. . . . These all look to you to give them their food at the proper time. When you give it to them, they gather it up; when you open your hand, they are satisfied with good things. . . . When you send your Spirit, they are created, and you renew the face of the earth" (Ps 104:24-31).

◆ Jesus revealed the basic problem of unbelief and ingratitude when He said to the Pharisees and Sadducees, "When evening comes, you say, 'It will be fair weather, for the sky is red,' and in the morning, 'Today it will be stormy, for the sky is red and overcast.' You know how to interpret the appearance of the sky, but you cannot interpret the signs of the times" (Matt 16:2-3).

Gratitude, design, purpose, hope, belief, analogy of experience, wonder, possibilities, free will, common sense, instinct, and God's revelation of Himself are all avenues by which we can discover the existence of our Creator and His values. Some of these avenues to truth are used by scientists and philosophers, but some of them are ridiculed as wishful thinking and the source of superstition.

It's natural for children to have gratitude toward their parents. It's just as natural for people to have gratitude and to give thanks to their Creator. The unnatural thing is to despise God and to deny His existence. Why be angry with God, when it is much wiser to explore what the Bible and the universe can teach us about Him?

God may be invisible, but He confronts us dramatically with His wonders. We can blame Him, deny His existence, and take for granted the wonderful things He gives to us. We can focus on the bad and completely overlook the good and our need to feel and show gratitude.

Why are many people unwilling to come to grips with life, face up to problems, *do* great things and *become* great? Facing future challenges and changes leads to personal greatness. Why then do we attach ourselves to unhealthy traditions and precedents, and why do we find it so easy to criticize and judge others? It's so easy to say "they" instead of "we," or to blame "our parents," "society," "the government," and "the church" when we should be looking inside of ourselves. Instead of being motivated by gratitude we often act out of anger or react wrongly to a challenge thrown at us by someone else.

Why do many people immerse themselves in resentment, cynicism, blame and jealousy when there are so many wonders in life to be happy and show gratitude for? Leo Buscaglia writes:

> We complain that our relationships are dull. We act as if these things [joy and happiness] are to be found *out there somewhere*. We seldom come to terms with the idea that happiness is in *us*. . . .
>
> We never stop to think that there is nothing in the world which can be given or denied us that will bring us happiness unless we decide it. In fact, the happiest people in the world would probably still be happy if stripped of everything except life. . . .
>
> All who so desire should be able to rise above whatever social condition in which they were born and attain whatever prize they want for what they believe to be their betterment or happiness. What I'm saying is that nothing but *life itself* is necessary for humans to know joy and happiness.

Buscaglia experienced these things in his work with handicapped people. He "saw quadriplegics who smiled and laughed their way through life." He was amazed that the healthy people working with them "were often miserable, unsatisfied and depressed." In his experience "those who seemed to have no particular cause to rejoice" were very happy. "They seemed to have in common a singular courage, a willingness to risk, to fail and to let go, a belief in themselves, a wonderful resourcefulness, a trust in their creative uniqueness and an ability to hold on to their dream."[32]

The authors have had the same experience with people everywhere. Those with the least to be thankful for often have great perseverance and optimism because they have learned to deal with misfortune and handicaps. The same circumstances that make one person a miserable complainer make others into thankful, productive overcomers. No small part of this is the decision people make to either see with gratitude or be blind with resentment to the wonders and hope all around them in God's Creation.

Why Be Angry at God?

Because there are many false religions and many false views of

God in the world, is it therefore wise to deny God's existence dogmatically? Is it wise for atheists and agnostics to insist that Christ's life and message are false and untrue? We agree that scientists have been criticized and opposed unfairly both in the past and present by dogmatic religious experts. Some criticism of dogmatic scientists (scientism) is justified just as some criticism of dogmatic theologians and religious people is justified.

We believe that people are unwise to react against and reject God. Everything ever designed, engineered, built, and maintained comes from intelligent people working in cooperation with other intelligent people. Mankind has developed and created technology through great intelligence, plenty of risks, much experimentation, tremendous cooperation and hard work. It can't be done any other way. Why then isn't it wise to believe in God by analogy? Why is it foolish to believe that what is greater and more complex than anything mankind can do is done by a personal Creator with higher intelligence, purpose and power? No one believes that what humans design and build (spaceships, TVs, race cars, computers, etc.) can come into existence by chance. Why then should we believe that life, reproduction, thought, and intelligence can come into existence by the blind forces of nature? Why should we believe that the "blind forces of nature" exist by chance? Creation calls out for gratitude!

Robert Schuller has said that it is instinctive for us to believe in God and in eternal life. Solomon wrote, "He has made everything beautiful in its time. He has also set eternity in the hearts of men; yet they cannot fathom what God has done from beginning to end" (Eccl 3:11).

What Do Churches Need to Discover?

◆ Belief in God is universal where gratitude exists. Most people naturally have gratitude for what they have received by just being alive.

◆ Analogy is powerful. We know of nothing that we have discovered, designed, or created that came without great wisdom, much experimentation, and knowledge used by thinking, living human beings. There is no evidence in existence that something can exist without being designed and created by wisdom and knowledge.

◆ Tunnel vision is common when we try to reconstruct history with limited facts. It's just not wise to limit ourselves to "nothing but" physical reality.

◆ We may throw out the baby with the bathwater when we aren't careful in our judgments and grateful for what we have been given by God.

◆ Lack of gratitude is a common failing in humans, but we in His church can help people rise above this problem.

What Can the Grassroots Christian Do?
The Baby and the Bathwater, and Tunnel Vision

Scott Peck asks the question, "What are we to do — we who are properly skeptical and scientific-minded — with this 'powerful force originating outside of human consciousness which nurtures the spiritual growth of human beings'? . . .Are we to operate with tunnel vision and ignore it because it does not fit in easily with traditional scientific concepts of natural law? To do so is perilous."[33]

Earlier he had pointed out,

Scientists are dedicated to asking questions in the search for truth. . . . In their desire for simple solutions, scientists are prone to fall into two traps as they question the reality of God. The first is to throw the baby out with the bath water. And the second is tunnel vision.

There is clearly a lot of dirty bath water surrounding the reality of God. Holy wars. Inquisitions. Animal sacrifice. Human sacrifice. Superstition. Stultification. Dogmatism. Ignorance. Hypocrisy. Self-righteousness. Rigidity. Cruelty. Book-burning. Witch-hunting. Inhibition. Fear. Conformity. Morbid guilt. Insanity. The list is almost endless. But is all this what God has done to humans or what humans have done to God? . . . Is the problem, then, that humans tend to believe in God, or is the problem that humans tend to be dogmatic? Anyone who has known a died-in-the-wool atheist will know that such an individual can be as dogmatic about unbelief as any believer can be about belief. Is it belief in God we need to get rid of, or is it dogmatism?

. . . Many scientists simply do not look at the evidence of the reality of God. They suffer from a kind of tunnel vision, a psychologically self-imposed psychological set of blinders which prevents them from turning their attention to the realm of the spirit. . . .

It is as if they were to say, 'What we cannot measure is unimportant and unworthy of our observation.' Because of this attitude many scientists exclude from their serious consideration all matters that are — or seem to be — intangible. Including, of course, the matter of God.

. . . This strange but remarkably common assumption that things that are not easy to study do not merit study is beginning to be challenged by several relatively recent developments within science itself."[34]

The grassroots Christian can thank God for the marvels of science. We can understand that everything in this world belongs to God. Everything has been designed and created by Him, including the very possibility of science. Even scientists themselves have God to thank for their very existence. Loving God and showing gratitude to Him by the way we live doesn't mean that we have to be dishonest or superstitious. Our lives and our work matter to God, and we can lead others to the joy of knowing Christ.

We don't have to second guess God. We can accept reality like it is and expect that God will be able to handle all of the things that we do not understand. Job was very upset with God because of the terrible pain and suffering he was experiencing, but God did not give plain answers to any of Job's questions or complaints. What God did do was reveal Himself to Job and let him understand that He created everything and that He could handle anything. Job was overwhelmed by God's appearance and was sorry that he had misjudged God. God knows what He is doing and why. We can trust Him to deal with all of His creation with complete fairness and unconditional love.

Philip Yancey, in discussing the "tunnel vision" or "reductionism" of the physical scientist, points out that reductionism is a powerful force, but it can be a curse as well as a blessing:

> And if we reduce behavior to *merely* hormones and chemistry, we lose all human mystery and free will and romance. The ideals of romantic love that have inspired artists and lovers through the centuries suddenly reduce to a matter of hormonal secretions.
>
> Reductionism may exert undue influence over us unless we recognize it for what it is: a way of looking. It is not a True or False concept; it is a point of view that informs us about the parts of a thing, but not the whole.
>
> Spiritual acts, for example, can be viewed from both a lower and higher level. One does not supplant the other; each merely sees the same behavior differently (just as looking *at* a beam of light differs from looking *along* it). From the 'lower' perspective, prayer is a person talking to himself. . . . The 'higher' perspective presumes that a spiritual reality is at work, with human prayer serving as a contact point between the seen and unseen worlds. . . .

Perhaps the continuity between natural and supernatural is a continuity of design from the same Creator. That, at least, is the 'higher' view of faith. The one level of viewing does not exclude the other; they are two ways of looking at the same event.[35]

It is amazing the amount of writing there has been defending hopelessness, cynicism, nihilism (life has no meaning), "nothing-butism." Dr. Viktor Frankl, a survivor of Auschwitz (the very name stood for all that was horrible: gas chambers, crematoriums, massacres) wrote:

The existential vacuum which is the mass neurosis of the present time can be described as a private and personal form of nihilism; for nihilism can be defined as the contention that being has no meaning.

. . . There is a danger inherent in the teaching of man's "noth-ingbutness," the theory that man is nothing but the result of biological, psychological and sociological conditions, or the product of heredity and environment. Such a view of man makes a neurotic believe what he is prone to believe anyway, namely, that he is the pawn and victim of outer influences or inner circumstances. This neurotic fatalism is fostered and strengthened by a psychotherapy which denies that man is free.[36]

What we recommend is that grassroots believers look at and see the wonders of their own bodies and minds, the wonders all around them in God's Creation, and the wonders of wisdom found in Christ. If all we had was life, nothing could keep us from bouncing back and becoming all that God wants us to be. (See Col 2:2-4.)

An Agenda for Small Groups

1. *Icebreaker (20 minutes)*: Ask each person in the group to tell of his or her most thankful relationship or experience between the ages of five and ten. Describe the details of what, when, where, who, why, and how.

2. *Read related Bible passages (10 minutes)*: Ask each person to participate in reading Luke 17:11-19 (ten lepers) and Matthew 26:6-13 (Mary's adoration).

3. *Discuss Jesus' teaching (30 minutes)*: Invite each person to discuss their own gratitude. Ask questions such as,

◆ What does God do to make us thankful?

◆ How does gratitude motivate us to grow in faith, hope and love?

◆ How do gratitude and wonder relate to each other?

4. *Prayer for needs (20 minutes)*: Invite each person to express personal needs and then pray.

5. *Vision (10 minutes)*: The leader summarizes how gratitude can expand the group's vision of the future.

Conclusions

Wisdom teaches us to aim at God's top priorities, not rely on God only as a last resort. Christ has done and is doing great and wonderful things for each of us. We have every reason to be thankful. Our gratitude should not be marginal, and we should make ourselves aware of the things that we take for granted.

No matter what our troubles, obstacles, and adversity, God uses them to teach us lessons that we can learn in no other way. We don't develop maturity by proxy. We can be grateful even in hardship since our victory is assured.

Gratitude has great power. Let's open our eyes and hearts to the numerous gifts and wonders that God has designed and created for us. We often close our eyes and hearts to Him and live in quiet desperation. Are we making the mistake of the cynic and skeptic by taking God's great gifts and love for granted? Tunnel vision is common, but we don't need to be a victim of it. We can concentrate on what we are thankful for, and not on what we despise and are against.

REFERENCES

1. Tate, *Habits of the Loving Heart*, 37-41.

2. Jim Lovell and Jeffrey Kluger, *Apollo 13*, (New York: Pocket Books, 1994), 88.

3. Ibid., 91.

4. Ibid., 94.

5. Ibid., 384.

6. Ibid., 102, 378.

7. Ibid., 107.

8. Ibid., 108.

9. Ibid., 112.

10. Ibid., 112-114.

11. Ibid., 141-143.

12. Ibid., 180-181.

13. Ibid., 143, 178-179.

14. Ibid., 182-183.

15. Ibid., 144.

16. Ibid., 264-266.

17. Ibid., 181, 233.

18. Ibid., 274.

19. Ibid., 272.

20. Ibid., 276-278, 384.

21. Ibid., 278.

22. Ibid., 307, 384.

23. Ibid., 319, 321.

24. Ibid., 322, 325.

25. Ibid., 334.

26. Ibid., 342.

27. Ibid., 344-346.

28. Ibid., 354.

29. Ibid., 358-360, 384.

30. Ibid., 360-361.

31. Batten, *Tough-minded Leadership*, 181.

32. Leo Buscaglia, *Loving Each Other*, (Thorofare: Slack Inc., 1984), 114-115.

33. Scott Peck, *The Road Less Traveled*, 261.

34. Ibid., 222-226.

35. Yancey, *Disappointment With God*, 161-164.

36. Frankl, *Man's Search for Meaning*, 152-153.

CHAPTER TWELVE
WONDER

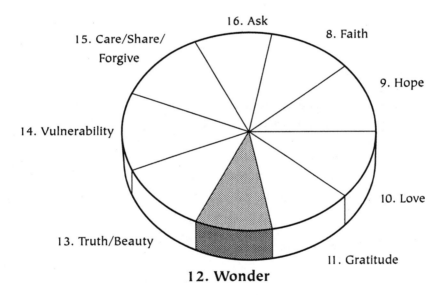

15. Care/Share/
Forgive

16. Ask

8. Faith

9. Hope

14. Vulnerability

10. Love

13. Truth/Beauty

11. Gratitude

12. Wonder

12

GENERATE AN APPETITE FOR WONDER, CURIOSITY, AND ADVENTURE

It's wonderful that I think;
It's even more wonderful that God thinks higher thoughts than I.
It's marvelous that I'm a living creature;
It's even more marvelous that God is my Living Creator.
Warren Howard

Jesus will come "to be glorified in his holy people and to be marveled at among all those who have believed. This includes you, because you believed our testimony to you."
Paul (in 2 Thessalonians 1:10)

Every good and perfect gift is from above, coming down from the Father of the heavenly lights, who does not change like shifting shadows.
James (in James 1:17)

Key Points

What causes people of all ages to lose the sense of wonder so crucial in retaining a zest for life? What has happened to their capacity for dreaming, for seeing visions? In this chapter we explain how to let ourselves "loose" and recapture our sense of wonder. What fills us with joy and motivates us? Based on what God has designed, created, and maintained, we see the marvelous wonder of what He is preparing for us.

People and organizations who succeed the most have an innate capacity for wonder at the great possibilities in life. Jesus commended childlike wonder as a great motivating power in His Kingdom.

Churches can greatly improve their awareness of the wonder designed into God's universe. He created it to be a place where He could prepare us for heaven. Christians who have learned from excellent organizations can glorify God in His church. Small groups have numerous and endless examples of God's love and wonder to marvel at. By this He motivates us to love and good works.

****

Wonder results in curiosity, enthusiasm, excitement, adventure, and discovery. We experience life when we see and feel the wonder of the world around us. True wisdom learns great lessons from the wonders of Creation. Fools fall back into skepticism, cynicism, negative thinking, and tunnel vision. To learn new truths we must concentrate on possibilities, not the risks and the dangers. We imagine what does not yet exist. We take risks. We experiment. We discover much more in life than first meets the eye. We receive great dividends when we listen to those with more experience than we. Humble and naive listening opens doors to new and wonderful ideas. People who know-it-all don't always appreciate the wonder all around us. We can learn when we ask and seek with open eyes and hearts. Excellent organizations keep on asking, keep on seeking, keep on knocking. They understand the rewards that come from giving and serving.

The Challenge of Wonder

The sense of wonder is developed through a positive outlook on life. It is a full-time, lifelong quest that persists in seeking out the wonder, the beauty-*enhancing* qualities of people, events, and things.

Perhaps this definition of *wonder* may be useful to you: "To sense, to reach, to hunger and thirst for further assurance of the possibilities in all things. This is the enhancement of a sense of wonder."

Can you think of anything more calculated to retain the emotional resilience and mental elasticity of youth and creativity than a sense of wonder? Out of this vital quality flow many very practical things: greater creativity, innovation, methods improvement, job performance, customer service, unity of family and fellow team members.

Joe Batten[1]

How Do Secular Organizations Show Wonder?

Nothing produces joy like a wonderful vision of the future. Excellent leaders envision and strive toward such wonders. They persuade others to follow their dream. They enable others to share the wonder.

Successful people follow their dreams. They overcome what is difficult. They see beyond what seems to be impossible. Others may look and be stopped by the obstacles, the troubles, and the not-so-wonderful. They prefer to complain about their lot. They object to, criticize, and mock the vision. The excellent companies give their people the choice to believe in, commit to, and get involved in the revolutionary vision, but the choice must be made.

The best organizations develop a wonderful and stretching vision and persuade people to work toward it with curiosity, adventure, and expectation. What could be more exciting than such a journey? What could have more lasting value? What could enable us to triumph over boredom, futility, and frustration? To answer these questions we need to appreciate just how wonderful Christ and His message are.

Examples of Wonder in Great Organizations:

1. *Stew Leonard's* sells dairy products in Norwalk, Connecticut. In one store Stew brings in more than $85,000,000 per year. Most single stores turn over about $300 per square foot of floor space, but Stew Leonard's does an amazing $3,000 per square foot. He simply delights his customers with the way he sells chicken, cheese, eggs, and muffins. He runs a petting zoo for kids. A Mechanical Chicken in the egg department lays eggs faster than any other chicken in the world.

He creates amazing wonder and loyalty in the minds of his customers. A funeral director wrote to him of a woman who left instructions that the belongings she wanted put in her casket should be in a Stew Leonard's shopping bag.[2]

This answers well Tom Peters' question about service and products: "Do any stand out in a flash? Or do you need an electron microscope to tell them apart?" How you serve or what you sell should produce wonder like Stew Leonard's. People should say "Wow!" in wonder and surprise at your obvious excellence in quality. Peters tells us that a visit to Stew Leonard's will show us "what is possible in a striking and dramatic fashion." We will see for ourselves how wonder and excellence are exceptions because, "Thinly Disguised Contempt is found everywhere."[3]

Stew also builds wonderful lifetime relationships with his suppliers. He had a banner year selling 25,000 Christmas trees in 1988. After the season one of his suppliers on a very tight margin lost $2,000 because a trucker took no responsibility for trees damaged in transit. The supplier asked Stew, "Will you split the cost?" Stew knew that these were "the most beautiful Christmas trees we've ever seen." When he agreed, the vendor responded, "Boy, I'm looking forward to doing business with you next year." Stew looks for long term relationships, so he concluded, "He'll be a supplier for life."[4]

Another supplier of eggs repackaged his eggs from flats into cartons for shipment to Stew. Stew then transferred the eggs to metal containers. He visited this supplier and saved him one process step by asking him to package directly into cartons. Later Stew asked him if he could package his eggs directly into the metal containers. Elimination of these two steps saved money for both the supplier and Stew Leonard's. Wonderful experiences and valuable results come from long term and excellent relationships, supplier and customer working as a team.[5]

Tom Peters tells us not to just "cope" or "deal with" our problems, but see them as opportunities, "Welcoming, laughing at, enjoying." We need to put wonder, curiosity, and adventure into our relationships to make them for life.[6]

2. *The Information Society*: Famous companies like *IBM, Apple, HP, Microsoft, Intel,* and *AT&T* catapult our society through the *Knowledge Age.* Joel Swedlow, Louie Psihoyes, and Allen Carroll describe this exciting adventure graphically as a ride on the *Information Highway.*[7]

◆ From little kids to senior citizens, from parents to scientists we, the drivers, have access to the wonders of this trip by computer and a telecommunications device. For "vehicles" we listen to a phone, watch a TV, instruct a computer, use a cellular phone, or operate a digital notebook.

◆ Our major "thoroughfares" include the phone system, cable TV, the Internet, etc. Communications companies battle for the traffic. Nine out of ten US companies use computer local area networks (LANs) to link their employees, their hardware, and their databases together. The telephone subscribers in a given area communicate by computer. People in cities and counties link up by computer, satellite, and high capacity fiber-optic lines.

◆ One out of every three US homes have computers. They tap into a variety of services. Businesses and individuals buy, sell, and advertise on-line. Churches reach out to members. Museums, schools, and libraries do research on-line. Hospitals transfer X-rays; governments share database records. Banks make instantaneous electronic transfers of assets.

◆ For the public to take advantage in larger numbers, the ride will be made much easier and more worthwhile than it now is. *Electronic mail (E-mail)* can be transferred in seconds. *Hypertext* for information on a certain subject will give immediate access to other documents in databases located anywhere in the world. Individuals working miles apart can *collaborate* in creating a common document, editing it jointly and instantaneously. *Intelligent Agents* can be available to search existing networks on specific topics. Using *remote control devices* professional and amateur astronomers can observe distant stars. Doctors can operate at a distance. *Shoppers* even now are purchasing by credit card, selecting products by computer and being charged or credited instantly. *Video on demand* movies will be available to families.

◆ Who makes the cutting-edge technological developments? Who is on the front lines? According to Bill Gates, CEO of Microsoft, CD-ROMs make tremendous amounts of information available on a single disk, more than 330,000 single-spaced pages. Hal Rosen of IBM, who led the development team that invented the CD-ROM, says that we can now have "a full public library on your desktop." Internet now links more than 20,000,000 users in 180 countries. AT&T in Bedminster, New Jersey, scans the news around the world with multiple TV screens to reveal trouble spots in communications. They reroute calls around trouble so that "each of 190 million weekday calls goes through in seconds."

◆ In designing car bodies, managers can watch full sized sketches generated by a designer painting on a computer. Engineers make crucial changes. With 3-D computer images plastic foam models can be made automatically. Design and manufacturing can be completed in three years instead of the usual five years. Soon it'll be only two years.

◆ In modern warfare, soldiers with a video on one eye see each member of their squad. The video links tanks, helicopters, command posts. They assess the battle continuously, make troop movements more effective, and target artillery more accurately.

◆ Technical assistance can be given to the disabled. A blind person walks in a virtual world of audio cues. On the left he hears "McDonald's," on the right "I'm the library," and in the distance "I'm Kentucky Fried Chicken." A computer teaches a boy in a wheelchair by virtual sights and sounds how to cross the street safely. He practices until he's got the knack, then he tries it on the street.

3. *Intel Corporation*: According to Brent Schlender, CEO Andy Grove dreams of making the PC more important than the TV. Computers have long been used for word processing and spreadsheets. Now with Intel's Pentium and P6 microprocessors PCs can do much more without the cost of added hardware: stereo sound, digital video, 3D graphics, fax, voice, and data communications.

Grove grew up in Hungary. At age 21 in 1957 he escaped to the West right after the Hungarian uprising against Stalinism. As a refugee Andy crossed the Atlantic in a former troop ship and landed in the Brooklyn Navy Yard. He went to live with an uncle in the Bronx and studied chemical engineering at City College of New York. He graduated first in his class and traveled across America to obtain a Ph.D. from UC Berkley in 1963.

After graduation he started working with Fairchild Semiconductor with Gordon Moore and Robert Noyce. Noyce had invented the integrated circuit. When Moore and Noyce started the company to become Intel four years later, Grove became their director of operations. Moore believed strongly that chip performance should double every 18 months.

Moore also believed in the "Cannibal Principle" that new chips should include the functions previously done by separate electronic components. This means that the user, according to Moore, gets "them back for free, or at least for a lot less money than what they cost as individual parts."

Since Grove became CEO in 1987 Intel's sales have multiplied six times to $11.5 billion in 1994. They are expected to reach $16 billion for 1995. Since the microprocessor is the heart of the PC, Grove wants it to set the agenda for the PC industry. He says, "We can make it so superb as an entertainment machine, and so vital as a communications medium for both the home and the workplace, that it will battle with TV for people's disposable time."

Existing software, including Microsoft Windows, doesn't take full advantage of the Pentium's capabilities, so Grove is developing software to enhance the performance of Windows. Grove wants "to inspire the development of software applications that make PCs much more engaging and useful." He wants "the whole pie to grow."

Intel is number one in the world as a producer of microprocessors. They build 80% of the microprocessors used in personal computers. The wonderful growth of computers since the early 1980s has revolutionized the way organizations are run throughout the world. There is no sign of slowdown in the changes taking place. Electronic communications with computers is making a world of virtual communication a reality. This makes relationships among people all the more important. With the advance of high-tech, organizations that develop high-touch and excellent people relationships will flourish.[8]

4. *IBM*: Apple computer started the PC revolution with the Apple II, the hobbyist computer. IBM came out with its PC in 1981 and soon took a major share of the market. IBM allowed other companies to produce clones and this enabled the IBM type PC to become the standard both in homes and in offices. They asked Microsoft to design and produce their Disk Operating System, allowing Microsoft to sell a modified version to companies that produced compatible computers.

Today Intel has 80% of the microprocessor chip market and Microsoft has 80% of the software market. IBM is struggling to be the leading producer of PCs because there are numerous producers of compatibles, Compaq Computer being one of the most successful in the business market. Apple with its various Macintosh models is especially strong in the Desktop Publishing field. IBM produces a lot of application software and can become a market leader with its recent purchase of Lotus Development Corporation. Lotus Notes has the potential to compete with Microsoft's Windows which now, with MS DOS runs on IBM compatible computers.

It's hard to underrate the wonder of the personal computer. It dominates business communications. Computers generate openness since many companies have opted to make virtually all information available to all employees. Middle managers no longer can hoard information to control either their subordinates or their superiors. Computers set teams of employees free to accomplish unbelievable innovations. With freedom and trust most people thrive. It's not the workers that have the problems with this newfound freedom and responsibility. It's the middle managers who often end up subtracting value instead of adding it.

With the takeover of Lotus, IBM may come to dominate the PC market once again just as Intel dominates microprocessors and Microsoft dominates operating systems. The application software market is wide open with numerous companies of all sizes. With the demise of communism, the universal use of computers strongly supports the growth of worldwide democracy. There is no better climate for the advance of God's kingdom on earth since the good news of Jesus also flourishes in a democratic world.

5. *Excellent Organizations* experiment with processes, products, and people relationships. These lead to great innovations and progress. Here is what Tom Peters says about organizations that excel in creating wonder:

◆ Delegation to teams reveals that people can take great responsibility and accomplish wonders by working together.

◆ A challenging vision for the future motivates their people.

◆ Teams must have a variety of people with needed skills.

◆ Close communication and cooperation dramatically increases effectiveness. Suppliers, workers, and customers can share all information and work together in exciting new ways. This encourages dramatic improvements and revolutionary innovations. They share all databases over common computer networks to eliminate paperwork duplication, speed up deliveries, reduce costs, and improve quality of products, processes, and the number of hand-offs in their relationships.

◆ Success comes from experimenting with fast feedback. The more trials run the more learned, the more useful mistakes made the more discovered.

◆ Wonderful things happen when we combine high touch with high tech. The universe responds to creative technology and great relationships among people.

What is great about excellent organizations? They believe in and understand the tremendous wonders that are to be discovered and developed by curiosity, enthusiasm, and visionary work. Every job has its dimension of wonder. Every person feels important and wonderful. Every challenge provides excitement and adventure. "Wow!" exclaims Tom Peters. Nothing is boring when you see the wonder.

◆ The best consider that the universe is wonderful, amazing, and great.

◆ They have great visions for the wonderful things possible in this physical universe. For example, look what intelligence and wisdom went into putting a man on the moon.

◆ They don't want "nay-saying" and pessimistic people in their organizations.

The Astronomers, God, and the Wonders of Nature

The astronomers, physicists, and mathematicians are turning to the wonder of creation as the only reasonable explanation for the universe as we know it. According to the latest scientific evidence for a beginning, creation of the universe happened about 16 billion years ago. Although some doubt, many astronomers believe that the universe and the solar system had to be designed and created on purpose and intelligently.

More than 40 physical constants are very finely tuned for living organisms. These physical constants could not even be slightly different or life on earth could not exist. Again these facts have convinced many astronomers, physicists, and mathematicians of the universe's design and creation. The evidence for intelligent design is very convincing.[9]

Even Stephen Hawking denies that he is an atheist and asks, "What is it that breathes fire into the equations and makes a universe for them to describe. The usual approach of science . . . cannot answer the questions of why there should be a universe for the model to describe." He goes on to say that if we had a complete theory of the universe, "why it is that we and the universe exist" ought to be discussed by ordinary people and not just philosophers and scientists. He thinks the answer to that question "would be the ultimate triumph of human reason — for then we would know the mind of God."[10]

Our intelligent Creator provides a rational and reliable universe operating by wonderful and consistent laws. People use these laws to invent ways to design and create machines, processes, products, and automated factories. Belief in a created universe allows considerable freedom for us to make choices and vary the experiences of our lives as individuals and organizations. Belief in creation and in an intelligent creator does not need to handicap legitimate science or any type of investigation and invention. "It is possible to love God and practice science."[11]

It's reasonable to see the need for and to accept God by analogy. We as humans use our intelligence to design, work creatively, and maintain what we create. Why shouldn't that be very plausible evidence that God does the same even though we can't see Him? (See Heb 11:1-3; Rom 1:21-23.)

Everything Jesus Said and Did Was Full of Wonder

Jesus provided a wonderful vision for all who are willing to see. He came into the world so the blind could see, so the prisoners could go free, so the poor could inherit true wealth, so the weak could become strong, so mortals could put on immortality. Many who saw and heard Him chose to hang onto their present status and to reject His wonderful message. They didn't see and weren't impressed by the wonders that God had always been supplying since the beginning of Creation. They were blind to both the marvelous design in nature and our responsibility to understand it and use it for good not evil.

Others weren't sure the prize was worth the responsibility, but they gave Him a try. Some jumped at the opportunity to serve and know their Creator. They went with His inspiring vision of the wonder that their lives could become. To them His message and His life demand a wonderful and enthusiastic response:

◆ God has a great purpose for each of us. Don't miss the basic reason for life. If there is one thing to be learned, it's that God exists and He rewards the people who seek to know Him (Heb 11:6,10).

◆ Use the temporary life you now have to gain an eternal life that you can't lose. Many will come and try to deceive you, leading you away from the way of life. Jesus is the way, the truth, the life (John 14:6). Those who lead His "little ones" astray would be better off if they had never been born, better off if they had been drowned in the depths of the ocean (Matt 18:6).

◆ God created us for a wonderful future but we must believe that Jesus is the One He claimed to be. If you can't believe His words, then believe in His miracles. His miracles speak of God, of heaven, and of eternity. Blindness is common, so we must open our eyes and look for the proof of God's wonders and wisdom. There is no excuse, because the universe plainly displays the glory of God and speaks to us clearly though not with human words. (See John 5:16-47; 8:12-59.)

◆ Jesus teaches primarily love: Love God, love your neighbor, love your enemy, and love each other. This is the road to wonderful living and the life that is eternal. Total integrity, gratitude for what God freely gives to us, and willingness to give ourselves freely to Him and to others bring tremendous wonders to us. We win when we love, because love unlocks the wonders of God's world. God created everything by, for, and through Jesus. He alone came down from heaven, lived on earth, and went back into heaven. If we don't believe what He tells us about earth, how will we believe what He tells us about heaven? God's revelation of Himself in and through nature is so easy to understand that little children can see it while the wise and educated cannot. (See John 1:1-10; 1 Cor 8:6;

Rom 11:36: Col 1:15; Heb 1:1-4, 10; Rev 10:6 and Matt 11:25-30.)

◆ The greatest wonder of all comes when you lay down your life for your friends. There is no greater love than this. Jesus said "You are my friends and I am laying down my life for you. I tell you this that your joy may be complete." (See John 15:13-27; quotation here is author's paraphrase.) Joy comes from being aware of the fantastic wonders that surround each of us. We can focus on what seems evil and bad, but if we do then we lose much. Why do children see the wonder and we adults miss it? Isn't this why Jesus praised children and used them as examples of who heaven belongs to? (Matt 18:1-5; 13-15) Isn't this why the lack of faith of His hometown people amazed Jesus? (Mark 6:6) And wasn't this why the blind man was amazed when the religious leaders showed no wonder when Jesus healed him? The leaders said, "We know this man [Jesus] is a sinner."

The man said in wonder, "Whether he is a sinner or not, I don't know. One thing I do know. I was blind but now I see!"

A little later Jesus told this man, "For judgment I have come into this world, so that the blind will see and those who see will become blind."

The leaders who heard Him said, "Are we blind too?" Jesus replied, "If you were blind, you would not be guilty of sin; but now that you claim you can see, your guilt remains." (See John 9:24-41.)

Those who knew Jesus were constantly amazed with wonder:

◆ Mary was amazed when she was chosen to be the mother of God's Son (Luke 1:29, 46-55).

◆ The teachers in the temple were amazed at His questions and answers at age 12 (Luke 2:41-52).

◆ The disciples were amazed enough to leave everything and follow Him (Matt 4:18-22; 9:9-13).

◆ People in His hometown were amazed at His wisdom because He was only the child of a carpenter. They knew He was nothing special because they were acquainted with His whole family (Matt 13:53-58; Luke 4:22-30).

◆ The leaders attributed His miracles to the devil showing how blind they were to the wonders of God and Jesus (Matt 12:22-49).

Why should we consider it incredible that Jesus has created all things in participation with God? Where do we get our evidence? Skeptics, doubters, and atheists can be blind and prejudiced like the religious leaders of Jesus' day. It should not seem incredible that the miracles and wonders of Jesus were planned and made possible from the Creation. His miracles were great but not as wonderful as the Creation of the universe and nature that we live in and experience constantly. His miracles and wonders were the signs of His times. They are consistent with the wonders of the Creation and result from the same wisdom and power (Matt 16:1-3).

Just as the wonders of the universe and nature speak, the miracles speak, telling us who Jesus is and why we need to listen to Him. One day we will all come face-to-face with the wonders of Jesus' birth, transfiguration, death, and resurrection although we may ignore them for the time being (John 10:24-39).

His message is vital and essential:

◆ He designed it to be received by honest seekers. He does not expect us to be foolish, superstitious, partial, or snobbish.

◆ He designed it to enlighten children and childlike people. He does thwart and frustrate people who are cynical and unbelieving.

◆ He teaches our hearts first, and then our intellects. God does not honor or encourage ignorance. He desires humble gratitude and wisdom in our scholarship, science, and living.

◆ His foolishness is wiser than human wisdom; His weakness is stronger than human strength. We have to work through what looks foolish and weak and not make the mistakes of tunnel vision or throwing out the good because we have experienced something bad (1 Cor 1:18-25).

Faith, Hope and Wonder

To have faith is to be sure of the things we hope for, to be certain of the things we cannot see. By faith people of ancient times won God's approval. It is by faith that we understand that the universe was created by God's word, so that what can be seen was made out of what cannot be seen (Heb 11:3).

When we believe in someone else, we see beyond their weaknesses. We forgive the things we see in them which we don't like. We want to give something better to them, not only receive something from them. In other words, we can see good things that are unseen and invisible. When we are blind to the unseen things that are really there, we find it difficult — maybe impossible — to have a sense of wonder. Children have a marvelous sense of wonder because they see the good and the wonderful. That's why Jesus praised them and told adults to become like children.

We have a choice! We are free to make a decision. We can choose to remain blind and dead to the unseen wonders around us, or we can open our eyes of faith and hope. We make this choice ourselves, one by one. No one can do this for us. Those who have cultivated faith and hope and wonder can expect the best of others, look beyond their weaknesses, and accept people where they are — warts and all. Let's give away as much of our own wonder as we can. Faith, hope, love, gratitude, and wonder all grow the more that we give them away to those around us. We never know when other people will respond to our example.

What Do Churches Need to Discover?

◆ We don't have to apologize for God. *He is the only reasonable explanation for reality*, and He is whatever it takes to explain the wonders of reality. It's in our best interest to give priority to what is wonderful and not to what is mean, bad, and unfruitful.

◆ The message of Christ is wonderful and nothing to be ashamed of. It does divide people with different attitudes, but this is to be expected. There are "good trees" and there are "bad trees." Our top priority must be to develop the wonderful capabilities and spiritual gifts of people. We do people a great favor when we expect the best from them. We need to free them with our encouragement and support. We need to express our love for those who don't share our wonder. We need to *expect the best* from God. He will work wonders with us if we allow Him to.

◆ All good things developed by secular organizations have been made possible by God. There is no reason for Christians to resent this. We need to learn from others. That's why Jesus used outsiders as the main characters of His parables. Let's realize that *the wonders of science are God's wonders.*

◆ We've commanded and controlled people long enough. Let's follow the wisdom of excellent organizations that give people freedom, authority, and responsibility. People can do great things in God's kingdom when they penetrate their relational networks with the wonderful message and lifestyle of Jesus. Let's leave the 99 and focus all our attention on reaching people and building relationships with those who show an interest. We'll have to know their traditions and de-emphasize our own. We can't afford to raise up barriers and obstacles to the people Christ has asked us to invite into His family.

◆ Above all we must get rid of our fortress mentality. We must be willing to risk our comfort and security to help others know Christ. If Jesus asks us to lose our lives in order to find them, we need to take that risk in reaching out to our neighbors. Being all things to all people simply means that we learn about the interests and traditions of the people we meet. Let's put our own desires and interests on the back burner until we understand those Jesus came to save.

◆ Science gets a better grasp on God's wonders every day. Without being arrogant and conceited, let's be proud of the fact that God is the God of science. *He designed and created everything that scientists will ever discover.* We should encourage science, because every discovery uncovers a wonder that God Himself has created. How else will we ever persuade agnostics, skeptics, cynics, and atheists that their blindness to God's existence, design, and creativity is hurting themselves more than anyone?

Grassroots Christians Can Encourage Wonder

◆ What can pull us out of the pits of sorrow, adversity, and despair but a touch of wonder, a vision of what can and will be? When do we need wonder the most? We need it when we are down, and we need it to hold us up. We need it to give the vision to others. We can't do that if we don't experience wonder for ourselves.

◆ We need to appreciate that all the treasures of wisdom and knowledge are found in Jesus. By daily study and prayer we can see how the Bible relates to our daily lives. There is really "no other game in town." God alone has the secret of eternal life. Without continuous input from Jesus we stifle our growth to become like Him.

◆ Many have never heard what Jesus taught plainly. They are *filled with the baggage of superstition, wrong priorities, and false knowledge.* Let's love others enough to keep people aware of what's important and what's happening in our world. According to Jesus, we are the salt of the earth and the light of the world. This is no small role to play in making others aware of God's wonderful message.

Keep learning more about how God works constantly in the universe. He is behind all the wonders of nature that we see, hear, and experience every day of our lives. We can be curious, enthusiastic, and excited about what He is teaching us. If this world is actually made in the image of heaven in order to prepare us for life with Him, then we can see value in everything we learn. God can use our lives, so we need to be enthusiastic about His plan. Though we can have the mind of Christ, this calls for humility, and also for a great sense of responsibility. Christ is using us if we are willing to be used by Him (John 5:17; 1 Cor 2:10-16).

◆ We can appreciate church leaders and encourage them to have greater vision and greater trust in the capability of God's people. We need to build on the people who are dedicated to growing and not turn our initiative over to the naysayers and complainers. Jesus was very emphatic and toughminded with those who did not share His vision and His love.

Where do we find wonder and how do we find it?

◆ Associate with those who have it.
◆ Read the Psalms where David speaks eloquently of God's wonders.
◆ Read Isaiah who writes of the great future God has prepared for us.
◆ Read the stories of Jesus' life on earth in Matthew, Mark, Luke, and John.
◆ Read Acts to see what happened to the disciples after Jesus went back into heaven.
◆ Read from the letters of Paul and Peter and John, the entire New Testament.
◆ Dare to *become all you can be* (a phrase Joe gave to the U.S. Army years ago).

Never Lose It!

Joe was walking through the woods with Wendy, his nine-year-old daughter. We were holding hands, as fathers and daughters will.

Suddenly Wendy stopped and said, "Listen, Dad."

I listened, but couldn't hear a thing.

Then Wendy ordered, "Listen more closely, Dad. Do you hear that bird singing? Isn't it beautiful?"

At last I could hear it — and it was beautiful.

"Do you hear the wind in the trees?" Wendy asked next, "Isn't it beautiful?" And again I hadn't heard it before, but now I did and it, too, was beautiful.

As I stood there in the woods — I could still picture the scene clearly years later — the sun was streaming down on the face of this young child, whose face was completely devoid of cynicism or defense. She was vulnerable; she was letting in the wonder, the joy. I reflected, as we walked on, that possibly this was what Christ meant when He said: "Except ye . . . become as little children, ye shall not enter into the kingdom of heaven."

The Prime Requirement

Never lose your sense of wonder.

Wonder is the prime requirement of the tender heart and tough mind: the open, questing, eager heart and mind. It can provide the key to a wonder-full life. Perhaps, too, it may be the real secret of retaining enthusiasm, so that life may be longer and richer and we may be able to relate much more meaningfully to the world around us.

Hope is essential if we are to relight the real dreams, the eternal wonder, the questing spirit, the restless wonder-full innovative thrust so badly needed at all levels of our society. Many have become prisoners of their own tensions and frustrations and their self-imposed isolation from other people. They can never relax long enough to respond naturally to what is wonderful in the world in which they live.

Those who use sophisticated instruments like radio telescopes and electron microscopes sometimes overlook the meaning of the very wonders they study. Even our minds and brains are so wonderful that understanding them is still a scientific frontier. It's easy to take the simple but profound facts of everyday experience for granted. Leo Buscaglia has said,

> . . . We are living in a society in which such words as love and commitment have been relegated to sentimental, old-fashioned nonsense. . . . This flippant attitude has had much to do with the breeding of a society of detached, non-committed persons too sophisticated to admit to their confusion and unhappiness and too caught up in ego to risk doing anything about it. It has perpetuated isolation and devalued basic human values.[12]

He states later, "Scientists almost totally avoid the study of joy, laughter, humor and happiness and its relationship to human well-being.[13]

In our experience this same lack of interest blinds us to the knowledge that comes from our personal study of wonder, purpose, design, creation, creativity, free will, revelation, spirituality, trust, faith, hope, gratitude, values, responsibility, etc. Atheists and cynics call these nonsensical.

In *Darwin on Trial* Phillip Johnson, who has taught law for more than twenty years at the University of California at Berkeley, asks the question, "What if Darwin was wrong, and natural selection doesn't have the fantastic creative power Darwinists credited it with?"

What is the difference between biblical religion and evolutionary religion? One begins with belief in a Creator who designed and created all things, who communicates with us through His Creation and through the Bible. The other begins with the assumptions that there is no invisible spiritual world, no creator, and that there was no creation. Darwinism assumes that everything came about only through evolution, and mankind is evolution's natural product.

Darwinism is a mythology. It is the evolutionist's "story of humanity's liberation from the delusion that its destiny is controlled by a power higher than itself." But what if Darwinism is false and God is no illusion? We should be open to both God's revelation and scientific truth.

But we tend to find the evidence that we look for. Johnson writes,

> Darwinists sometimes find confirming evidence, just as Marxists found capitalists exploiting workers and Freudians analyzed patients who said that they wanted to murder their fathers and marry their mothers. . . .What they never find is evidence that contradicts the common ancestry thesis, because to Darwinists such evidence cannot exist. The "fact of evolution" is true by definition, and so negative information is uninteresting, and generally unpublishable.

What if there is no such thing as a beneficial mutation? Everyone agrees that mutations are accidents and overwhelmingly harmful. Not only that, God undoubtedly included the process of mutation in His design for the reproduction and survival of all living things from one generation to another. It's certainly only an hypothesis that "beneficial mutations" can accumulate over billions of years to bring about creative changes. Remember, mutations are accidents, and *natural selection selects against and eliminates the mutant organisms*. How great a miracle it would be if all living things came from stringing together beneficial accidents over billions of years. Accidents do occur, but why not see genetic variability as designed in? Natural selection works to maintain variability in organisms and to eliminate the accidents that harm. This is survival of the fittest *by design*.

Many Darwinists don't want a Designer and Creator to exist. The wonders of nature call out for a Creator, but this makes us accountable to God. If we let God exist, we also run the risk that dogmatic believers in God will be "a threat to liberal freedom, and especially as a threat to public support for scientific research. As the creation myth of scientific naturalism, Darwinism plays an indispensable ideological role in the war against fundamentalism."

No matter what Darwinists believe, "Common ancestry is a hypothesis, not a fact, no matter how strongly it appeals to a materialist's common sense." According to Johnson, "The leaders of science see themselves as locked in a desperate battle against religions fundamentalists." To them this means "anyone who believes in a Creator who plays an active role in worldly affairs." To many Darwinists there are no good or honest believers in creation or in God. Darwinists see their purpose "to persuade the public to believe that there is no purposeful intelligence that transcends the natural world." This means that scientists cannot "consider all the possibilities, but must restrict themselves to those which are consistent with a strict philosophical naturalism. For example, they may not study genetic information on the assumption that it may be the product of intelligent communication."

These scientists admit that their colleagues in the past have been dogmatic and fanatic. It's true that "whenever science is enlisted in some other cause — religious, political, racialistic — the result is always that the scientists themselves become fanatics. Scientists see this clearly when they think about the mistakes of their predecessors, but they find it hard to believe that their colleagues could be making the same mistakes today."[14]

There is a need for humility. There are dogmatic and fanatic scientists. There are dogmatic and fanatic Christians. Grassroots believers can help Christians see both sides of an issue. We can appreciate the wonder of God's creation, and we can separate the facts from the fiction in the dogmas that naturalistic scientists and scholars try to impose on society.

An Agenda for Small Groups on the Subject of Wonder:

◆ Icebreaker on the wonders all around us in God's creation.
◆ Scriptures teaching us the source and meaning of these wonders (Ps 19:1-3; 104:1-35; Rom 1:18-25).
◆ Discussion of how these wonders increase our faith.

◆ Prayer for God's blessings with our thanks for everything.
◆ What God is doing and what He will do — His vision for the future.

Conclusions

Wonder cries out from every leaf on every tree, from the beauty of every rose, from the excitement of every baby's birth, and from the baby's development into a full grown child. The stars, the planets, our sun, and our moon speak eloquently about our Creator. When we design, build and operate an automated factory to produce complex products we have sufficient proof that God exists. We exist and we do many wonderful things. Therefore God exists.

We need a wondrous and wise view of the past, the present, and the future. God has made known His feelings and His desires. Our prayer and our hope is that Christians will see and grab every opportunity to light up the dark world with the enthusiasm that comes from wonder:

Do everything without complaining or arguing, so that you may become blameless and pure, children of God without fault in a crooked and depraved generation, in which you shine like stars in the universe as you hold out the word of life . . . (Phil 2:14-16).

REFERENCES

1. Batten, *Tough-minded Leadership*, 182.

2. Peters and Austin, *Passion for Excellence*, 66-67.

3. Tom Peters, *The Pursuit of Wow*, (New York: Vintage Books, 1994), 129. Peters, *Liberation Management*, 690. Peters and Austin, *Passion for Excellence*, 129.

4. Oster, *Vision-Driven Leadership*, 131-132.

5. Ibid., 133.

6. Peters, *Liberation Management*, 677-678.

7. Joel L. Swedlow, Photography by Louie Psihoves, and Art by Allen Carrol, *Information Revolution*, (National Geographic Magazine, October 1995), 5-36. Also read Robert X. Cringely, *Accidental Empires*, (New York: HarperCollins, 1992, 1996).

8. Brent Schlender, "Why Andy Grove Can't Stop." *Fortune*, 1995, *132* (1), 88-98.

9. Hugh Ross, *The Creator and the Cosmos*, (Colorado Springs: NavPress, 1993), 129-132.

10. Stephen Hawking, *A Brief History of Time*, (New York: Bantam Books, 1990), 174-175.

11. Maitland A. Edey and Donald C. Johansen, *Blueprints*, (New York: Little, Brown and Company, 1989), 291.

12. Buscaglia, *Loving Each Other*, 11-12.

13. Ibid., 111.

14. Phillip Johnson, *Darwin on Trial*, (Downers Grove: InterVarsity Press, 1991), 109-110, 128, 131, 152-154.

CHAPTER THIRTEEN
TRUTH/BEAUTY

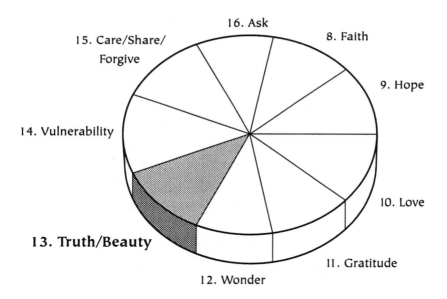

16. Ask

8. Faith

15. Care/Share/
Forgive

9. Hope

14. Vulnerability

10. Love

13. Truth/Beauty

11. Gratitude

12. Wonder

13

ARE OUR VALUES BASED ON TRUTH AND BEAUTY?

If you hold to my teaching, you are really my disciples.
Then you will know the truth, and the truth will set you free. . . .
I am the way and the truth and the life.
No one comes to the Father except through me.
Jesus (in John 8:31-32 and 14:6)

Together we have walked the walk
from sorrow to joy, from despair to victory,
Together we have seen and lived
the truth of our Lord's beautiful Be-Happy Attitudes.
Robert Schuller

Key Points

The search for truth and beauty has led to more breakthroughs in technology and human understanding than anything else in history. We humans are walking bundles of blessings, strengths, and possibilities. The world in which we live provides many more beautiful opportunities for growth, change, and enrichment than we can perceive. We open our eyes to truth and beauty when we feel grateful for what we have been given.

Most excellent organizations appreciate truth and beauty. God and Jesus designed a beautiful universe to move us to faith. The Creation is not only good, but it is full of truth and beauty. God gives us science, technology, and Creation. Christians involved in excellent secular organizations can use their successes to illustrate the beautiful truths of Christ. He is the author of every beautiful thing that happens in our world. Small groups are places for cultivating the joy of knowing God's eternal truth and amazing beauty.

∗∗∗∗

How Do Secular Organizations Use Truth and Beauty?

1. *James Kouzes and Barry Posner* surveyed close to 1,500 managers in various parts of the United States in cooperation with the American Management Association. They asked each person, "What values (personal traits or characteristics) do you look for and admire in your superiors?" More than 225 different answers were given but the judges classified them into fifteen categories. The top three most frequent responses were:

◆ Truthful, trustworthy, has convictions and character: *Integrity*.
◆ Capable, productive, and efficient: *Competence*.
◆ Inspiring, decisive, and gives direction: *Leadership*.

They did a similar exercise with 800 senior executives in the federal government. These executives responded in the same way. They admired in their superiors *integrity, competence, and leadership*.

Later in a two-year study at Santa Clara University and other corporate locations they had 2,615 top-level managers describe what they admired in leaders. The rank and percentages for the top five characteristics looked very much like the previous studies:

◆ Honest - selected by 83% of managers.
◆ Competent - selected by 67%.
◆ Forward-looking - selected by 62%.
◆ Inspiring - selected by 58%.
◆ Intelligent- selected by 43%.

AT&T conducted a similar study using their modified version of Kouzes and Posner's checklist. The AT&T employees came out with results similar to the studies mentioned above. Top five characteristics of admired leaders were, (1) honest, (2) competent, (3) inspiring, (4) courageous, and (5) forward-looking.

From the above we can see that truth and integrity is vital in our motivation. If we don't trust people, then we won't believe what they say or follow them. How do we decide that others are worthy of our trust? We watch what they do. We want to see if their actions follow their words, if they practice what they preach. If they do, we consider them to be honest and trustworthy. Kouzes and Posner also point out for courageous actions: "We appreciate people who take a stand on important principles. We resolutely refuse to follow those who lack the confidence in their own beliefs. Confusion over where the leader stands creates stress; not knowing the leader's beliefs contributes to conflict, indecision, and political rivalry. We simply do not trust people who will not tell us their values, ethics, and standards."[1]

Truth and beauty are more than just being honest although honesty and integrity take first place in importance. Credibility comes from modeling greatness of heart and spirit. We need to be competent, forward-looking, and inspiring as well as honest and courageous. Beauty may be only skin deep, but where we have truth we usually have beauty. True goodness is lovely and beautiful. "How beautiful are the feet of those who bring good news" (Rom 10:15; Isa 52:7).

Credibility involves "trustworthiness, expertise, and dynamism." These three characteristics are much the same as those found in the above-mentioned studies. Later we will show how Jesus taught and lived the same principles. Kouzes and Posner refer to a study by Charles O'Reilly of the University of California, Berkeley regarding credibility of top management. When leaders are "perceived to have high credibility and a strong philosophy," their followers will usually:

- ◆ "Be proud to tell others they are a part of the organization."
- ◆ "Talk up the organization with their friends."
- ◆ "See their own values as similar to those of the organization."
- ◆ "Feel a sense of ownership for the organization."

When leaders have poor credibility, employees will often have the following beliefs:

- ◆ Workers will "produce only when watched."
- ◆ They "are motivated primarily by money."
- ◆ People "say good things about the organization at work, but feel different in private."
- ◆ They "would consider looking for another job if the organization were experiencing tough times."[2]

2. *Innovation is the systematic development and use of new truth.* Peter Drucker points out that "miracle cures" are "real enough," but they can't be replicated, taught, or learned. The same is true of innovations

that "are the result of a 'flash of genius' rather than of hard, organized, purposeful work." Flashes of genius can't be replicated, taught, or learned. He also says, "bright ideas are the riskiest and least success-ful source of innovative opportunities. The casualty rate is enormous." Less than 1% of patents for bright ideas "earns enough to pay back development cost and patent fees." And "as low as one in five hundred makes any money above its out-of-pocket cost."

Leonardo da Vinci, the greatest inventor in history, had great ideas — "submarine or helicopter or automatic forge. . . . But not one of these could have been converted into an innovation with the technology and the materials of 1500."

Drucker lists seven areas that he calls "sources of innovative opportunities":

1. *"The unexpected* — the unexpected success, the unexpected fail-ure, the unexpected outside event." This area brings the greatest opportunities, but it is the one most neglected or deliberately rejected.[3]

2. *"The incongruity* — between reality as it actually is and reality as it is assumed to be or as it 'ought to be.'" These are mostly hidden opportunities due to "changes *within* an industry, a market, a process."[4]

3. *"Innovation based on process need."* This has to do with what already is. "It perfects a process that already exists, replaces a link that is weak, redesigns an existing old process around newly available knowledge."[5]

4. *"Changes in industry structure or market structure* that catch every-one unawares." These changes often lead to disaster and extinc-tion, but are also major opportunities. New answers have to be given to the question, "What is our business?"[6]

5. *"Demographics."* Population shifts are often very sudden, and they "often defy explanation." If companies are "willing to go out into the field, to look and to listen, changing demographics is both a highly productive and a highly dependable innovative opportunity."[7]

6. *"Changes in perception, mood, and meaning."* Success here comes from being close to the customer and alert to opportunity. Changes such as seeing the glass "half full" instead of "half empty," bring "major innovative opportunities."[8]

7. *"New knowledge,* both scientific and nonscientific." This type of innovation gets most of the attention and money. Both scientific and social knowledge can produce important innovations. These are the "super-stars" of entrepreneurs. "And like most 'super-

stars,' knowledge-based innovation is temperamental, capricious, and hard to manage."[9]

To discover, develop, and successfully use the above sources of new and important truths we need "analysis, system, and hard work." Drucker describes some simple "Do's" and "Dont's" that he calls "the principles of innovation, representing the hard core of the discipline." First the "DO'S":

(1) Innovation means analyzing the opportunities conceptually. The innovator must think through the seven sources of opportunity listed above. Analysis and study must be done systematically, the search organized and done on a regular basis.

(2) Innovators have "to go out to look, to ask, to listen." They have to look at the people involved as well as the figures. It is important to perceive "the expectations or the habits of the people who have to use" the particular approach to innovative truth. You have to make sure "that the people who have to use it will *want* to use it, and see in it *their* opportunity." You could have "the right innovation in the wrong form." Great computer programs have often been "not used by teachers scared stiff of the computer, who perceived the machine as something that, far from being helpful, threatened them."

(3) An effective innovation "has to be simple and it has to be focused." If it is too complicated, it's too hard to use and to fix. It should be so simple that "people will say: 'This is obvious. Why didn't I think of it?'"

(4) The best innovations "are not grandiose. They try to do one specific thing." Small, fast experiments give the fastest feedback, the most practical information, and are less costly. Mistakes are always made and changes "are almost always needed for an innovation to succeed." This can happen only if the scale is kept small and the investment modest.

(5) Plan to be the leader and not a follower. You can't "foretell whether a given innovation will end up as a big business or a modest achievement." If leadership isn't the goal, the innovation may not get established and may not be innovative enough. It may "simply create an opportunity for the competition."[10]

THE IMPORTANT DONT'S:

(1) Don't "try to be clever. . . . Anything too clever . . . is almost bound to fail."

(2) Don't "try too many things at once . . . there has to be a core of unity to innovative efforts or they are likely to fly apart." The people involved have to be united in understanding.

(3) Don't "try to innovate for the future." Do it for the present. Unless "there is an immediate application in the present, an innovation is like the drawings in Leonardo da Vince's notebook — a 'brilliant idea.'"[11]

Innovation is work. Talent, ingenuity, and predisposition are important "as in any other work." But these will not be sufficient if there is not "hard, focused, purposeful work making very great demands on diligence, on persistence, and on commitment."

Innovators must build on their strengths. Which opportunities fit me and fit the company? There must be a temperamental "fit." Knowledge and performance capacity are vital. If the opportunity doesn't make sense to those working on it, they won't be "willing to put in the persistent, hard, frustrating work that successful innovation always requires."

Innovation changes the behavior of customers and people in general. To be successful the innovator must be close to the customer, focused on the market, and dedicated to meeting needs and wants of people.[12]

3. *True principles used by effective people*: Stephen Covey tells us of his experience in organizations working with people who are successful but frustrated. These people are "struggling with an inner hunger, a deep need for personal congruency and effectiveness and for healthy, growing relationships with other people."

He discovered that prior to the 1920s much of the literature on success "focused on what could be called the *Character Ethic* as the foundation of success — things like integrity, humility, fidelity, and the Golden Rule." These are the truest principles of life, and people can't be successful or happy unless "they learn to integrate these principles into their basic character."

People working productively in excellent organizations tend to follow principles that apply to all successful people. According to Covey, "principles are deep fundamental truths. . . . They apply to individuals, to marriages, to families, to private and public organizations of every kind. . . . When we value correct principles, we have truth — a knowledge of things as they are." These true principles for guiding our behavior tend to be self-evident, fundamental, and "have enduring, permanent value.

"One way to quickly grasp the self-evident nature of principles is to" look at the foolishness of living by their opposites. Covey says, "I doubt that anyone would seriously consider unfairness, deceit, baseness, uselessness, mediocrity, or degeneration to be a solid foundation for lasting happiness and success." The apostle Paul said a similar thing about the true principles or fruit of the Holy Spirit: "Against such things there is no law."[13]

4. *The Wow of Beauty*: Tom Peters really hits beauty and fashion as keys to success in his recent book, *The Pursuit of WOW!, Every Person's Guide to Topsy-Turvy Times.* The "Wow," or what we call beauty, has mostly to do with a truth that has been kept secret for millennia. People in the front lines are what make things happen with speed and excellence. Middle managers have for years hoarded information and prevented frontline workers from doing all they can do. People working together, managing themselves, can do ten times as much as they can when they are held back by supervisors and middle managers.

He describes the beautiful way De-Mar treats its people to provide the best in plumbing service. De-Mar makes $3.3 million revenue, employs 40 people called Service Advisors rather than workers. When they get complaints they figure out ways to improve their service, not cut their prices. Their Advisors work in teams: "'There's so much peer pressure, there's no need for supervisors, just team leaders,' says Randy Newman, a Service Advisor and leader for the heating and air-conditioning team." Everybody on the team jumps on a person who doesn't fit in. They give people a fair chance, and they try hard to work things out. "The team does the counseling. If you have a grievance, you go to the team leader. People speak right up, and we work anything out." One worker who got fired appealed to the group, and he was voted back in.[14]

Who needs supervisors if people can handle their own problems and do better without them? Peters has shown how management layers subtract value by preventing people from using their own knowledge, ingenuity, and resourcefulness. People want to be responsible, and they work much more effectively when they are free. In today's world, organizations are discovering the beautiful methods and truths that Jesus taught and practiced with His disciples 2,000 years ago.

The Challenge of Truth and Beauty

Since we become what we think and say, the nutrients to enrich and toughen our minds are crucial. No matter how skillfully we develop and chart our process of planning and goal setting, we can achieve and sustain the necessary momentum only by thoughts that flow out of truth and beauty. Since the search for truth and beauty has fueled more breakthroughs in technology and human understanding than anything else in history, and since thoughts are the quintessential tools of the future, the tough-minded leader feeds and develops the capacity to think in all logical and feasible ways.

Our Most Priceless Gift

We human beings are walking bundles of blessings and possibilities, and the world in which we live provides vastly more opportunities for growth, change, and enrichment than we can perceive.

The greatest gift of all is the ability and opportunity to learn! We must constantly alter our paradigms, our visions, our values, and what we are becoming. Central to the Total Quality Culture is the opportunity to share learning so that all group activity is synergistic. The great corporations of tomorrow will, above all, be *learning corporations*. They will consistently move toward a culture that provides alignment, creativity, and empowerment.

Joe Batten[15]

What Did Jesus Teach About Truth and Beauty?

John told to us most of what Jesus said about truth and light and life. Jesus chose practical, hard working men to preach His truths to the world. Jesus called John and his brother James "sons of thunder." Later, both of them, along with their mother, asked Jesus to give them seats of honor on his right and left when He came into His kingdom. (See Matt 5:18-22; 20:20-28; Mark 3:17.)

Jesus came to reveal truth, beauty, and joy that had been missed and misunderstood since the Creation of the world. Jesus was with God in the beginning: "Through him all things were made; without him nothing was made that has been made." With regard to eternal life and spiritual truth John said, "In him was life, and that life was the light of men. The light shines in the darkness, but the darkness has not understood it" (See John 1:3-5, 9-11, 14,17.)

Very early in His public teaching Jesus confronted the heavy-handed dogmatism and hypocrisy of the religious leaders. John tells us how angry Jesus was when He saw what was going on in the temple. Jesus "found men selling cattle, sheep and doves, and others sitting at tables exchanging money." He made a whip and drove out the people and animals. He turned over their money tables, scattered their money, and said, "Get out of here! How dare you turn my Father's house into a market?"

The religious authorities were incensed and demanded, "What miraculous sign can you show us to prove your authority to do all this?"

Jesus shocked them with this answer: "Destroy this temple, and I will raise it again in three days."

Jesus actually meant the raising of His own body after His crucifixion. Naturally, they missed His point. John tells us in great detail the constant verbal battle that Jesus had with those who were in positions of religious and political power but not loyal to God's word. Jesus' battle is not a beautiful picture, but it does help us to appreciate how important God's truth really is. (See John 2:13-25.)

Nicodemus came alone and at night to talk with Jesus. He was a prominent member of the Jewish ruling council and one of the few leaders who listened to Jesus. He told Jesus, "we know you are a teacher who has come from God. For no one could perform the miraculous signs you are doing if God were not with him."

Jesus explained how he must be born again, born of the Spirit, and this amazed Nicodemus. He didn't get Jesus' meaning and took Him to mean literal rebirth from a mother's womb. Jesus called for a change of heart, mind, and perspective. It takes great humility and good judgment to see things from God's point of view, and Nicodemus suffered from dogmatic, legalistic thinking, "tunnel vision." (See John 3:1-21.) There is really "no other game in town" as important as God's game of life. John the Baptist said, "The one who comes from above is above all . . . . He testifies to what he has seen and heard, but no one accepts his testimony. The man who has accepted it has certified that God is truthful. For the one whom God has sent speaks the words of God; for God gives the Spirit without limit. The Father loves the Son and has placed everything in his hands" (John 3:31-35).

John's biography of Jesus reveals the tremendous battle that Jesus had with the religious and political authorities over the beauty and value of God's truth and God's will. Secular organizations give us a good model, a parable, for illustrating the importance of seeking and finding both truth and beauty. But we should go further than physical, political, psychological, and social science. We need to take the eternal dimension of life seriously and consider ourselves created for and worthy of eternal life.

One early confrontation that Jesus had resulted from his healing an invalid on the Sabbath. This man had been crippled for thirty-eight years and Jesus told him, "Pick up your mat and walk." The man did just that, but the Jews criticized him by saying, "It is the Sabbath; the law forbids you to carry your mat."

When they found out it was Jesus who healed him, they began to persecute Him. Jesus told them plainly,

> I tell you the truth, the Son can do nothing by himself; he can do only what he sees his Father doing, because whatever the Father does the Son also does. . . .
>
> For the very work that the Father has given me to finish, and which I am doing, testifies that the Father has sent me. . . . You have never heard his voice nor seen his form, nor does his word dwell in you, for you do not believe the one he sent. You diligently study the Scriptures because you think that by them you possess eternal life. These are the Scriptures that testify about me, yet you refuse to come to me to have life. . . .
>
> I know that you do not have the love of God in your hearts. . . . How can you believe if you accept praise from one another, yet make no effort to obtain the praise that comes from the only God? (John 5:19-47).

Later in Jesus' ministry John tells us how Jesus spoke up in the temple courts. The Jews were amazed and asked, "How did this man get such learning without having studied?"

Jesus answered, "If anyone chooses to do God's will, he will find out whether my teaching comes from God or whether I speak on my own. He who speaks on his own does so to gain honor for himself, but he who works for the honor of the one who sent him is a man of truth; there is nothing false about him" (John 7:14-18).

The religious leaders sent temple guards to arrest Jesus, but the guards went back to the leaders without arresting Jesus. They said, "No one ever spoke the way this man does," when they were asked why they didn't bring Him in. The rulers and the Pharisees really got on their case. They accused them of being deceived, and they also insulted the people: "this mob that knows nothing of the law — there is a curse on them." (See John 7:32-52.)

Jesus' most violent exchange of words with the religious leaders came after He spoke of freedom based on the truth. Some Jews followed Him, and He told the ones who believed, "If you hold to my teaching, you are really my disciples. Then you will know the truth, and the truth will set you free."

This offended them, and they responded with, "we . . . have never been slaves of anyone. How can you say that we shall be set free?"

Immediately Jesus revealed their inmost attitudes: "I am telling you what I have seen in the Father's presence, and you do what you have heard from you father. . . . You belong to your father, the devil, and you want to carry out your father's desire. He was a murderer from the beginning . . . he is a liar and the father of lies. Yet because I tell the truth, you do not believe me! . . . The reason you do not hear is that you do not belong to God." (See John 8:31-59.)

When Jesus was tried before the high priest, John reports that one of the officials struck Jesus in the face. Jesus responded, "If I said something wrong, testify as to what is wrong. But if I spoke the truth, why did you strike me?" (John 18:23). A little while later before Pilate Jesus said, "for this I came into the world, to testify to the truth. Everyone on the side of truth listens to me."

That's when Pilate asked the question for which he is famous: "What is truth?"

Jesus had shocked him by saying, "My kingdom is not of this world. If it were, my servants would fight to prevent my arrest by the Jews. But now my kingdom is from another place." (See John 18:35-38.)

Pilate eventually gave in to the pressure of the religious leaders and had Jesus crucified. God raised Jesus back to life three days later. After His resurrection Jesus stressed the importance of believing truth based on eyewitness testimony when he told Thomas, "Because you have seen me, you have believed; blessed are those who have not seen and yet have believed." (See John 20:24-29.)

John tells us that Jesus did many other miraculous signs. John wanted us to believe that Jesus is the Christ, the Son of God, and to have life in Jesus' name. (See John 20:30-31; also 21:25.)

Our Creator has revealed Himself with overwhelming evidence. The story we have of Jesus' life is beautiful and true. Philip Yancey shows the powerful impact of God's truth when he writes of Dostoevsky's hard labor in Siberia. He had a New Testament given to him as "he boarded the convict train toward Siberia. . . . Dostoevsky poured over that New Testament during his confinement. After ten years he emerged from exile with unshakable Christian convictions. . . . 'If anyone proved to me that Christ was outside the truth. . . . Then I would prefer to remain with Christ than with the truth.'"[16]

God has not left us without reliable eyewitness evidence and a thoroughly adequate record. He sent His Son, Jesus, to live among us. He has communicated with us since the Creation of the world, but we haven't listened very well.

Jesus gave two reasons why people had no excuse for hating Him and His Father: what He said to them and what He did among them. "If I had not come and spoken to them, they would not be guilty of sin. Now, however, they have no excuse for their sin. . . . If I had not done among them what no one else did, they would not be guilty of sin. But now they have seen these miracles, and yet they have hated both me and my Father" (John 15:22-24).

What Do Churches Need to Discover?

Leaders need to give top priority to truth and beauty in the same way that Jesus did. We can learn much from the advances made by secular organizations when they stress truth-seeking and sensitivity to beauty.

Integrity is the number one character trait of excellent leaders! Jesus also chose followers by character rather than by scholarship, wealth, or power. He could be more successful training people whose hearts were right. We can learn great things from His example. Kouzes and Posner's leadership qualities and Covey's seven habits are certainly in tune with Jesus, and the churches can learn from them.

Jesus brought with Him great opportunities totally unexpected by His people. "He came to . . . his own, but his own did not receive him. Yet to all who received him . . . he gave the right to become children of God" (John 1:10-12). Virtually every truth Jesus practiced and taught was an innovation to the blind and corrupt religious leaders and even to His followers. Drucker's emphasis on innovation and entrepreneurship certainly can be applied to churches today. (See 1 Cor 1:18-2:16.)

Tom Peters has been the modern champion of liberating the frontline workers to manage themselves, take responsibility, and accomplish ten times what has been expected and experienced in traditional command-and-control organizations. Peters champions bureaucracy-busting in secular organizations. Jesus chose ordinary people and freed them from the chains of stifling and untrue traditions. He led them to beautiful truths about God and God's kingdom, astounding things that had been hidden from the beginning of Creation. The disciples amazed the established religious leaders. "When they saw the courage of Peter and John and realized that they were unschooled, ordinary men, they were astonished and they took note that these men had been with Jesus" (Acts 4:13).

As God's leaders and children we need to discover the practical truths taught by Jesus. We need humble, wise, and courageous attitudes that will motivate us to challenge our preconceptions of God's truth and God's will.

Children of God as individuals need to keep learning and growing in the life-changing truths of Jesus' message. Jesus constantly used examples of common people and events for parables illustrating spiritual truths and hidden beauty. He made it clear that nobody profits from gaining temporary wealth if that person eventually loses what is most important of all, life. Covey's first three habits are like our first six chapters on Dynamics of Achievement in Part One. Be proactive, personally responsible: discover your gifts and strengths. See the end from the beginning: have vision and set goals. Put first things first: develop an action-plan, understand excellence, and work on a timetable of priorities. (See Matt 13:52; 16:24-26; John 3:21; 14:6,17; 15:26; 16:13; 17:17; 1 Cor 5:2; Phil 2:12-13; 1 Thess 3:2; 1 John 1:3.)

We need to cultivate true and beautiful relationships in the lives of believers. God's truth teaches us first of all about good relationships — integrity, true friendship, and beautiful intimacy with each other. Individuals learn and mature best by being free to discover for themselves, to follow Jesus and learn from their own study and mistakes. *God has us all in His school of experience to teach us truth and beauty.*

Small groups and project teams work well in secular organizations. Jesus also used the small group as the key fellowship for training leaders and disciples. This is undoubtedly the best and most effective medium and context for learning and practicing God's will.

It is highly effective also in reaching people within our circle of influence and exposing them to Jesus, the way, the truth, and the life (John 14:6).

Our hope is that more churches can see the connection between intimate small learning groups and doing what Jesus did in the first century. Nothing is more beautiful than a group of Christians working together and loving each other as they accomplish the mission and vision of Christ. (See John 15:1-17; 17:17-26; Rom 12:1-8; 1 Cor 12:12–13:13; Eph 4:1-28.)

What Can Grassroots Christians Do?

◆ *We can center our lives in Christ*: read His Sermon on the Mount as His goals to be studied and worked into our lives over our whole lifetime. They are not impossible commands. (See John 14:16,23; 15:7; 15:26; 16:13; 1 Cor 2:6-16 and Phil 2:12-13.)

We should perceive the truth as beautiful, not limiting and burdensome. We must continue in the word as a lifelong training school. Jesus asks us to come to Him and learn from Him. He is humble in heart and gentle. The yoke we share with Him is easy. At three minutes per page we can read a 500-page New Testament in less than two months, if we read it one hour per day. Reading ten minutes per day we can read through the NT once per year. God provides us with *gourmet food for the soul*. (See Matt 11:25-30; 2 Tim 2:22-26; James 1:21-25; 1 Pet 1:22–2:3; 3:13-17; 1 John 2:27 and 5:1-5.)

◆ We can continue to learn truth and beauty from our secular experiences and see how they fit in with the teachings of Jesus. We can lead and teach others by example. The message of Christ spreads through society like leaven, and we don't know who will respond, or for that matter how, when, where, or why. Our example can have a great effect on those in our circle of influence, because Jesus makes us His light — the light of the world. (See Matt 5:13-16; 9:12; 13:31-33; 21:28-32.)

◆ Perhaps the most effective way to walk in the way of Christ is to actively participate in a small group. John tells us that God's command is to believe in Jesus and to love one another. What better way can we demonstrate our love for each other than by associating together on a regular basis. (See 1 John 3:23; John 13:34-35; 15:9-12; Gal 6:2; Heb 10:23-25.)

Conclusions

◆ Through Paul Jesus explains that the wisdom from above appears foolish to people with "tunnel vision," those who are blind to the spiritual realm. God's wisdom is beautiful to people who grow spiritually mature by allowing the Spirit of Truth to guide and teach them. There is great beauty in childlike openness and humility. We can learn the meaning of truth by personal experience. Let God open your eyes and the Holy Spirit teach you. (See 1 Cor 1:18-30 and 2 Cor 2:10-16.)

◆ God hates partiality and snobbery in His people. He loves everyone in the world. We should set priorities for discovering vital, great, and central truths. God expects us to investigate the beautiful truths designed for eternity.

◆ God has invested much in the great beauty of the truths that He has designed into nature. All science and technology come from God even though they are developed by human research. The statement sometimes made "There is no evidence whatever for the existence of God" is way off base and an example of terrible blindness. Really, the evidence for God's existence is overwhelming, all around us, and in us.

REFERENCES

1. Kouzes and Posner, *The Leadership Challenge*, 16-18.

2. Ibid., 22-23, quoting O'Reilly, C., "Charisma as Communication: The Impact of Top Management Credibility and Philosophy on Employment Involvement." Paper presented at the annual meeting of the Academy of Management, Boston, 1984, 15.

3. Drucker, *Innovation and Entrepreneurship*, 35-56.

4. Ibid., 57-68.

5. Ibid., 69-75.

6. Ibid., 76-87.

7. Ibid., 88-99.

8. Ibid., 99-106.

9. Ibid., 107-129.

10. Ibid., 134-136

11. Ibid., 134-138.

12. Ibid., 138-140.

13. Covey, *The Seven Habits of Highly Successful People*, 15, 35 and Galatians 5:23. Also read Anita Thompson, *Habit Forming*, The PriceCostco Connection, January 1996, 1,12.

14. Tom Peters, *The Pursuit of Wow!*, (New York: Vintage, 1995), 98-101.

15. Batten, *Tough-Minded Leadership*, 183, and *Building A Total Quality Culture*, 67.

16. Philip Yancey, *The Jesus I Never Knew*, (Grand Rapids: Zondervan, 1995), 141. He quotes from Joseph Frank: *Dostoevsky, The Years of Ordeal, 1850-1859*, (Princeton: Princeton University Press, 1983). Psalm 104:24-30 and Romans 1:18-23.

CHAPTER FOURTEEN
VULNERABILITY

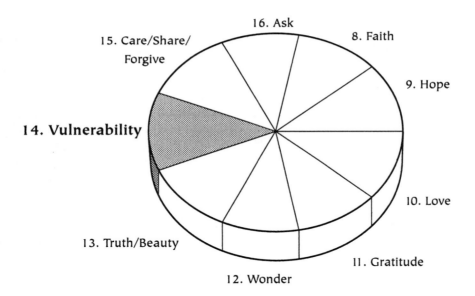

14

BE VULNERABLE WITH
COURAGE AND CANDOR

You know that the rulers of the Gentiles lord it over them, and their high officials exercise authority over them. Not so with you. Instead, whoever wants to become great among you must be your servant, and whoever wants to be first must be your slave — just as the Son of Man did not come to be served, but to serve, and to give his life as a ransom for many.
Jesus (in Matthew 20:25-28)

Do not be overcome by evil, but overcome evil with good.
Paul (in Romans 12:21)

Vulnerability is invincible! The courage to become and remain vulnerable in relations with others requires both tenderness and toughness. That kind of humble confrontation and courageous vulnerability develops strength of character.
Joe Batten

Key Points

Cooperation brings greater achievement than competing with others, but this means being more vulnerable and less defensive. We gain by admitting and facing our errors and our faults. The greatest advances of science and technology come through making mistakes, learning from them, and going on to success. God enables each of us to rise far above faults, troubles, and handicaps.

Excellent companies make the most of change and opportunity because they listen vulnerably to others, to their associates, customers, and suppliers. Jesus teaches us humility and respect for others' ideas. The churches need to avoid snobbery and self-righteous pride. These blind us to the good things others say and do. Christians can learn from the good we find in others, especially from those who have discovered many of Jesus' principles. In small groups we learn to appreciate a healthy variety in perspective when we listen vulnerably to what others are saying and where they are coming from.

****

How Do Secular Organizations Practice Vulnerability?

VeriFone is a $259 million Redwood City, California, company that we mentioned briefly in chapter four. CEO Hatim Tyabji believes in being vulnerable with his associates. He cultivates a climate of courage and candor. "Open communications is one of the foundations" of his business. He expects everyone to talk with him either personally or by e-mail. New employees are often skeptical of this openness, but when he cracks "through the self-protective shell" of the "inhibitions and fear they bring" into the job, "the rewards can be enormous!"

One new employee gave lip service to Tyabji's invitation to talk with him. Six months later his supervisor told the CEO that this person "had developed an attitude problem." Tyabji took him to lunch to hear his point of view. He encouraged him to speak frankly and told him that he had to open up and risk rejection. Otherwise his action was a self-fulfilling prophecy. He had to let down his defenses and allow himself to be vulnerable. Tyabji said, "If you choose not to say anything to anybody, then you screw up. Nobody can help you."

He told Tyabji that they were making costly mistakes by shipping products from Taiwan to other Asian factories and modifying them only after delivery to the customer's plant. They would have much better control of quality if they configured products in Taiwan to the specific customer's needs before shipping.

He had devised a worldwide system that would improve quality, reduce problems, and save money. Tyabji saw the wisdom of the person's plan, and they tried it out. It was very successful. His plan reduced build-to-order time from three months to 15 days. This shows how important it is to encourage candor and courageous vulnerability. VeriFone "created — and kept working on — an environment that encouraged him to speak up." And then they listened.[1]

We develop people and increase their effectiveness when we

encourage them to confront reality with courage and vulnerability. No one grows when they defend, flee, or desire safety and comfort. We must avoid the expedient of defensiveness. We must open our hearts and be interested in what other people think and say. This requires courage, humility, openness, and vulnerability. When we stick our neck out and take risks, rally from rebuffs and failures, that's when we motivate ourselves and grow. Vulnerability brings synergy — true cooperation.

Semco SA: President Ricardo Semler practices vulnerability to an unusual degree. He laughs at the consequences because his associates take him so seriously. After an extended trip, he returned to his office only to be advised, "Your office is not here anymore." It was now on the first floor and "reduced . . . to one third of what it used to be, and . . . I have never found the Persian carpet that used to be under my sofa."

Semler says that this means people no longer consider closed offices, Persian rugs, lots of secretaries, or special parking spaces that important. The important thing is "respect for competence." People no longer hoard information and power. "Power within the organization will have to come from the additional value that they are able to provide."[2]

For leaders to help their organizations constantly renew themselves like Ricardo Semler does, they must lead with vulnerability and openness. Only then will people grow and develop new abilities. Flexibility and versatility prevents rigidity and rigor mortis. Freedom to live and grow thrives in such a climate.

Steelcase: President Frank Merlotti and Chairman Bob Pew have decentralized and started small project teams on a voluntary basis. They made themselves available and vulnerable. They insisted that all employees be free to call them anytime, even at home. They made all home phone numbers available to everyone.[3]

One supervisor tells how hard it was to get used to the more open ways of doing things. So much change made him very skeptical. He thought, "Boy, I don't know if I can change like that. This is completely different." He struggled at first, but he decided to be more vulnerable and to give it a chance. He knew that they had to change if they were going to move ahead.

Now after two years he sees the improvements. "Fantastic — a lot of good things, a lot of cost-saving ideas. . . . The people are happier. . . . They put out the small fires and give me extra time to work on cost-saving projects and do the things I really should be doing."

Garfield quotes Merlotti on "the importance of training and of taking one step at a time in overcoming the resistance of plant supervisors to self-management and teamwork." Merlotti points out that "the line supervisors . . . were the most reluctant, the most concerned, and the most threatened." Creating a climate of vulnerability and openness takes time but it yields great results.[4]

Union Pacific Railroad: Railroads have a pronounced cost advantage over truckers, but often they've lost it due to unreliability and arrogance. According to Tom Peters, the Union Pacific Railroad before Mike Walsh served as CEO "was stiff, hyper-formal, bureaucratic, stodgy, sluggish, militaristic." It had 180,000 cars on the tracks and received more than $5 billion annual revenue. They did everything by the book. Leaders had little desire to be vulnerable and open to either employees or customers. One manager who supervised $22 million in business couldn't spend more than $2,000 without written authorization. That kind of approval required eight weeks.[5]

Walsh heard of a "drug raid" they made on workers in Louisiana about four months after he became CEO. He was outraged when he found out that they had scheduled a "safety meeting," but had made the workers lay on the ground while dogs sniffed for drugs. They found nothing. Walsh told the heads of engineering and operations, "We're going to meet with those people . . . and apologize publicly to them. . . . We're going to tell them that we don't tolerate drugs . . . we don't tolerate this kind of management either."

His managers were "aghast" and said, "You can't do that." Walsh not only did it, but they all went with him. The workers were amazed and accepted their "apology in about ten minutes." Walsh asked for any other comments, and one fellow told them how dangerous the steps on the bunk cars were: "You don't have adequate safety precautions. The steps are a mess . . . we're going to get hurt."

Walsh got after one manager who started to give the worker a lecture on how much money they spent maintaining bunk cars. He said, "Look, that's got nothing to do with this guy's question." He made everyone walk three blocks in the pouring rain to look at the bunk cars. "They were unsafe and they were embarrassing."

That showed management's willingness to be vulnerable, to listen to their people, and to do what was right rather than give people lectures.[6]

In 90 to 100 days Walsh created "a brand new railroad." Even against the counsel of Union Pacific's former chairman he pushed "the needle all the way over." He took away five of the eleven layers in the operations structure. Before the changes they were "playing trains." Afterwards, decisions that took months now took hours or days. Walsh centralized the collection of information, but he decentralized "'running the railroad' — taking care of day-to-day customer needs."

He gave much more authority to those close to the front. He made the major goal "learning how to cooperate and operate 'horizontally' — across functional barriers." Lower level teams became the key to cooperating "horizontally." UPRR put major effort into preventing the growth of new bureaucracies. He made leaders learn to delegate and made it very clear that high-level committees were not to "develop any permanent staff."[7]

Today when customers have problems they talk with "the crew foreman on the scene." The foreman resolves the problem right there on the spot. The Union Pacific Customer Action Team has developed processes for "getting people together at the ground level and giving them the responsibility and the control necessary to solve the problem."

What happened before this? When a customer wanted to trace a railcar the railroad usually traced the wrong car or the right car wasn't where the customer needed it to be. The customer went to his sales rep, who went to the district traffic manager, who went to the regional traffic manager. The next step was from sales and marketing across an enormous barrier "to the operations department general manager." This person had to now start going down the ladder to the superintendent, who went down to the train master to find out what went wrong. Then the whole process had to be reversed which all together took several days. People tried to cover themselves and place the blame. All this drove "the customers up the wall."

On top of all this, "there was a sense of frustration. People knew what to do, but they weren't being allowed to do it."

After Walsh's changes "on-time deliveries improved from about 40 percent to about 70 percent." Business volume went up 18 percent. Annual revenue went up 25 percent. Employees were reduced from 45,000 to 30,000. "Productivity per employee — 25 percent more revenue with 25 percent fewer people — has nearly doubled."[8]

Walsh in a speech to security analysts showed how all these changes went against "conventional management wisdom":

- All-at-once-change was possible.
- Great change did occur in a "very tough union environment."

◆ Even with massive job cuts people were kept "spirited and motivated."
◆ Top management doesn't have to be cleaned out. Some took a shine to liberation.
◆ It was done in a semiregulated environment.
◆ There was no reduction in financial performance.[9]

Asea Brown Boveri: ABB brings in about $30 billion in annual revenue in 140 different countries. It has about 215,000 people with many at the "bottom" organized "into 10-person, multifunction High-Performance Teams." Each profit center averages between 40 and 50 people.

CEO Percy Barnevik hates bureaucracy. He gave most of the staff members in their headquarters three months to find a job on-the-line where they could contribute more directly to the value and success of the profit centers. They would still be available as consultants on an as-needed basis. He reassigned 3000 staff members to operating units and this left only 250 on the permanent staff. He asked people to be vulnerable, to be servants, to work where they are needed the most, and to give up traditional management perks. "Live 'where it makes sense,' and move when it makes sense."

Barnevik believes that "two-thirds of Europe's giant companies will fail in the wake of European economic integration." He's making sure that ABB doesn't fail. This "means more clever products, and intertwining with customers in ever more intimate ways." Vulnerability, openness, and the courage to serve others are the motivational keys for the future.[10]

Peters summarized the four convictions that had to be present in the various stories he told of companies that asked their people to be vulnerable to change, change designed to make the company more healthy and serve its customers with openness and sensitivity:

1. You have to believe in "Stalk and Hout's '0.05 to 5 rule." That means we spend "95 to 99.95 percent waste time" on things that are not as important as what is never done at all. No wonder reinventing the organization can make people ten times more productive.
2. People can "handle all that change." People actually *"want* the opportunity." The conductors at UPRR knew "all along that it makes sense to do" what they already wanted to do. And it's not all middle management. Peters says that "the principle problem is a failure of nerve on the part of top management."

3. Unfortunately "most managers have added negative value to our corporations." In the UPRR the frontline workers were humiliated and "the customer tuned out."

4. There has to be awareness that major change is needed. Many old organizations need to be obliterated and totally new organizations created in their place. Survival depends on it."

To avoid defensiveness and ultraconservative dogmatism we have to make vital changes and *take the necessary risks.* We need to listen to others, receive valuable feedback, and continue to grow. In a fast-changing world, discovery and innovation are essential to survival and productivity. We need to be vulnerable, sensitive, aware, and cooperative without losing our own initiative to do our best.

◆ Leaders encourage change by delegating and trusting people to innovate, discover problems, cooperate, and be loyal to the needs of the organization and its customers:

1. It's a greater risk to not trust, not delegate, and not encourage.

2. Command and control type of leadership stifles growth in a society that is changing fast. Leaders must have vision, be competent, and have great character values. They control best by group peer pressure and accountability rather than by directing, telling, and closely supervising. They motivate best by promoting freedom, dignity, inspiration, cooperation, hope, and humility.

3. A fortress mentality shuts off feedback and discovery. It slows down innovation and action that eliminates roadblocks and blind spots. It is defensive, selfish, fearful, blind, and doomed to failure. It fears failure in even small experiments and it cuts off the learning necessary for big victories.

4. We learn the most and grow the most when we are vulnerable to everyone who has something to teach us. If being vulnerable, listening humbly, and learning constantly have worked well in secular organizations, how much more should they work well in Christ's eternal family.

◆ Here is what excellent organizations do:

1. *Delegate most things to teams.* Allow mistakes because people must experiment constantly to discover valuable truths and better ways of doing things. People must be vulnerable to mistakes and failures or nothing new and valuable can be learned.

2. *Let teams manage themselves* because this leads to greater effectiveness than the defensive command and control management style. Freedom motivates, and over-control de-motivates.

3. *Encourage teams to contact customers and suppliers directly*. This opens up valuable opportunities.
4. *Allow peer pressure to provide most of the required control*. This motivates team members effectively and also reveals who needs encouragement or reassignment. Insist mainly on firm character standards, on integrity, positive thinking, and enthusiastic participation.
5. *Reward performance* with bonuses that the team itself decides how to use. Base rewards on results and not on activity.
6. *Reduce headquarters staff* and give them the option of finding line jobs where they can contribute directly. Make valuable know-how available to all parts of the company by encouraging experts to travel and to communicate by computer.
7. *Allow a free flow on information* with no secrets. This produces faster innovation and problem solving. It encourages valuable participation by those who may have had no previous opportunity to contribute. Openness leaves the organization vulnerable, but this produces far greater advantages and motivation than the stagnation of stultifying secretiveness.
8. *Challenge the status quo*. Change upsets, but improvement is impossible without constant innovation. New opportunities come only to those who seek and develop better products, better services, and better solutions.

The Challenge of Vulnerability

We cannot truly love anyone — ourselves or others — unless we let ourselves be vulnerable. We can sometimes be emotionally hurt in the process, but if we never let ourselves be open to another person — family member, colleague, or friend — we cannot grow as a human being. When we let ourselves be open with others, we can discover in them good qualities we never suspected. As a result, we grow stronger and are able to bounce back from the times when we are rebuffed or hurt by someone. We become more tough-minded in our vulnerability!

I have often used the phrase "Vulnerability is invincible" and I mean precisely that. If you find that hard to believe, give me just one example of significant growth or gain that was not preceded by some testing, trying, tough circumstance.

A major breakthrough becomes possible when we equate emotional vulnerability with courage and strength. What happens to a mental muscle when it encounters *no* stress or resistance? Do you begin to see the self-destructiveness of a lifestyle rooted in defensiveness, safety, and *in*vulnerability?

Can a marathon runner develop toughness and stamina without going through many long, aching hours of effort? Can any man or woman, boy or girl, develop social skills, confidence, poise, and grace without vulnerably engaging in a wide assortment of social activities? Can the timid become courageous in *any* endeavor if they live behind a safe wall of nonconfrontation? Can your team develop unity, synergy, and esprit de corps without undertaking some tough and stretching objectives — and *winning*?

Joe Batten[12]

What Did Jesus Teach about Vulnerability?

A rough but vulnerable fisherman: Let's look at the story of Peter's life. Jesus emphasized Peter's strengths but He left Himself vulnerable to Peter's impulsive nature. He never gave up showing him the greatness of God's possibilities. We challenge you to read through Peter's two letters and from Matthew through Acts in the New Testament. Follow the amazing events in the life and development of Peter. His brother Andrew first introduced him to Jesus. Later, we see him as a fisherman in business with Andrew and with James and John, two brothers called *sons of thunder* by Jesus. They all leave their nets when Jesus asks them to start training for the more important job of catching not fish, but the real thing: *people*, for entry into the eternal kingdom of God! (See John 1:35-51; Matt 4:18-21; Luke 4:38-39; 5:1-11; 6:12-16.)

As an apostle to the Jews, Peter became a key messenger in spreading the wonderful news: *"The Messiah has come* and is ushering in the kingdom that will never end."* Peter made many mistakes and put "his foot in his mouth" constantly. When Peter objected strongly to Jesus' prediction of His coming suffering and death, Jesus told him, "Get behind me, Satan! You are a stumbling block to me; you do not have in mind the things of God, but the things of men." But Jesus never gave up on him.

Peter climbed a mountain in northern Palestine with Jesus to see Him transfigured into His glorious body. He saw Moses and Elijah appear and talk with Jesus about His final days in Jerusalem. Then Peter heard God speak from heaven: *"This is my beloved son. Listen to*

Him." (See Matt 16:13–17:27; also Matt 14:22-36; John 6:60-71.)

As a rough and tough fisherman Peter never dreamed that the Messiah would choose him to learn and serve as one of His ambassadors. He never expected to hear God's voice personally. Yet here he was standing on the mount, and all these things were happening to him. Christ gradually weaned Peter away from defensive and reactionary thinking. He released the chains of human tradition and dogmatism. *He opened up to Peter an ever-expanding vision of God's purposes and possibilities.*

Peter still had problems with Jesus' teachings on vulnerability and servant-leadership. He reacted when Jesus' knelt to wash his feet during their last Passover meal, where Jesus gave the Twelve encouragement before His death. Then came Peter's greatest disappointment, the arrest and death of Jesus. When Judas brought the temple guards and chief priests to arrest Jesus in the Garden of Gethsemane, Peter struck out with his sword. Jesus told him to put his sword away, because "all who draw the sword will die by the sword." Peter ran away and abandoned Jesus along with all of the other disciples. However, he regained enough courage to follow Jesus to the High Priest's home to see Him on trial before the Jewish leaders. In this Peter showed courageous vulnerability. But even though Jesus had forewarned him, his courage faltered, and he denied three times that he knew Jesus. In less than one day, Jesus was tried, crucified and buried! All Peter's dreams were hopelessly shattered. (See Matt 18:21-35; 19:23-30; 26:31-56; Luke 22:24-38; John 13:1-17; 31-38; 18:10-27.)

But wait! Three days after His burial Jesus came back to life! It happened just as He had predicted, and Peter saw Him in His resurrected body. Forty days later after many appearances Jesus ascended back into heaven to resume His position of glory at the Father's right hand. Before He left His disciples, He asked Peter three times, "Do you love me?" Each time after Peter assured Him of his love, Jesus told him, "Feed my sheep!" Jesus was letting Peter know that He was still an apostle of the kingdom of heaven, but he could also expect to suffer much before realizing the eternal dimension of his dream. Jesus also showed Peter that he would die in a way he would not want to go. (See John 20:1-9; 21:1-25; Mark 16:1-8; Luke 24:1-35; Acts 1-15; Gal 1-3; the two epistles of Peter, especially 2 Peter 1:5-8.)

Peter's two letters show his transformation from an impulsive fighter into a mature and patient servant. He tells us that God "has given us new birth into a living hope through the resurrection of Jesus Christ from the dead, and into an inheritance that can never perish, spoil or fade — kept in heaven for you." Peter says that in this living hope "you greatly rejoice, though now for a little while you may have had to suffer grief in all kinds of trials. These have come so that your faith — of greater worth than gold, which perishes even though refined by fire — may be proved genuine and may result in praise, glory and honor when Jesus Christ is revealed. Though you have not seen him, you love him; and even though you do not see him now, you believe in him and are filled with an inexpressible and glorious joy. . . (1 Peter 1:3-8).

Remember Charles Sheldon's best seller, *In His Steps*? Sheldon describes people who became vulnerable by asking "What would Jesus do?" He based his book on Peter's statement that we should be willing to endure suffering for doing good, "because Christ suffered for you, leaving you an example, that you should follow in his steps." Jesus lived out what He preached:

> "He committed no sin, and no deceit was found in his mouth." When they hurled their insults at him, he did not retaliate; when he suffered, he made no threats. Instead, he entrusted himself to him who judges justly (1 Peter 2:21-23).

Peter teaches us that we learn things through vulnerability that we could learn no other way. We don't usually volunteer for trials that bring suffering and sacrifice. But God enables us to conquer many obstacles that we fear and avoid. He leads us through great trials and over impossible hurdles to help us develop maturity. We don't learn very much by always taking life easy, avoiding challenges, and reacting defensively. Christ showed Peter that nothing is impossible. With God all things are possible (Matt 17:20; 19:26).

Peter gives us the secret of constant growth through making ourselves vulnerable to God and others. We have been born again, "through the living and enduring word of God. '. . . the word of the Lord stands forever.' And this is the word that was preached to you.

"Like newborn babies, crave pure spiritual milk, so that by it you may grow up in your salvation, now that you have tasted that the Lord is good. As you come to him, the living Stone — rejected by men but chosen by God and precious to him — you also, like living stones, are being built into a spiritual house. . ." (1 Peter 1:23–2:5).

As you examine the life of Peter you can see how *Christ developed his vulnerability* to enable him to learn the tremendous value of doing

God's will. Peter changed his focus radically from the bleak human viewpoint to the *eternal big picture*, God's viewpoint.

Jesus came into this world as a vulnerable little baby born into a poor and vulnerable family. What could be more risky than a birth in a stable more than 70 miles from His hometown? When King Herod learned of His birth, he immediately killed all the baby boys in the neighborhood of Bethlehem. Joseph and Mary had to flee to Egypt with the new baby. (See Matt 1:18–2:23; Luke 1:26-38; 2:1-20.)

Jesus made Himself vulnerable by choosing a small group and teaching them to accept sinners, tax collectors, prostitutes, and other outsiders. He infuriated the religious experts by reaching out to all people with God's love. He may have hated the sin, but he certainly didn't hate the sinners like those leaders did. He gave people the freedom to serve God. He kept telling His disciples that God would do anything they asked. On one occasion He astonished them by asking them to give 5,000 people something to eat. Then He went ahead and fed them all with five loaves of bread and a few fish. (See Matt 9:9-12,35-38; 14:13-21; 17:20.)

When He preached and trained His disciples, He had no headquarters, no corporate facilities, no wealth or million dollar endowments. He offended those in power by associating with the worst of sinners. He healed people of all manner of diseases: blindness, deafness, leprosy, paralysis, insanity, possession, etc. He used no violence except for driving the "robber" money changers and animal merchants out of the temple, His Father's House. (See Matt 21:12-15; John 2:13-16.) He conducted no rebellion, but His message was a threat to the religious authorities. He challenged the religious power structure by drawing the people away from them. He admitted that He was a king. Even though His kingdom was from another place and not of this world, Pilate was intimidated enough to crucify Him (John 18:33-39).

At Jesus' arrest, trial, and crucifixion one disciple betrayed Him, one denied that he knew Him, and they all abandoned Him. He even felt forsaken by His heavenly Father as He hung on the cross. His own nation and the Gentiles conspired to kill Him, and He was vulnerable enough to let it happen. He actually controlled the whole series of events. (See Matt 26:14–27:66; John 10:14-18.)

By His earthly weakness and *vulnerability* He displayed spiritual *invincibility*. He let Satan do his worst and kill Him. On the third day He arose from the tomb. He appeared many times to His disciples before He ascended back into heaven 40 days later. By His vulnerability He became the source of eternal life for all who believe in Him and follow Him. (See Luke 24:1-53; John 20:1–21:25.)

During His earthly ministry Jesus sent His disciples out in twos several times to contact the people in ways no one else was doing. He asked them to announce the nearness of God's kingdom. He taught His disciples to use their own judgment since He was to be with them for only three years. The Holy Spirit would live in them to encourage, teach, and guide them, but they would still face terrible temptations. (See Matt 10:1-20; Luke 10:1-17; John 14:16-17; 15:26-27; 16:12-15.)

Jesus conferred on them His kingdom and promised them that they would receive 100 times as much in that kingdom as what they had previously had. In the end they would receive eternal life. His kingdom would be known for being vulnerable. He taught His followers to turn the left cheek when someone hit them on the right one. Go two miles with those who force you to go one. Give your cloak to the person who takes your coat. In other words, love your enemies and those who mistreat you. His way was revolutionary but not rebellious. He avoided the use of physical violence, but He spoke the truth plainly to those who needed to know it. He argued constantly with the religious leaders because they needed radical correction. They were in danger of speaking against the Holy Spirit. (See Matt 5:43-48; 12:22-37; 23:1-39.)

He introduced the priesthood of all believers. He created a fluid organization based on personal relationships and predicted the end of the centralized system of temple worship and control (Matt 24:1-35). Nothing could have made Him more vulnerable to the power and hatred of the corrupt and dogmatic religious leaders! They had temporary power, but Jesus showed how wicked that power could be by allowing them to crucify Him. He triumphed over all the powers and authorities by being vulnerable even to death on a Roman cross. (See Matt 20:17-19; 26:52-56,64; Acts 3:13-26.)

Jesus told His followers that nothing would remain hidden. Everything would eventually be revealed, and they were to preach from the housetops everything they learned. God wanted to give all people the opportunity to hear, believe, and obey. Jesus did not make organizational control the key priority (Matt 10:26-27).

Christ's Wonderful Choice of Vulnerability, Service, and Courage: Paul

Saul of Tarsus persecuted Christians to their death. Trained in the law under Gamaliel, he was a leading Pharisee and "extremely zealous for the traditions" of his fathers (Gal 1:13-14; Phil 3:4-6).

We see him for the first time supervising the stoning of Stephen, one of the Christian leaders in Jerusalem. After this he immediately began to destroy the church, putting both men and women in prison and voting against them when they were put to death. He searched fanatically from house to house and from one synagogue to another for people to punish and kill. He even traveled to foreign cities in this reign of terror. (See Acts 7:54–8:3; 22:5-11.)

Then unexpectedly, Jesus appeared to Saul in a blinding light as he neared the city of Damascus. Jesus instructed him to go into the city where he would be told what to do. "For three days he was blind, and he did not eat or drink anything." Finally a Christian named Ananias told Saul that Christ had chosen him to preach His good news to both the Gentiles and the people of Israel (Acts 9:5-17).

Saul recovered his sight, regained his strength, and astonished the people as he preached in the synagogues that Jesus is the Son of God. Because he had persecuted Christians so severely in Jerusalem, the Jews of Damascus were baffled. He proved with great power that Jesus is the Christ (Acts 9:18-22).

Rather than accept Saul's logic and experience, his people plotted to kill him. So he escaped death by going down the city wall in a basket and traveling to Jerusalem. He continued to speak boldly about Jesus and amazed the people of Jerusalem. Some Grecian Jews argued with him and tried to kill him, but again he escaped and went to his hometown of Tarsus (Acts 9:23-30).

Years later many Gentiles had become Christians starting in the city of Antioch of Syria. The disciples sent Barnabas to preach and teach at Antioch, and he in turn went to Tarsus to bring Saul back with him. In Antioch he and Saul were preaching (along with several other prophets and teachers) when the Holy Spirit chose them to be sent out to spread the great news about Jesus to the Jews and Gentiles of Cyprus and Asia Minor (Acts 11:19-26).

From the time that Saul, Barnabas, and Mark arrived on the island of Cyprus Saul became known as Paul (the Greek for Saul). He made two more missionary trips that went as far as Macedonia and Greece. He established churches in many cities of Asia Minor and Europe including Galatia, Ephesus, Philippi, Thessalonica, and Corinth.

Luke wrote the history of the early church and described many of the trials that Paul endured. Paul also described his "light and momentary troubles":

1. In prison often and flogged severely.
2. Beaten with 39 lashes five times.
3. Three times beaten with rods.
4. Once dragged outside a city, stoned, and left there as dead.
5. Shipwrecked three times (not counting his shipwreck on the island of Malta).
6. Spent a night and a day in the open sea.
7. Constantly on the move and exposed to persecution and death.
8. In danger from rivers, bandits, his countrymen, Gentiles, and false Christians.
9. In danger in the city, the country, at sea.
10. Worked very hard to support himself while preaching and went without sleep often.
11. Suffered hunger, thirst, cold and nakedness.
12. Sick with a disability that he called a thorn in the flesh.

He boasted about his vulnerability and sufferings for Christ because some of the people he loved the most needed to understand the significance of vulnerability, physical weakness, and humility in serving Christ. All these "light and momentary troubles" and "sufferings" showed that Christ's "power is made perfect in weakness." (See 2 Cor 4:7-18; 11:21–12:10.) Christ turns *vulnerability* into *invincibility*. Paul delighted in being vulnerable, "in weaknesses, in insults, in hardships, in persecutions, in difficulties." When he was weak, he learned true strength. This is a hard lesson to learn, because our society often trains us from youth to avoid all pain, struggle, and challenge. Paul shows us that "in all things God works for the good of those who love Him" (Rom 8:17-28; see also 1 Cor 4:8-13; Phil 4:13).

Finally, Paul was beheaded in Rome. He mentions his imprisonment in that city many times in his letters written from prison to church members and the fellow preachers he had trained. Luke describes the frightening boat trip and shipwreck as they sailed to Italy where Paul the prisoner was to be tried there before Nero. Paul's life illustrates and proves dramatically God cares for us in the midst of weakness, suffering, and vulnerability. (See Acts 27 and 28; also James 1:3; Heb 10:32-36; 12:1-11.)

What Do Churches Need to Do?

1. *Risk mistakes*: Based on what Jesus did to please His Father in

heaven, we must be willing to take more risks for Him. He risked persecution and eventually death in order to follow the will of God. Churches must encourage the same kind of risk taking. We are plagued by spectatoritis. This goes right along with dogmatism and a critical spirit. We can learn from excellent organizations who have freed people to learn from their mistakes rather than cover them up and criticize others. We in churches can learn to avoid over-control by dogmatic experts. We can provide an encouraging climate that stresses our need to examine our traditions and make changes that put us closer to the way of God's Spirit.

2.   *Grant freedom*: Churches can allow members in small groups and task forces to make their own decisions. Leaders need to review performance periodically but not prevent or discourage participation, group discussion, and group action. Christ wants His people to be free to follow Him and grow to maturity in Him.

3.   *Reach out*: God wants all people to come into His kingdom. By encouraging small groups we can help all members to develop relationships that make friends, family members, and fellow workers acquainted with Jesus. Small groups will help us get away from either the country club or the fortress mentality.

4.   *Promote* the character of Jesus as the standard. We should be willing to walk as He walked and love as He loves. Members can learn to counsel each other and not depend on or be stifled by too much criticism from authority figures. We must be free to follow Jesus as His Spirit leads and teaches us.

5.   *Encourage members* to share resources to meet the real needs all around us. Such generosity is very pleasing to God and gives Him a good name. We have much greater resources in today's world than the early disciples had.

6.   *Teach leaders* to reduce control and delegate most things. Leaders can work right alongside of members as servants much in the way that Jesus did with His disciples. We need less command and more example. We can hold people accountable without leaders doing everything or using leadership methods that excellent secular organizations reject as ineffective and de-motivating.

7.   *Promote openness* which is vital. Participation, involvement, commitment, and conviction will be greatest where there is freedom. Churches should discourage gossip and a critical spirit. We can create a climate where confessing faults is healthy, where we can truly forgive and help each other grow spiritually.

Churches need to understand and practice vulnerability in our society in order to be *invincible* in God's society. The Romans destroyed Jesus' nation. Jesus predicted this destruction. He never intended to create an organization to compete with or to fight secular kingdoms and governments. He wants His people to fight spiritually and penetrate society like leaven. He wants to bring people to faith, not fight against them.

Jesus created a kingdom of relationships. He predicted that we would be persecuted for righteousness' sake and for His sake. We share in His sufferings. That makes us *vulnerable*, but it also makes us *invincible* in the long run. He makes us invincible because no secular society can successfully fight against God.

Jesus asks us to be vulnerable and liable to persecution for only one lifetime. Since we labor for a kingdom that will never pass away, the pain and vulnerability of this earthly life is not worth comparing to the glory that God will reveal to us. Jesus' disciples at first focused on restoring the secular power and glory of Israel, so they had a hard time understanding the kingdom priorities of Jesus. We need to take the example and teachings of Jesus seriously. We certainly don't want to make the same mistakes all over again, and we ought to learn from the mistakes of church history.

If we understand the invincible power of vulnerability, we should be able to see how easy it is to understand the road that Jesus asks us to walk. But it's been often misunderstood because it's so very hard to practice vulnerability, humility, and love. Walking as Jesus walked requires great faith in God. It was a lifetime job for Peter, John, Paul, and the other disciples to develop spiritual maturity. Jesus also wants to transform each of us.

What Can the Grassroots Christian Do?

1. *Take risks*: Be willing to facilitate and lead small groups and task forces. Help train people with no experience. Show others how to be vulnerable and take risks like Jesus, Peter, and Paul did.

2. *Utilize freedom*: Christ has set us free, and we should use our freedom to please Him. How do you share the good news of Christ with people in your own circles of influence? Take the initiative to be a self-starter and not depend on full-time professionals to do everything.

3. *Make personal contacts*: Show others how to reach out and develop relationships. How it's done in the business world can be a parable for the kingdom.

4. *Help each other*: Encourage church leaders to trust members and encourage members to help each other in building Christlike relationships. Avoid the judging, critical spirit.

5. *Work together*: Have living relationships with other believers. There is great reward from helping other believers to grow in their faith. Encourage staff leaders and members to share responsibilities. Use business methods of delegating and decentralizing as a parable for the church.

6. *Study Christ's message*: Learn together. The excellent companies are all learning companies. Christians should see the value of studying Christ's message for themselves. Full-time pastors should see the importance of grassroots faith. Members should be encouraged to discover their own views. In small group discussions no one should be made to feel that their questions are foolish.

Conclusions

The religious authorities considered Jesus insane and rebellious. He amazed Pilate with his courage. Pilate knew that Jesus did not deserve the death sentence. But His enemies and His "streetwise" disciples never considered Jesus to be a coward. His courage, power, and vulnerability stood out to all of them. He taught and lived courageously, with vulnerability and humility.

We please God when we live vulnerably, humbly, and courageously. But people often think that both vulnerability and humility are cowardly, especially people who misuse wealth, strength, and authority. Vulnerability may be hard to sell to people with little faith, but it is the only route to spiritual maturity. To follow after Jesus and walk *in His steps* we have to *be vulnerable with courage and candor*. Our next chapter will show that vulnerability leads directly to caring, sharing, and forgiving.

REFERENCES

1. Peters, *The Pursuit of Wow*, 254-256.

2. Garfield, *Second to None*, 158.

3. Waterman, *The Renewal Factor*, 175.

4. Garfield, *Second to None*, 114-115.

5. Peters, *Liberation Management*, 87-88.

6. Ibid., 99-100.

7. Ibid., 90-94.

8. Ibid., 88-90.

9. Ibid., 101-102.

10. Ibid., 44-55. *Tom Peters' Seminar*, 162-164, and 66. *The Pursuit of Wow*, 279-281.

11. Peters, *Liberation Management*, 101-102.

12. Joe Batten, *Tough-Minded Leadership*, 183.

CHAPTER FIFTEEN

CARE/SHARE/FORGIVE

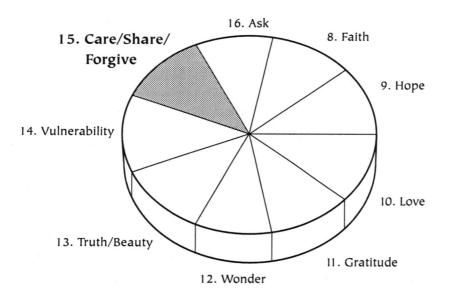

15

DO YOU CARE ENOUGH TO
HEAR ME AND FORGIVE ME?

I want them to know that when they're hurting we care for them — that's first. . . .
You don't necessarily have to hire folks who have been in the industry;
more important, you hire folks who care. As long as they care you can teach them
the job skills. If they don't have a caring view, you can't change them.
Bob Denckhoff[1]

As apostles of Christ we could have been a burden to you, but we were gentle
among you, like a mother caring for her little children. We loved you so much that
we were delighted to share with you not only the gospel of God but our lives as well,
because you had become so dear to us.
Paul (in 1 Thessalonians 2:7-8)

What we are forgiving is not the act. . . . We are forgiving the actors. . . .
Forgiveness is required of us in rich measure, not because the hurts that come are
not painful but because it is forgiveness that sets us free, that heals the unspeakable
wounds, that allows us to grow in heart and spirit. . . .
When we forgive one another our clumsiness, we are set free of the past,
we are free to be born fresh into this moment. . . .
Wayne Muller[2]

For if you forgive men when they sin against you, your heavenly
Father will also forgive you. But if you do not forgive men their sins,
your Father will not forgive your sins.
Jesus (in Matthew 6:14-15)

273

Key Points

We cannot overemphasize the cleansing, freeing-up, growth-inducing value of learning to truly forgive. There are far too many to whom revenge is sweet and vindictiveness is a crutch. Can we put ourselves in the shoes of others? By perceiving those around us with mercy — by truly listening to them — we come to understand how it is that God forgives us.

How do caring, sharing, and forgiving enable excellent organizations to motivate their people to excellence and high productivity? Jesus is our model, and He motivates us through His serving and forgiving message and life. Christians can show churches how to learn much from secular organizations. This kind of caring and generosity in His people pleases God. Small groups enable effective relationships to develop where caring, sharing, and forgiveness take place.

✳✳✳✳

The Challenge of Caring, Sharing, and Forgiving

These are some of the most profound keys to success in life as a whole. To care, share, and forgive is to live at life's cutting edge. As we care, we reach out beyond ourselves. Caring suffuses all superior leadership and full functioning. If we do not care much about others, we will ultimately not care much about ourselves. When we care, we become vulnerable. When we do not care, we become *in*vulnerable and *die* a little inside.

To share is to express caring tangibly. It is a further expression of vulnerability, wonder, faith, hope, love, and gratitude. It is the here-and-now hands-on practical way we help enrich the human condition. Remember, too, that an excellent and appropriate *expectation* is one of the finest things we can share.

Forgiveness is a requisite for happiness and peace of mind, for a liberated and energizing approach to life. The all-too-rare ability to forgive is best developed as part of an overall lifestyle. A lifestyle based on being *for-getting* sets up a collision course with rigidity. Actually, we never truly forget; we simply tuck the "forgotten" feelings into our subconscious. They are still there. In truth, we must remember in order to forgive. As we then develop a lifestyle that is based on *being for-giving* we become capable of *forgiving*.

Joe Batten[3]

How Do Secular Organizations Handle Caring, Sharing, and Forgiveness?

Mary Kay Ash Cosmetics: Mary Kay wants her company to be a caring one. One of her executives began to have trouble with being late to work and to meetings, not participating much, and getting reports in late. In the past he didn't have these problems so she told him, "Bill, . . . you're one of our key people, you've been with us for twelve years, and I feel we have become good friends in that time."

He said, "I feel that way, too, Mary Kay."

She mentioned that he hadn't been himself lately, and he agreed. Mary Kay then asked, "Is something wrong at home?"

He nodded his head, and she asked, "Is there anything I could do to help?"

Then he told her how his wife had a tumor in her upper back. They talked for more than an hour. Mary Kay tells how he felt much better from the talk, "and later his work improved immensely. While I didn't solve his personal problem, it was good for the two of us to talk about it."

Above all she wants her people to be caring and demonstrate concern — "listening will always be a top priority."[4]

Mary Kay wants her associates not only to care but to share their time and expertise. She has over 300,000 "beauty consultants who operate as independent retail businesses dealing directly with their customers." From the start her company had no assigned territories. When she had worked for direct sales companies she lost her sales commissions built up over many years. Why? Simply because she moved to a new territory when her husband's job location changed.

With no territories in *Mary Kay Cosmetics* a director can recruit people from anywhere she wishes; "a director who lives in Chicago can be . . . visiting a friend in Pittsburgh, and recruit someone while there. It doesn't matter where she lives in the United States; she will always draw a commission from the company on the wholesale purchases made by that recruit." The sharing comes in when the director in Pittsburgh trains the new recruit. The new recruit will attend her sales meetings. But the Chicago director will get the commissions. This is called their "adoptee" program.

Outsiders said, "Your adoptee program can't possibly work!" It does work for the reason that each director receives the benefits from her recruits in other cities. People in Mary Kay Cosmetics think this way right from the start. Instead of, "What's in it for me?" they think,

"I'm helping them, but someone is helping *my* recruits in another city."

Mary Kay knew that the adoptee program "would work because it was based in the Golden Rule." She believed that a philosophy of caring, sharing, and giving could penetrate "every aspect" of her business. Her company has become famous for being a caring family.[5]

The Printer, Inc.: Merrill Oster tells about Bill Benskin's vision to make his company a caring one. Bill's company has grown from a two-person business to one of more than 100 people. The Printer is a leader among US "database" publishers. Customers order by computer, and The Printer fills the order without the traditional paperwork and verbal communication. This avoids typical errors and eliminates the typing of orders, specifications, etc. It requires teamwork, trust, and complete access between The Printer and its customers.

Bill Benskin wants caring to begin at the top. He wants each group of people in the process to see themselves as customers of each other. "We wanted to end up with a set of teams that cuts across departments and conventional boundaries." This means:

◆ We treat "customers as the most important people in the world . . . from the heart." We must have a servant attitude.

◆ The top leaders maintain constant contact with customers. They go overboard to see things from the customer's point of view.

◆ Customers want to be shown that their supplier cares for them. The environment needs to be one "you would want your own family to work in." It's only common sense that both employees and customers "need to be loved."

◆ Caring service means being available when a customer needs help. The best companies drop "everything to help."

◆ It's important to be sensitive to the little things, especially when a customer calls for information. How you handle telephone calls tells how much you care.

◆ The overall long-range vision must be motivated by a desire to serve other people. Servant-leadership must filter down from the top to all people in the organization.

◆ What are some specific attributes of a caring company?
  1. Enlist caring, quality people who readily adopt the company's vision.
  2. Develop workers who are committed to growing and learning. The company should be interested in all dimensions of its people's lives: physical, emotional, and spiritual.

3. Don't be afraid to love — develop win/win attitudes.
4. Make changes even though this means taking risks. The greatest risk comes from failure to change, cultivating a climate of fear instead of love.
5. Customers as well as workers should be made to feel that they are members of a family.
6. Develop long range vision. Make customers want to stay customers for life. By caring it's easy to keep customers, but it costs a lot to get them back once they leave.
7. Pulling together with synergy and teamwork makes for a smooth machine. Only through caring relationships can you stay on the "cutting edge of the field." With synergism "customers truly participate in the birth and development of a new idea." The future hope of any business depends on new ideas and constant growth through innovation.[6]

Federal Correction Institution McKean, in Bradford, Pennsylvania: Tom Peters tells us how a caring attitude works great in a "federal pen." What better place could we find to illustrate Jesus' principle of treating others as you want to be treated (Matt 7:12), or Paul's statement, "Don't be overcome by evil, but overcome evil with good" (Rom 12:21)?

In 1992 this facility took care of 1,261 inmates with a staff of 334. Warden Dennis Luther opened the prison in February of 1989 with the philosophy that a prison doesn't have to be a "constant negative experience." He said that "punishment is being *sent* to prison," not punishing prisoners while they are in the prison. Some of his staff opposed this caring philosophy. Luther allowed popcorn at movies, and some guards said, "Inmates would stuff the popcorn in the locks." They went ahead with the popcorn, and no locks were stuffed. Two associate wardens had to be transferred because of their continued opposition.

One staff member who experienced "constant fighting and harassing" at another prison said, "Inmates here have a choice . . . and that choice is a high degree of self-management. . . . They're not getting any more" than those in other prisons. He thought one of Luther's secrets was complete honesty.

Warden Luther expects every staff member to contribute ideas. No one ever cared like this before. Every two weeks he expects each person to make at least "one concrete suggestion for improvement." One of the inmates said that he had never "seen people get along together regardless of race, creed or color except here." He was awestruck by the freedom, and by the fact that the prisoners could "use their skills and talents to benefit themselves and the institution."

The caring climate amazes new inmates. Abdul Adam spent ten years in Leavenworth where he had a reputation of being "a first-class troublemaker." At McKean incoming Muslim inmates looked for him often to ask "him for a knife." Adam has them sit down and tells them "how it's run around here. They can't believe it."

The Inmate Benefit Fund "raises money, then spends it on charities, cultural affairs, leisure activities, and special programs." This allows them to help out in "running the internal affairs of the prison." Warden Luther reported with pride that the Inmate Benefit Fund in 1991 had raised "$2,000 for needy local children. Overall, the IBF has raised more than $20,000 for local charities."

Even a hunger strike at the opening of the prison "was a wonderful training experience." It turned into an opportunity to practice "communication and responsiveness." Luther said that he would "open every prison with something like this!"

McKean's credo includes the following points in its list of "Beliefs About the Treatment of Inmates":

◆ "You must believe in a man's *capacity* to change his behavior."
◆ Be "sensitive to personality differences, cultural backgrounds, lifestyles and educational levels, and treat inmates as individuals."
◆ "*Be responsive* to inmate requests for action or information . . . the first time an inmate makes a request."
◆ "*Be dependable* when dealing with inmates." Do what you say you are going to do.
◆ The staff should "*model* the kind of behavior they expect" from the inmates.
◆ Treat inmates "*respectfully and with basic dignity.*"
◆ "Inmates will cooperate" if they are "motivated by *respect rather than fear.*"
◆ "Inmate discipline must be consistent and fair."[7]

What better example can we find of using a caring climate to turn around a culture that is normally full of hatred, animosity, violence, and injustice? It reminds us of how Jesus responded when the Pharisees asked His disciples, "Why does your teacher eat with tax collectors and 'sinners'?" Jesus said, "It is not the healthy who need a doctor, but the sick. But go and learn what this means: 'I desire mercy, not sacrifice.' For I have not come to call the righteous, but sinners" (Matt 9:12-13).

The importance of all members sharing the same values, mission, and vision: Leaders and followers share the same values in highly successful organizations. Excellent leaders give people every opportunity to share the values and the stretching vision of what can be. But they don't allow people into the organization if they oppose the values, mission, and vision. Merrill Oster writes of "ruthless hiring" practices that must be maintained to keep nonproductive and divisive people from joining a dynamic, caring company.[8] This is like Paul's advice: "Warn a divisive person once, and then warn him a second time. After that, have nothing to do with him" (Titus 3:10). He also said, "watch out for those who cause divisions and put obstacles in your way that are contrary to the teaching you have learned. Keep away from them" (Rom 16:17-18).

Covey on interpersonal relationships: Caring, sharing, and forgiving relationships undergird what Steven Covey describes as habits 4, 5, and 6. If we expect both parties to gain valuable Win/Win results from a relationship, then we must care enough to explore all avenues that are mutually advantageous (Habit #4). We have to care about someone to understand them. If we want them to listen to us and understand our point of view, then we must care enough to understand others (Habit #5). Synergism that brings unexpected and dramatic results comes only from intimate and cooperative work (Habit #6).[9]

Reasons For Caring, Sharing, and Forgiving

1. *Caring provides an inspiring, nurturing, and opportunity climate*:
   - ◆ Leaders in this climate consider the value, strengths, dignity, and amazing potential of all people — suppliers, workers, and customers. The organization cares responsibly for its contribution to society. It gives top priority to the wonder of Creation and motivates itself by gratitude to its Creator.
   - ◆ They cultivate a culture of learning from others. All excellent organizations are growing, productive, learning companies. They stay dynamic and on the cutting edge of the information society by using effectively the best in computer technology. They provide constant opportunity and encouragement to keep their members learning essential new truths and principles.
   - ◆ They understand that everyone's interest, commitment, and involvement is increased and optimized by wide open, two-way communication. Leaders have a vulnerable, open-door

policy with very few levels of middle management. More than 50% of leaders' time is spent on relationships — leadership by walking around, being totally aware of reality, and coaching people. Freedom creates the best kind of climate, and people are trusted to take responsibility and perform with enthusiasm and excellence.

◆ Leaders search out unexpected opportunities. They value serendipity (providence) and synergism (total results greater than sum of individual efforts). Both leaders and people motivate themselves to excellence by honest, competent, and inspired caring. All involved in the organization give top priority to uncovering and exploiting hidden problems and opportunities. The organization values experimentation and does all work with new discoveries in mind.

2. *Caring results in sharing*:

◆ Leaders and workers share facts, possibilities, vision, and values. No one hoards vital information or follows restrictive job descriptions. Teams cross-train, and everyone chips in and cooperates to get maximum effectiveness.

◆ A climate of giving stimulates generosity and mutual appreciation. More blessings and advantages come from sharing and giving rather than withholding cooperation for selfish reasons. Organizations that have learned to share everything produce ten times more than those that don't trust each other and restrict the flow of information. Everyone loves and cooperates with a giver.

◆ Cooperation always wins over competition in a climate of innovation. Organizations keep winning if they keep stretching and cannibalizing their successful products and services to deliver astonishing improvements — with "WOW." Xerox failed to do this with their copiers and left the door open to competition. Open, information-sharing companies always out-perform those who slow down innovation, enslave customers, and keep everything secret. Various studies prove this to be true.

◆ Caring, sharing teams produce much more value than bureaucratic structures. Excellent companies have prospered by eliminating middle manager positions that have slowed down progress and subtracted value. Front office staff have been asked to find jobs where they contribute directly to operating units. Brainstorming, goal-setting, and fast development work great in this more intimate climate.

3. *Sharing and cooperating bring synergism and serendipity*:
   - ◆ Unanticipated and unexpected opportunities usually produce better results than centrally planned projects. They come from many inexpensive, fast experiments and avoid the slowness and unpredictability of expensive mammoth projects. Necessary changes can be discovered and exploited quickly.
   - ◆ Those projects that need planning become more timely and effective. Routine and well understood operations still need planning and improvement. But it's primarily a numbers game. Numerous, more revealing experiments bring quick, valuable feedback and result in more breakthroughs and better service to markets and customers.

4. *Change is the one thing we can count on*:
   - ◆ People in a caring community help each other meet change as opportunity. With good relationships, adventure, excitement, and value come from constant change. Not everything changes at once, but most products and processes can stand improvement.
   - ◆ To stay ahead and survive the pain and trouble associated with change we have to innovate constantly. Endurance and perseverance make the difference between winners and losers. We always learn the most from change, from new facts and new truths. Opportunity comes where most people don't expect it. And it comes to those who prepare the best for it.

5. *Caring means forgiving*:
   - ◆ Mistakes and failures should be looked at as necessary trials in an experiment. Being afraid of mistakes will stop experimentation and prevent valuable innovation. We must encourage experimentation and forgive failure in order to stimulate valuable research and courageous action. Excellent companies reward good tries as well as the successful ones. Failed experiments often reveal vital truths that can be discovered in no other way.
   - ◆ Forgive quickly but don't accept deliberate violation of integrity and character values. This is what Peters and Waterman call "Tight and loose values," tight on character and loose with the freedom to try things and fail. It takes good leadership judgment and character to know when discipline is necessary and when thanks are appropriate.
   - ◆ Remember, nothing new will ever be discovered if leaders try to avoid all failures and mistakes. Others will do the experimental work and make the valuable breakthroughs. This is the

essence of having a vision and creating the inspired, involved, and highly motivated organization of people that will commit to the mission and believe in the vision. Edison never would have invented the light bulb if he had to get it right the first time!

Caring, Sharing Ourselves and Being Aware

To communicate at the high level at which we genuinely share ourselves, it is important that we:

◆ Avoid presentations. Invite every kind of question, comment, anecdote, experience, suggestion, and recommendation.

◆ Listen. Get behind the person's facial expressions and sense what they *really want* and *need* and *mean*.

◆ Be vulnerable. If there is even a smidgeon of defensiveness in your voice, words, manner, and posture, you will probably turn someone off. You'll never know why, and perhaps they won't know either.

Superior cultures are of, by, about, and for people who care enough to share. They are aware of the wonders, uniqueness, strengths, and possibilities of everyone with whom they associate. They enjoy helping others fulfill their highest values and become all they can be.

These people are at a premium. We need more of them. Do you care, share, and dare enough to be aware of the infinite possibilities just waiting to be discovered in others? I'm going to bet that you do.

Joe Batten[10]

What Did Jesus Teach and Do about Caring, Sharing, and Forgiving?

His life tells us how much God cares. Jesus came into this world because He cares for us. God supplies our very existence and all that we have and need to live our lives. Jesus shared with His disciples all that they needed to know — about life, about God, about eternity. Caring comes directly from love and results in sharing with others.

We often forget or overlook that God shares everything with us, and He gets nothing in return. The world we live in belongs to Him. We belong to Him. Jesus not only shared His life with His disciples, but He also makes His life available to each of us. The kingdom of heaven can belong to us, and we can inherit the earth. He tells us that our Father in heaven knows our every need. We don't have to worry about our clothes, our food, or our lives, because God already knows what is best for us. He provides for our needs before we even ask Him. (See Matt 5:3-12; 6:25-33.)

When we pray, "Give us today our daily bread," we acknowledge the fact that this is what God has been doing throughout our lives. Gratitude for His gifts motivates us to care for others, to share with them, and to thank our Father in heaven. (See Matt 6:11; 25:34-40; Acts 20:35.)

Jesus shared strong words with the religious leaders of His nation, and they hated Him for that. He told them exactly what they needed to know, because they were moving fast in the wrong direction. He called them snakes and hypocrites. They strained out a gnat and swallowed a camel. They missed the weightier matters of the law, such as justice, mercy, faithfulness, and the love of God. They stressed meaningless ceremonies and failed to hear what God really wanted them to stress (Matt 23:1-39; Luke 11:37-54).

The religious leaders persisted in their wrong attitudes, and they eventually conspired to have Jesus killed. Jesus predicted His suffering and death many times to His disciples. He said to them, "The Son of Man is going to be betrayed into the hands of men. They will kill him, and on the third day he will be raised to life" (Matt 17:22-23).

Jesus motivates us to love one another by the tremendous love He shared with all of us. He demonstrated God's love for us, and He showed us that we don't have to fear death or anything else in this world. God knows the number of the hairs on our heads. He makes us joint heirs with Jesus as members of His eternal family. In dying for us, Jesus provided for our forgiveness. (See Matt 10:24-31.)

Jesus told the parable of the Prodigal Son to illustrate how much God loves and how quickly He forgives our mistakes and sins. He asked us to pray, "Forgive us our debts, as we also have forgiven our debtors." Then He added the comment, "For if you forgive men when they sin against you, your heavenly Father will also forgive you. But if you do not forgive men their sins, your Father will not forgive your sins" (Matt 6:12-15).

To illustrate the above warning more clearly, He told the parable of the Unmerciful Servant. He showed us God's attitude toward people who desperately need His forgiveness but will not forgive others who owe debts to them. God forgives readily, but He will not forgive people who are unforgiving. He forgives all the sins common to human beings except one. He will not forgive us when we insist on continuing in rebellion against the very Spirit of Truth (Matt 12:31,32).

His story of the Good Shepherd shows how Jesus leads His followers. He cares, shares, and forgives. These are attitudes that come from love, and they motivate us to service in God's church on earth. In this book we've shown that many excellent leaders in secular organizations have discovered some of the wonderful things Jesus taught and practiced. They've learned to motivate themselves and their associates to follow *the Leadership Principles of Jesus.* (See John 10:1-21.)

Caring, sharing, and forgiving are practical applications of faith, hope, love, and gratitude, (our chapters 8-11). Jesus constantly modeled and taught these motivational attitudes. He gave these a high priority and called them the more important principles of God. His chief enemies (the Pharisees and teachers of the law) neglected these leadership principles, and Jesus condemned their corruption to their faces (Matt 23:24).

While dying on the cross Jesus asked God to forgive those who killed him. He realized that they didn't really know what they were doing. He knew that many of them would eventually be sorry for what they had done to Him. They would come to know how far He was willing to go in caring, sharing, and forgiving (Luke 23:34).

On the night Jesus was arrested He prayed for the unity of all those who would believe in Him. He asked God to care for His close disciples who would soon be experiencing the same persecution and hatred that He was experiencing. He and the Father share the same Spirit, Truths, and Vision. (See John 17:1-26.)

◆ Examples of Jesus' mercy, love, and forgiveness to those in adversity:
   1. Lazarus and the rich man (Luke 16:19-31).
   2. The thief on the cross who asked Jesus to remember him (Luke 23:39-43).
   3. The man possessed by a legion of demons (Luke 8:26-39).
   4. The woman caught in adultery (John 8:1-11).
   5. The Samaritan woman at the well (John 4:4-42).

What Jesus' Disciples Did and Taught

◆ Just as Jesus prayed for His killers, Stephen prayed for those who were stoning him (Acts 7:60).
◆ The apostles met in Jerusalem to show their concern for both Jews

and Gentiles. They were overjoyed (except for some legalists) that God was showing His love (His caring, sharing, and forgiving) to the whole world. (See Acts 15:1-31; 21:17-25.)

◆ Paul was Jesus' great example of caring, sharing, and forgiving. Where Paul could do it, he practiced being *all things to all people.* This is not impossible or impractical. He related to people where they were for their own good. With all his heart he wanted to help as many people as possible to accept Jesus as the Savior of the world. (See 1 Cor 9:19-23.)

◆ Paul constantly explained how God loves both Jew and Gentile. By His love Jesus broke down the wall of separation between Jew and Gentile. He created one body, one family. Paul's prayers were for the same kind of unity that Jesus prayed for on the night before He was crucified. (See John 17:20-26; Rom 9–11; Eph 2:14-22.) He reminded the believers in Thessalonica how he loved them and cared for them like a mother and father care for their children (1 Thess 2:7-8).

Old Testament Examples of God's Love

◆ God showed great concern for Abraham's descendants when they were enslaved in Egypt. With His mighty power He led them out of slavery and guided them into a land He had promised long before to Abraham. He forgave them except when they refused to repent and persisted in rebellion. We see this throughout Exodus, Numbers, and Deuteronomy.

◆ God loved those outside Israel. All the prophets told God's people to treat foreigners right as well as widows, orphans, and those who were oppressed. (See Ps 94:6; 146:9; Jer 7:6; 22:3; Zech 7:10; Mal 3:5. Especially consider Ezekiel 22 on how God stresses character standards and Ezekiel 34 on leaders and followers.)

What Do Churches Need to Discover?

◆ God wants us to help save the people of our culture, not fight them. In order to be heard and understood, we must work hard at *understanding* those in our circle of influence. We and our families should demonstrate caring for others by being willing to give up comfort and face adversity. We can avoid a fortress mentality by seeing ourselves as pilgrims looking forward to an eternal home in heaven. We need to listen to God and choose His priorities for being His light to our world. God wants all people to know Him intimately, not coddle or show favoritism to those who already know Him. This key to excellent leadership is a good reason for us to accept partnership with God and accountability to Him.

◆ God wants all of us to change our hearts and lives. If we provide a caring climate, God will draw people to us as His family on earth. Perhaps we can help others to know what pleases God and He will change their hearts.

◆ How can we unite to help God in saving the people of the world? That's what Jesus prayed for! People see our lack of unity and wonder why we don't take Jesus' principles and His wonderful prayer in John 17 more to heart. (Read John 17:20-26.)

What Can the Grassroots Christian Do?

We can show the churches that "sinners" often are just as caring and more ready to repent than "righteous" people:

◆ Practice caring on our jobs and help church groups see how Jesus cared. Use our own job situations (whether good or bad) as parables when we have opportunities to teach others. This is how Jesus used thought-provoking parables. Most of His parables illustrate God's priority of caring for others.

◆ Since we all sin, we need to be tenderhearted with others. If we lead with a tender heart then our intellects will be more likely to follow. Our heart helps us to get our head in the right place — in the attitude of humility and service. According to Pascal, "The heart has its reasons that reason knows nothing about." Jesus praised God because He had "hidden these things from the wise and learned, and revealed them to little children" (Matt 11:25).

We can learn from our jobs how sharing is more effective than being secretive or competitive. We must be dedicated to continuous growth, learning, and excellence.

◆ Volunteer to lead or facilitate in a small group, teaching and showing the group how to discuss sharing in various areas of life. We learn to lead and facilitate best in small groups because the climate is friendly like it is in a family.

◆ Study Jesus' life for ideas on what God thinks of sharing. Be prepared to share Jesus by being close to Him. Don't neglect God's wisdom. James said, "If any of you lacks wisdom, he should ask God, who gives generously to all without finding fault, and it will be given to him" (James 1:5).

◆ Allow God to motivate us, and motivate ourselves to reach our circle of influence, relatives, friends, fellow workers, etc. Use our chapters 8-16 for principles of motivation.

We can learn the value of innovating, experimenting, and correcting mistakes:

◆ Become aware of what Jesus taught on forgiving sins. (See Matt 6:12-15; 18:21-35.) Compare His words with how this works out in secular organizations. Discuss some of the church's problems in the past with failure to forgive and examine how Jesus worked with His disciples on forgiveness. Make changes, and take the risks involved to get others to see how Jesus taught. Study and discover how some excellent organizations treat people better than many churches do.

◆ Explain why character standards are vital, but don't criticize or punish unintentional sins, errors, or differing opinions. We should be free to learn from Jesus, free to be taught by His Spirit. Paul said, "It is for freedom that Christ has set us free. Stand firm, then, and do not let yourselves be burdened again by a yoke of slavery" (Gal 5:1).

◆ Expect trials, temptations, and tests to challenge our attitudes, priorities, and goals. We need to avoid the fallacy of trying to be perfect by doing nothing. We can't grow spiritually without trying to learn new things and better ways to do old things. Experiments and honest mistakes provide us with the knowledge and wisdom that we need for growth. The greatest errors and risks come from not trying to learn.

Small Group Agendas

On Caring:

◆ Icebreaker on caring experiences when you were younger.
◆ Have the group take turns reading Matthew 6:19-34, Luke 12:13-34, 2 Corinthians chapters 8 and 9.
◆ Discussion on caring in Scriptures and caring in everyday life.
◆ Prayer with each taking part.
◆ God's vision and our vision for the future.

On Sharing:

◆ Icebreaker on the sharing you experienced when you were a child.
◆ Have the group take turns reading Matthew 5:43-48; 25:31-46; Luke 10:25-37; 12:32-34 and 14:12-14.
◆ Discussion on sharing in Scriptures and sharing in everyday life.
◆ Prayer with each taking part.
◆ God's vision and our vision for the future.

On Forgiving:

◆ Icebreaker on forgiveness you received when you were a teenager.

◆ Have the group take turns reading Matthew 6:12-15; 18:21-35; Luke 23:34, 39-43.
◆ Discussion on forgiveness in Scriptures and forgiveness in everyday life. God forgives us through Jesus' great love. He died to take away our sin.
◆ Prayer with each taking part.
◆ God's vision and our vision for the future.

Conclusions

God demonstrates His care, His giving, and His forgiving love. When people we know show the same attitudes, we need to give them credit. Many people may be close to God's will and not even know it. In our experience with secular organizations we see some of the excellent ones applying *The Leadership Principles of Jesus*.

We Christians need to examine ourselves to see if we are part of God's answer or part of His problem. Jesus prayed that we might be led by God to be His answer, that we all might be united as He and God are united. We have read about how intimate small groups practice Jesus' leadership principles effectively. In small groups we have a great opportunity to learn from others, because unleashing people and giving them the freedom to care, share, and forgive will certainly help God to attract people into His Family.

Will you do it?

Caring Enough To Forgive

A personal philosophy of forgiving if diligently practiced, ultimately allows one to feel a healthy measure of forgiveness *toward* and *from* one's God, one's fellow person, and oneself.

I cannot overemphasize the cleansing, freeing-up, growth-inducing value of learning to truly forgive. There are far too many to whom revenge is sweet and vindictiveness is a crutch. This can, and has, countless times caused all forms of bitterness, conflict, personality disintegration, and just plain unhappiness.

To truly lead, will you respond to this challenge?
**Will you build a life-style of being forgiving
and shun the expedience of seeking only to take and get?
You decide!**

Joe Batten[ll]

REFERENCES

1. Oster, *Vision-Driven Leadership*, 55.

2. Wayne Muller, *Legacy of the Heart*, (New York: Fireside, 1993), 11.

3. Batten, *Tough-Minded Leadership*, 194.

4. Ash, *People Management*, 32-33.

5. Ibid., 2-3.

6. Oster, *Vision-Driven Leadership*, 116-127.

7. Peters, *Liberation Management*, Ibid., 249-255.

8. Oster, *Vision-Driven Leadership*, 78.

9. Covey, *The Seven Habits of Highly Effective People*, 204, 235, 261.

10. Batten, *Building A Total Quality Culture*, 60, 62.

11. Batten, *Expectations and Possibilities*, 170.

CHAPTER SIXTEEN
ASK

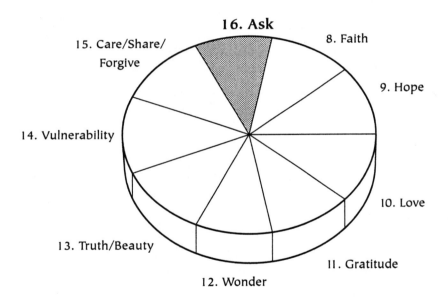

16. Ask

8. Faith

15. Care/Share/
Forgive

9. Hope

14. Vulnerability

10. Love

13. Truth/Beauty

11. Gratitude

12. Wonder

16

ASK FOR THE WISDOM AND COURAGE TO CHANGE

If any of you need wisdom, you should ask God, and it will be given to you. God is generous and won't correct you for asking. But when you ask for something, you must have faith and not doubt. Anyone who doubts is like an ocean wave tossed around in a storm. If you are that kind of person, you can't make up your mind, and you surely can't be trusted. So don't expect the Lord to give you anything at all.
James (in James 1:5-7, CEV)

Ask, and you will receive. Search, and you will find. Knock, and the door will be opened for you. Everyone who asks will receive. Everyone who searches will find. And the door will be opened for everyone who knocks.

Jesus (in Matthew 7:7-8, CEV)

We are certain that God will hear our prayer when we ask for what pleases him. And if we know that God listens when we pray, we are sure that our prayers have already been answered.

John (in 1 John 5:14-15, CEV)

Key Points

This final chapter shows that people achieve the most and the best with great expectations. People learn more from Jesus by achievement than by getting something for nothing. We have a high calling. Christ motivates us to continuous spiritual growth. We give life our best shot and know it. Remember, we learn by taking risks and making mistakes.

291

How does a person motivate self and others by asking much and expecting greatness and excellence? We ask God to help us, and with God's help nothing is too hard. Jesus asks great things of His disciples, and He inspires us to courageous and productive living. How do churches and church leaders sometimes miss this and get embroiled in fruitless politics, traditions, and legalisms? Grassroots Christians can achieve great things without fear and guilt, because Christ promises great things to those who truly love Him. Godliness has value both in this life and in the life to come. God's family on earth supports and motivates each of us by developing healthy expectations in communities of small groups.

✳✳✳✳

What Do Excellent Organizations Ask of People?

1. *Leaders ask for achievement:* They don't tell, dictate, or demand. They know their values, their mission, and their vision. They ask all people in the organization to share the values, mission, and vision. People who don't buy into a philosophy and vision of excellence won't contribute their wholehearted effort to the organization's success and health.
   - ◆ *People produce great results* when leaders give them freedom to succeed. People respond best when they are valued and loved. When they stretch towards great possibilities they develop wisdom and they learn valuable lessons from barriers and difficult problems along the way. Excellent leaders live by integrity. They ask people to experiment constantly, to accept failures in stride and learn from them. *Shared values are vital.*
   - ◆ *Leaders increase leverage* by trusting and asking others to do their best. People love a challenge when they can see the results and when their leaders appreciate them. Leaders and people together must know and pursue their *purpose, and mission.* People enjoy responsibility when they produce something valuable for society.
   - ◆ *Inspired people* contribute their best. They develop the wisdom and courage to change when they participate in *a great vision.* They expect their leaders to have a clear vision of the highest and best possibilities. People expect their leaders to have the courage it takes to lead through both good and troubled times.

2. *High expectations motivate people the best:*
   - ◆ We need leaders to ask and stretch us for our own good.

Why? Because many people spend more than 95 percent of their time and effort on things that are not as important as the things they never do at all.

◆ Capability, strengths, and maturity grow only with practice. We grow only when we seek out and make healthy changes. To accomplish great things we must expect and ask for great things.

3. *We harvest what we plant.*
    ◆ To do our best we need a vision of the highest possibilities.
    ◆ It's good for us to be responsible and learn how to handle still more responsibility. Given the opportunity, we can usually become servant leaders. All of us lead someone in one way or another.
    ◆ Cooperation and relationships bring more results than competition. Our leaders can decentralize authority and delegate virtually every task to intimate small groups.
    ◆ We reach the highest goals by steps. No one learns maturity overnight. We sow what we later reap over the course of our whole lifetime.

Leaders Ask People to Develop Their Capability to Achieve

In *chapter one* we told stories about a Japanese automaker, IBM, Matsushita (Panasonic), and Taco Bell. These all reached out for the best *possibilities and opportunities*, and they asked their people to own the *vision and mission* they adopted. In *chapter two* we highlighted a stutterer, a video products company, and Dataproducts. These exemplify the vital importance of *discovering spiritual gifts and building on strengths*, not weaknesses. In *chapter three* we used America West to demonstrate the power of *pursuing the best goals*, goals that came from adopting a transcendent vision and developing people's strengths and gifts. America West illustrates how inspired associates and leaders work together to make the goals of the company fit their vision and mission. They aim for their vision of the future and they implement their mission daily as they fulfill the company's purpose. Developing and reaching practical goals by constant experimentation and testing creates great achievements. No other approach works as well as this one.

These three chapters work together much in the same way that Stephen Covey's first two habits do. Covey's book *The Seven Habits of Highly Successful People* has been a runaway best seller (more than 250 million copies have been sold). He asks his readers to cultivate the seven habits and fundamental principles that highly successful people practice:[1]

Habit 1 — Be Proactive expects the same as our principle of *Building on Strengths and Gifts*. We take responsibility for ourselves. We live by our values rather than being led by our feelings. We decide what to do, rather than allow our actions to be programmed by the climate we find ourselves in. Reactive people allow the weather, other people, the circumstances to control their behavior. "Proactive people are still influenced by the same external stimuli, whether physical, social, or psychological." But they choose how they will respond to stimuli based on "carefully thought about, selected and internalized values."[2]

Habit 2 — Begin With the End in Mind agrees with our principle of searching out the best *Possibilities*. Leaders and their people develop a vision of what they want their life to be as a whole. They create a good "understanding of your destination . . . know where you're going so that you better understand where you are now and so that the steps you take are always in the right direction."

Leaders and employees jointly develop a vision and write a mission statement in which "you think through your priorities deeply, carefully, and to align your behavior with your beliefs. You have a sense of mission about what you're trying to do and you are excited about it."[3]

In chapter four we move on to the action plan that uses our first three principles to create a thrilling environment of constant experimentation to maximize each person's productivity and contribution. 3M, HP, EDS, Bell and Howell, Ogilvy & Mather, Bell-Atlantic, and VeriFone serve as excellent examples of companies who *motivate people to action* that benefits all people involved: themselves, suppliers, customers, and society in general.

Our chapters five and six ask for a standard of excellence and for giving top priority to the most important responsibilities. In *chapter five* we cite examples from Milliken & Co., Raychem, Data General, Mary Kay Cosmetics, Johnsonville Foods, and especially Honda. In *chapter six* we use Milliken again, HP, and Mervyn's. Covey's *Habit 3 — Put First Things First* goes right along with our principles of defining *excellence* in quality and developing a *timetable* that puts first things first. Stephen Covey, Warren Bennis, and Burt Nanus all say "leaders do the right things" rather than do things right. Covey's Habit 3 says to "schedule priorities rather than prioritize your schedule." Spend the most time on what's important but not urgent. Focus on important priorities in order to solve the long term problems that cause most of the urgent problems. Put no effort on unimportant non-urgent problems, and very little on urgent unimportant issues.[4]

Our chapter seven rounds out our Part One and stresses the need for work and discipline to create ongoing great achievements. Our first six principles (possibilities, strengths, goals, action plan, standards, and timetable of priorities) require a dedicated group of leaders and followers who buy into and share the values, the mission, and the vision of the leaders. Here we tell of research done by Scott Peck, Dr. Link, and Dr. Robert Eisenberger. Covey's *Habit 7 — Sharpen the Saw* deals with the discipline of continuing to improve all of his other habits just as we use *work and discipline* for continuous improvement of our first six principles.

How Do Excellent Leaders and Their Associates Create a Motivational Climate?

In our *chapter eight* we use Johnson & Johnson's Tylenol tragedy, Semco S/A, and Quad Graphics as examples of organizations that motivate by *faith and trust*. In *chapter nine* Apple Computer shows how a great company fought back from a crisis by creating *hope* in the future. *Chapter ten* stresses the Golden Rule, how *loving one another* supplies the greatest of all motivation. Organizations mentioned include the Green Bay Packers, Worthington Industries, Domino's Pizza, Celestial Seasonings, IBM, Milliken, and Mary Kay Cosmetics. Covey's *Habit 4 — Think Win/Win* parallels our principles of *faith, hope, and love*. Take sincere interest in the other party's welfare. Hear and understand the concerns of others. Arrange cooperative efforts so that all parties obtain what they want out of the partnership or contract. Don't enter into relationships when only one party wins and the other loses. It should be win/win or nothing.[5]

In *chapter 11 on gratitude*, we use the dramatic rescue of the Apollo 13 crew to demonstrate how strongly gratitude motivates people. In *chapter 12 on wonder*, we tell stories about Stew Leonard's, the Information Society, Intel Corporation, IBM, discoveries of the Astronomers, and Phillip Johnson's, *Darwinism on Trial*. In *chapter 13* we cover work done by Kouzes and Posner, Peter Drucker, and Tom Peters to show how *truth and beauty* motivates.

In *chapter 14 on vulnerability* we mention VeriFone, Semco S/A, Steelcase, Union Pacific Railway, and Asea-Brown-Boveri. Great illustrations on the motivating power of *caring, sharing, and forgiving in chapter 15* come from Mary Kay Cosmetics, The Printer, Inc., and the Federal Correction Institute McKean in Bradford, Pennsylvania. Covey's *Habit 5 — Seek First to Understand, Then to Be Understood* corresponds with our motivating principles of *vulnerability* and *caring, sharing, and forgiving* in chapters 14 and 15. Listen with the intent to hear, not with the intent to give them your reply. "Instead of projecting your own autobiography and assuming thoughts, feelings, motives and interpretation, you're dealing with the reality inside the other person's head and heart . . . the deep communication of another human soul."[6]

Our *final chapter on asking* deals with all of the principles in chapters one through fifteen. Leaders and associates together motivate themselves to great achievements by using all of these principles *synergistically*. The total results are much greater than the sum of the individual parts. Covey's *Habit 6 — Synergize* bring his first five habits together in concert. This true principle is to value differences because different people have a variety of talents, gifts, and strengths. Pooling strengths makes a group highly effective. Partnering with suppliers and customers brings tremendous results because of the synergistic effect.

Covey tells a story to illustrate this: He worked with a land developer with a desperate need. The developer's bank was foreclosing and "he was suing the bank to avoid the foreclosure." He couldn't make the payments, and he had to have more money to finish his development. He finally agreed to meet together with the bank officials. The bank's attorney "had committed the bank officials to say nothing." They wanted to win in court and the developer to lose. The bank officers gradually became less defensive as Covey taught the whole group "the principles of Habits 4, 5, and 6."

After three hours of discussion the bankers felt understood and realized how poor communications had led to "misunderstanding and unrealistic expectations." In four hours, the bank officers and the developer were making progress and felt positive about reaching a good agreement. Real synergism began to take place because everyone was thinking Win/Win. In about five hours the bankers and the developer left with a plan to submit to the city and Home Owners Association.

The land development was successful, but this would never have happened without the parties learning how to cooperate, understand, and synergize at a new and vital level.[7]

What Does Jesus Ask and Expect?

1. *He set the goals and possibilities high*; He had a strategy for accomplishing His mission and vision.
   - ◆ God is in the process of making us in His image. He wants us to ask, seek, and knock. He always gives us the wisdom we need and ask for. God helps us and teaches us. This life is a school of training for something far better. (See Matt 7:7; James 1:2-12; John 6:27-68; 2 Cor 4:16-18; Rom 8:18-39.)
   - ◆ God doesn't let us off cheaply. He rewards us according to our faith and judges us according to our deeds. Jesus is preparing a great and wonderful future for us. (See Matt 16:27; Luke 6:23; John 14:1-3; Eph 6:8; Heb 11:6.)
2. *Jesus asks us to volunteer ourselves.*
   - ◆ Since all that we are and have comes from God, we can only boast of God's greatness (1 Cor 1:31).
   - ◆ God never forces us to listen, but He really wants us to. Christ has set us free, but to become free like Him we must choose to live by His truths (Gal 5:1; John 8:31,32,36).
   - ◆ He gives us all that we have, to motivate us by faith, hope, love, and gratitude, not by selfish ambition, arrogance, conceit, or fear.
3. *Jesus created a team and a family climate.*
   - ◆ He asks us to treat others as we want to be treated by them (Matt 7:12). This one principle leads to loving God and loving others. We learn to ask the best for each other. This produces right relationships. What better place for cultivating and perfecting these relationships than in the small groups that we are asking you to get involved in? (See Matt 22:34-40; John 13:34,35; 15:9-17; Rom 13:10; 1 Cor 13:1-13.)
   - ◆ Love produces a spirit of giving, caring, sharing, and forgiving. These parallel and motivate our asking, seeking, knocking, and receiving. (See Matt 7:7; 1 John 5:14-15; Acts 20:35.)
   - ◆ Jesus keeps the family on target and sets the example. He modeled His leadership principles in the small group of disciples that He created and trained for the last three years of His life. He cared enough to live and die for us, even while we were still His enemies. He forgives every sin except rebellion against the Spirit of Truth (Matt 12:31,32). He saves us by His death, but even more He saves us by His life (Rom 5:6-10).
4. *We come to know God personally.*
   - ◆ God always hears us when we ask. He only requires that we

ask according to His will, not to spend what we receive on our own sinful passions. If we are seeking His kingdom and righteousness, He gives us what we need even before we ask (Mark 11:24; 1 John 5:14,15).

◆ In addition to giving us what we need He also gives us what we want, our heart's desire, provided we ask in agreement with His will (Matt 7:7, Mark 11:24, 1 John 5:14-15; Ps 37:4).

◆ He desires intimacy with each of us and asks us to desire intimacy with Him. He created us in the first place so that He could prepare us for eternal fellowship with Him. He created the universe as a training and testing place for all people and continues to transform us into the image of Christ (John 14:27).

5. *Jesus expects the best we are capable of. We can expect the best from Him.*

◆ He expects more from those who have been given more. He will take away everything people think that they have, if they don't use what they already have (Luke 8:18; 12:45-47; 19:26).

◆ We should aim for perfection as God is perfect (Matt 5:48). He knows we are weak and need to learn by His words and our experiences. We need trials and experience — perfection comes from practice, not from abstract theories. We should expect adversity and desire God's discipline to handle it. (See 2 Cor 1:3-11; Heb 12:1-13; 1 Peter 1:3-9; 2:19-21.)

◆ We need to deny ourselves so we can see things from God's point of view. He wants us to seek for truth rather than what feels good. We must take a stand for true principles rather than protecting our lives by compromising with evil. (See Matt 10:26-39; 16:24-27.)

◆ Seek first His kingdom and His righteousness and everything we need will be ours (Matt 6:33). God has designed, created, and sustained us. He knows what is best for us, and Christ came to earth to persuade us to live in His love. (Read John 13–17.)

6. *In many of His parables Jesus plainly illustrated what God expects from us*:

The parable of the tenants: God is like the owner of a vineyard. The owner rented it to some farmers but they refused to pay him his share of the production. When he sent servants to collect, they beat some and killed others. When he sent his son they killed him, thinking that they would take over the vineyard for themselves. But the owner had other plans. He took away the vineyard and gave it to those who would pay their share of the crops.

Jesus' own people and their leaders represent the tenants who killed the owner's son. Those who follow Jesus represent the new tenants who will respect and serve the owner. (See Matt 21:33-44.)

The faithful servant: Since we do not know when the Lord will come for us, we need to be prepared. The faithful servant does his job wisely and joyously. The unfaithful one beats the other servants and does not prepare for the master's return. Jesus asks us and expects us to serve Him and to share His mission to the world. (See Matt 24:45-51.)

The wise and foolish bridesmaids: Five prepared for the coming of the groom, and five did not. He came while they were sleeping, and the prepared ones had enough oil in their lamps to go with him. The five foolish ones weren't ready. Their lamps were going out, so they were unable to go with the groom. Christ asks us to be prepared. (See Matt 25:1-13.)

The talents: A man left on a journey and asked his servants to invest his money while he was gone. He gave one servant five talents of money, another two talents, and a third one talent. The first two servants doubled the amount of money entrusted to them. The one talent man hid his talent in the ground. When the master returned he rewarded the first two, but the third man he punished severely. Christ expects us to use our time and capabilities wisely. He asks us to work for Him in His kingdom. (See Matt 25:14-30.)

The sheep and the goats: The kingdom of Christ is like a king who judges his people. The king was pleased with those who saw the needs of others, had mercy on them, and did what they could do to help. The king severely punished those who neither saw nor helped others who had real needs. Jesus used this story to show that we help and serve him when we help others who are in real need. He asks us not only to see the needs of others, but to actively help them. (See Matt 25:31-46.)

Every perfect gift comes from God, so He does not hesitate to ask us to love Him and serve Him. Jesus asked great things from His disciples. He asks great things of us today. Do you want to lead successfully? Then ask great things from others. We have a high calling and we are not wise to neglect it. Ask God to motivate you in your desire to be like Jesus and walk as He walked? (See James 1:16-18; 1 John 2:3-6.)

God's perfect gift is Jesus. By His sacrifice of Himself Jesus provided forgiveness for us. He demonstrated God's great love. By His resurrection He demonstrated God's great power. He ascended to God's right hand to reign over the whole universe. He has eternal authority and He cares for us. (See Rom 5:6-11.)

7. *Jesus asks us to believe in Him.*

God sent Jesus to be His personal message to His creation. Jesus was with God before the creation of the universe. He participated with God in creating everything that was created — everything was created by, for and through Him. He came to live in a human body in order to make God known to us — He was the exact image of God. He came to earth to fulfil the prophecies about Himself and to teach us God's priorities and principles for living righteously and abundantly. (See John 10:10; Rom 8:1-39; Col 1:15-20; Heb 1:1-10.)

God prepared the descendants of Abraham and Sarah to be His people. He guided them through history and disciplined them through His mighty acts. Through the Old Testament prophets God revealed His principles and the planned coming of Jesus. But His people usually ignored or persecuted these prophets. (We can see this in the Psalms and Old Testament prophetic books.)

When Jesus came to earth as predicted, He grew up in Nazareth. He eventually selected followers and trained them to practice His way of life and lead His followers. The disciples recorded what He did and what He taught, and they spread this message all over the known world of the first century. Jesus taught God's principles for productive living and servant leading. He revealed that we are all eternal beings, made in God's image and designed to live forever with God. He asked for all people to believe in Him as the only One who ever came down from heaven and went back into heaven. He asks everyone living in every generation to believe in Him as the only Savior of the world. (See John 3:1-21.)

He taught of God's love, His own love, and our need to always love one another. He condemned the corrupt leaders of His own generation. He lived out His message and predicted that the religious leaders would persecute Him and finally have Him executed by the Gentiles. His message threatened the hypocritical leaders who loved the praise of men more than the praise of God. They decided that He must die or the Romans would destroy their whole nation. (See John 11:45-57.) He humbly submitted to this betrayal of justice because His own Scriptures predicted how He must die, for the sins of the whole world. By His death He has demonstrated for all time God's amazing and tremendous love for us. While we were still His enemies, Christ died for us. (See Rom 5:6-11.)

He predicted that God would raise Him, and three days after His crucifixion He arose from the grave. He appeared to His followers over a period of 40 days and then ascended back into heaven to rule over all people. He authored eternal salvation for all who believe in Him as God's one and only Son. He revealed Himself as the only person who was both the Son of God and the Son of Man.

Jesus asks us to believe only what is true, not what is superstitious and false. He asks us to live humbly with our neighbors and to love even our enemies. He wants us to believe in and expect the best possibilities, use our strengths and gifts for Him, and work towards only the goals that please God. He wants active followers and not mere spectators. His priorities should be our priorities, and His standard of excellence should be our standard. Jesus asks us not to work for the food that spoils, but to work for the food that endures to eternal life. This food is the message that Jesus, the Son of Man, gives us. God has placed on Jesus His seal of approval. God's work for us is "to believe in the one he has sent" — Jesus Christ (John 6:27-29).

All creation belongs to Christ. He is involved in the design, creation, and maintenance of all reality. He is the One who makes all true science possible, so scientists will only discover what God makes possible for them to discover. Scientists will never discover anything that is unknown to God, so Christians need not fear any threat from true science. No matter what scientists believe personally, they don't create the things or principles that they discover. They may advocate false theories and questionable hypotheses, but Christians should rejoice at the wonderful truths and technologies scientists actually discover. God makes true science possible, and the best scientists should be the most humble believers in Jesus.

We believe that God is always reasonable. His creation demonstrates His wisdom, understanding, intelligence, and power. He creates the very scientists who may deny His existence and reject Jesus as the One who makes God known and who participated with God in the creation. God and Christ not only make true science possible, but they bless the whole world with valuable technology when we humans use it as a way to love each other. When we hate each other and use science to destroy each other, it becomes a curse.[8]

When we use science to deny or disprove God's existence we fight a losing battle. There may be plenty of very evil people who profess to follow Jesus, but such a fact does not prove Jesus or God to be supporters of evil. God is the God of all truth, and all people who really love truth will come to know Him. God is always reasonable. True reason is spiritual as well as natural. The created universe cries out with overwhelming evidence that God exists. His invisible nature and divine power are made plain by the things that exist, the things and forces that He has designed, created, and maintains. (See Rom 1:18-25; John 1:1-3.)

We've tried to show in this book that excellent secular organizations practice *The Leadership Principles of Jesus*, often without realizing that they come from Him. In science especially, atheistic naturalists practice reductionism ("tunnel vision") in order to avoid belief in God or Christ. For them macroevolution by mutation and natural selection (or some variation of these, such as punctuated equilibrium) replaces any need for God. They define truth as only what can be measured by science — to them naturalism is the whole story and includes all truth. But God defines truth as all reality visible and invisible, measurable and immeasurable, physical and spiritual, temporary and eternal.[9]

Jesus asks us to hear whatever our ears are able to hear (Matt 13:9-17). We will know eternal truths that are beyond science if we listen to Him. Where science is true we can accept it with gratitude. Where scientists practice "tunnel vision" and reject the claims of Jesus (often because of the foolishness or wickedness of His human followers) we must be humble and understanding. God loves mistaken scientists just as much as He loves you and me, or tax collectors, prostitutes, and thieves on crosses. Most scientists are dedicated to searching for materialistic truth even though they may be very mistaken and biased in their understanding of God's truth. (See 1 Cor 1:18-2:16.)

There is no future in accepting the idols of atheistic scientists in order to please them or to avoid mockery and persecution for Christ. God's prophets and faithful people have always been mocked and persecuted by those who believe only in the idols of this physical world (Matt 5:11-12).

What Do Churches Need to Discover?

Throughout this book we've appealed to church leaders to expect greater things from the members of their flocks. We've called members grassroots Christians.

Leaders of many excellent secular organizations achieve great visions by unleashing all of their people to be *all that they can be*. Leaders and people cooperate together to develop the best vision. They decide on their mission and carry out a dynamic and viable action plan. Leaders develop great motivation throughout their organizations by using the same principles that Jesus uses.

All of this means that we must encourage greater freedom among grassroots Christians. We all need to follow Jesus personally and grow in our relationship with Him as our living Lord. Jesus amazed everyone by selecting and training common people to be His ambassadors to the world. Perhaps we would have chosen scholars, experts in the law, and those with reputations for righteousness and leadership performance. But, look who Jesus chose! He selected four fishermen (Peter, Andrew, James, and John, Matt 4:18-22), a tax collector (Matthew, Matt 9:9-13), a revolutionary (Simon), and other very common people to learn directly from hands-on experience in a small group (Matt 10:1-4). He even praised His Father, the Lord of heaven and earth, for hiding the marvelous things He was teaching from the wise and learned and revealing them to little children. He asked all who were weary and overburdened with life to come and learn from Him (Matt 11:25-30).

Excellent leaders expect everyone to *share* the same dynamic values, vision, and mission. Let us encourage church members to use their God-given freedom to listen to and follow Jesus. The Spirit of Christ motivates and teaches people to cooperate and to work together to reach the goals of Jesus. Churches that organize everything they do around the cell-group structure are highly successful in developing individual gifts and strengths. These churches reach outsiders effectively. Small-group members approach people in their natural circles of influence. Relatives, neighbors, fellow workers, and friends are much more likely to learn about Jesus in these meetings held in homes rather than in church facilities. Many people will come to a home who would never enter a church. Isn't this more like what Jesus did when He trained His followers to go and make disciples of all nations? (See Matt 28:16-20; Luke 24:24-49; John 21:15-19.)

What Do Leaders Need to Do?

1. *Focus on Jesus as the center of our concern, not themselves.*
   - ◆ Ask for growth in knowing God's will and pursue servant leadership as a top priority. Be servant leaders, not those who "lord it over the flock." Set priorities to follow the example of Jesus and especially to apply the lessons in His parables. Where the wisdom of secular leaders agrees with *The Leadership Principles of Jesus*, we ask church leaders to have the wisdom and courage to keep on learning how to lead like

Jesus. Jesus constantly showed that common people (even the tax collectors and prostitutes) were closer to God's heart than the religious leaders were. (See Matt 21:28-32; 23:1-12.)

◆ Oppose the intimidation and persecution of corrupt leaders. Encourage people to hold onto the freedom we all must have to follow Jesus personally. Jesus has set us free, so don't submit to legalistic slavery. Recognize that Jesus taught and modeled *principles of leadership* as well as *principles of living.* (See Matt 7:15-29; 10:24-42; 12:1-21; 15:1-20; 18:1-14; 23:13-39.)

◆ Reduce dogmatic intellectual control and trust our hearts. Hasn't theological snobbery and dogmatism created the 1,500 denominations we now have? We must decentralize, delegate, and avoid the sectarian spirit like the plague. May the Spirit of Christ teach us humility and acceptance as we study His Word. The Spirit can teach us all we need and He is reliable. (See 1 Cor 2:1-16; 1 John 2:20-27; also consider John 8:31-32; 1 Cor 12:3; Gal 5:1; Eph 4:1-24; Col 3:12-17; 1 John 4:1-3; 5:14-15.)

2. *Ask for what others need.*

◆ Sacrifice traditions, comfort, and control for the welfare of others, for "sinners." Avoid the "squeaky wheel" and listen to those God tells us to care for. Notice His priority to care for widows, orphans, strangers, etc. Remember that Jesus came as a "doctor" to heal the sick. He came to save sinners, not the righteous (Matt 9:9-13).

◆ Give higher priority to eternal, invisible, and spiritual wealth, power, and health. (See Matt 6:19-24; 2 Cor 4:16-18; 1 Tim 4:8.) Philip Yancey gives us the secret of helping others meet their desperate needs:

"I now easily understand why the Gospels repeat the one saying of Jesus more than any other: 'Whoever wants to save his life will lose it, but whoever loses his life for my sake will find it.' Jesus came . . . not to destroy life but that we may have it more abundantly, . . . We get it by investing in others, by taking courageous stands for justice, by ministering to the weak and needy, by pursuing God and not self . . . ."[10]

3. *The possibilities are unlimited.*

◆ Let God reveal His greatness. Seek His motivation. Keep on knocking. Ask Him to lead us toward His goals. Trust in the New Testament's priority for healthy relationships and small, family-like groups.

◆ Ask others to put the fruit of the Spirit on the top of their priority list. Motivate believers to trust in the wisdom found only by a lifetime study of God's word, especially the four letters on the life of Jesus: Matthew, Mark, Luke, and John.

4. *Challenge the status quo, the conventional and traditional process.*

◆ Be wise enough to see, hear, and understand what Jesus really did and said. Ask for the wisdom and courage to be true to His leadership principles. As servant leaders we should follow Jesus' advice to examine our traditions so that we won't nullify God's word by teaching what are merely the rules of men. Then we won't condemn the innocent and we won't strain out a gnat and swallow a camel. (Especially consider the accounts in Matthew, chapters 12, 15, and 23.)

◆ Be patient with those who love Jesus and want to know His will. Even if we differ, Christ is able to make each of us succeed. (See Rom 14:1-23.)

What Can the Grassroots Christian Do?

1. *Ask for more opportunities.*

◆ See the *possibilities*, develop more *strengths and gifts*, and work on *specific goals*. Have a servant's heart. Focus on the best and the highest. Work toward *standards of excellence* and use your *time* on the *top priorities*. All this takes tremendous wisdom and courage, but Christ gives these to us when we ask. (See Matt 10:24-31; 2 Tim 1:7; James 1:2-8.)

◆ Allow Christ to motivate you with *faith, hope, love, and gratitude*. Hunger for ways to increase these spiritual fruits. (See Matt 5:3-12; 1 Cor 13:1-13; Gal 5:22-26.)

◆ Increase your awareness and knowledge of the *wonders* of God's Creation. He has designed it to make us say "Wow!!" *The truth and beauty of Christ* includes all nature, science, and human ingenuity. Let's make ourselves *vulnerable* to the wisdom, love, and glory of God rather than always dwelling on what's bad, wrong, or unfair.

◆ When we ask God for His help we motivate ourselves towards His *high mission and vision*. We humble ourselves, and then He exalts us with unbelievable power and joy. All this means that we must be wise enough to learn from successful and excellent organizations. Their stories are parables of what Jesus taught and we can get great lessons from them. He teaches and motivates us to have a *caring, sharing,* and *forgiving* spirit.

◆ Also *ask God* to open the eyes of others who are so addicted to their comfort levels that they are controlled and blinded by inappropriate traditions. Change will be a threat to many, as it was to those who opposed Jesus and finally had Him crucified. (See Luke 23:34; Acts 7:60.)

2. *Ask for patience.*

◆ Don't seek or expect shortcuts to make life simple. Ask for strength to serve rather than be served. (See Matt 23:11,12; Luke 22:26,27; John 13:12-17.)

◆ Keep on studying the life and teachings of Christ and compare them objectively and subjectively to what excellent organizations do and teach. Talk with God about everything at all times in all places, especially while reading His word. We can't expect God's Spirit to teach us with new information if we don't listen to what He has already said over and over again. Study the Scriptures that deal with asking and that show how Jesus, Paul, John, Peter, and others asked.

3. *Ask for guidance.*

◆ God's Spirit will use us for the good of all. God will help us realize how He continues to sustain all life in the universe by supplying knowledge, wisdom, energy, food, clothing, and everything else, whether made by people or existing in nature.

◆ Humbly expect church leaders to follow Christ, not human traditions or inappropriate secular models. Study how the prophets and the disciples of Jesus had to constantly avoid being led away from God by philosophy that was not according to Christ.[11]

◆ Be aware of the fact that we have historically tended to ignore the methods and model of Jesus; in the crunch we've often resorted to the methods of Caesar. We usually think of Jesus as One who teaches us how to live, but we need to see Him as *One who also shows us how to lead.*

4. *Christ asks us to work hard at the exciting process of building relationships in the midst of change.*

◆ Christ makes us His partners. Give top priority to the real treasure, found only in Him and in His word. Let God teach us (1 John 2:27). Take the risks and be vulnerable to the inevitable changes that go along with asking for personal growth. All the victorious people of the Bible had to experience radical change in their lives. They got much more than they ever dreamed of asking for. God wants us to grow, and we can't grow mature in Christ unless we let Him change what needs changing. We can't do this without God's constant help and love. (See 1 Cor 1–2, Matt 11:25-30.)

◆ We need to work at believing in Christ. In Him are found all the treasures of wisdom and knowledge. Christ in us is our hope for glory (Col 1:27-2:3)! When those He fed miraculously asked what work God required, Jesus said, ". . . believe on the one he has sent" (John 6:28-29). He said in another setting, ". . . with God all things are possible" (Matt 19:26). Jesus and what He teaches are *gourmet food for our souls.*

◆ Encourage believers to cooperate with each other in small groups and in task forces. We learn best as we experiment with the process of asking, trying, failing, then trying again until God gives us success. Keep the example of Jesus before us — His life, arrest, trial, death, resurrection, ascension, and living presence. We are His family on earth and His Spirit leads in the direction we need to go. (See John 14:5-27; 15:1-16; 16:12-15; 17:20-26.)

Small Group Agenda on Asking

◆ Icebreaker inviting each person to tell a story of what they asked for as a child and what they actually received.

◆ Use Scriptures illustrating what Jesus and His disciples asked God for, what they received, and what they did not receive. Have each person take turns in reading through the following Scriptures: Matthew 6:24-34; 7:7; Mark 11:24; Luke 11:11-13; John 14:13,14 and 1 John 5:14-15.

◆ Discussion of how God gives us what we need and asks us to tell Him what we want. What part does knowing His will play in our asking?

◆ Have each person pray for individual and group needs, asking God according to His will even when we don't know His will.

◆ Have the leader explain his vision of how cooperation and intimacy with God and each other can bring unbelievers into God's kingdom.

The Challenge of Asking

The importance and power of *asking*, of clear expectations, has been neglected in the literature of effective living and leading. It is the one act that fuses and focuses all the rest.

Most people are unaware that a question is almost always a stronger and more effective approach than a declarative, directive, or commanding statement. Thoughtful, clear, firm, and tough expectives get better results, and allow the other person to retain self-respect and dignity. They are "open sesame's," the initiators of real productive actions. In the future, *telling* will be accurately perceived as obsolete, and *asking* will be understood as a real power instrument.

The power and importance of asking is beautifully illustrated by the following:

Ask and it will be given you.

Seek and you will find.

Knock and it will open unto you.

It can be tough and zestful — and isn't that what it's all about?

Joe Batten[12]

REFERENCES

1. Covey, *The Seven Habits of Highly Successful People*, 15, 35 and Galatians 5:23. Also read Anita Thompson, *Habit Forming*, 1,12.

2. Ibid., 65-94.

3. Ibid., 95-144.

4. Ibid., 145-182. See Covey, Merrill, and Merrill, *First Things First*.

5. Ibid., *The Seven Habits of Highly Successful People*, 204-234.

6. Ibid., 235-260.

7. Ibid., 261-284.

8. Read Phillip Johnson, *Reason in the Balance*, (Grand Rapids: InterVarsity Press, 1995).

9. Ibid., 7, 64, 65, 125-129.

10. Yancey, *The Jesus I Never Knew*, 125.

11. Read and study Matthew 24, Romans 1:18-25; 1 Corinthians 1-3; Colossians 2, 1 and 2 Timothy, 1 and 2 Peter, 1 and 3 John, and Jude.

12. Batten, *Tough-Minded Leadership*, 184.

APPENDIX

REPLY TO DARKNESS

THE following poem is written in the idiom of the rock opera *Jesus Christ, Superstar* and was intended as a relevant Christian "secularistic" response to what was felt to be the challenge inherent in the original lines.

Reply to Darkness
by Gail Batten

Hey there, Savior Jesus Christ,
What is it made you sacrifice?
That life we value You threw out.
But people didn't really shout.
They put You down — called You no king,
Said that your life meant not a thing.
We still live now in misery and wallow in our sin.

Oh, Jesus Christ, you crazy man . . .
What made You rise to live again?
Can You still love these lives we lead
Of pain and hate and greed?
Or is there something we don't know,
A fire that sets Your soul aglow?

Oh, come on, Jesus . . . You aren't king.
Where's that immortal life You bring?
If You're so great then tell us how
To find the answers to love — right now.

O.K., you call me Superstar. . . .
I don't get drunk or go too far.
But do I ever put you down
For taking time to mess around?
I don't condone the narrow life
All filled with toil and fear and strife.
My task on earth's no simple one,
To show you God can be great fun.

I know you laugh — you play it cool
And think me one gigantic fool.
But do you really understand
What it's like at God's right hand?
"Come on," you say, "Why should we pray?
Walk piously around all day?"
I fear you all don't really see
That gift God gave to you and me.
You've all been taught the Savior Man
Was words and love — a gentle lamb.

You're too hung up on all your needs
To see I was a man of deeds.
I roared with laughter, partied after,
For humor and jokes there was no one faster.
Too bad all my Biblical verse
Is destined to an endless curse . . . of misunderstanding.

We all had fun, the Twelve and I.
Not drugs — but love. We soon got high.
We talked with God — and loved ourselves
And didn't live in little hells.
I hope you hear now what I say,
Because I live with you today.

Yes, Jesus Christ, that fabled Man,
Dwells here on earth in every land.
In heart and mind — new peace you'll find,
If you see that Christ was not just kind!

But, full of vital energy,
He lives and loves life passionately.
And with Christ's sacrifice of self
He helps to save somebody else,
By bringing facts of life to you,
By showing you that God means Truth.
He gave his soul, came back from Hell,
Helped us survive our smothered shell.
He hopes to make us plainly choose
God above drugs and excessive booze.
Sure, you can still have sinful times
If God turns out to be all lies.
But try Christ first — give Him a chance
And know that life will be enhanced.

Transitioning To Cell Groups

Why Transition? Why Change?
Something is wrong with the way we do church.

A. Jesus expressed displeasure and outrage at the way "church" was done in His day:
Matthew 23:1-13
  1. Religious teachers don't practice what they preach.
  2. They require things they aren't prepared to do themselves.
  3. Things are done for show.
  4. The clergy separates itself from the masses.
  5. Jesus' position as Leader is usurped.
  6. There is self-exaltation which leads to a fall.
  7. Teachers block the kingdom of God to everyone, even themselves.
In this passage Jesus attacks inappropriate attitudes (especially of leaders), systems, structures, and traditions.

B. Current church problems experienced include the following:
  1. Excessive individualism (as in the Book of Judges).
  2. Excessive institutionalism — structures oppose change.
  3. Only a small nucleus of church members active.
  4. Church is irrelevant to the world and has little impact.
  5. Christians can't get along — lack of Christian fellowship.
  6. Lack of spiritual growth and commitment.
  7. Church lacks direction and concentrates on maintenance.
  8. Lack of discipline — worldly church members.

C. Churches need more of the following:
  1. Community and family spirit, love, belonging among Christians.
  2. Openness to change to engage and impact the world.
  3. Flexible structures for changing needs.
  4. Church members active.
  5. Accountability, growth, and discipleship.
  6. Evangelism and edification.
  7. Decentralization and simplicity.
  8. Cooperation among churches and church members.
  9. Vision and direction owned and supported by all.

D. Changes are needed:
  1. Where there are too many rules and regulations, concentrate on the majors according to Jesus.
  2. Where there are too many traditions, evaluate in the light of those majors.

3. Where there is too much structure, demolish it and let all believers minister.
4. Where there is too much talk, engage in action. (Gideon in Judges 6:1-32.)
5. Where there is too much institutionalism, decentralize into the neighborhoods.

Luke 5:36-39. The gospel of Jesus is always new wine in every generation, so it always needs new wineskins. Each generation has to study and apply Jesus' message in their own culture.

Used by permission. From a class taught by Robert Reese, missionary to Zimbabwe, Africa for the past 15 years where he participated in the planting of more than 55 churches.

Affirmations for the Tough-Minded Christian Leader

I will exemplify a passion for excellence.

I will ask, listen and hear — to determine the wants, needs and possibilities of my customers and my team.

I will provide an example of accountability, commitment and integrity.

I will follow a path of continual empowerment for myself and others.

I will constantly look for a focus on the strengths rather than the weaknesses of all with whom I come in contact.

I will cultivate optimum physical, mental and spiritual fitness.

I will lead as I would like to be led.

I will savor the flavor of each passing moment.

I will enfuse every thought and relationship with faith, hope, love and gratitude.

Abbreviations of Bible books

For those unfamiliar with the abbreviations used in references to Scripture, we offer the following. (Note that some books are not abbreviated.) E.g. Gen 10:13 means book of Genesis, chapter 10, verse 13.

Old Testament

Genesis	Gen
Exodus	Exod
Leviticus	Lev
Numbers	Num
Deuteronomy	Deut
Joshua	Josh
Judges	Judg
Ruth	Ruth
1 Samuel	1 Sam
2 Samuel	2 Sam
1 Kings	1 Kgs
2 Kings	2 Kgs
1 Chronicles	1 Chr
2 Chronicles	2 Chr
Ezra	Ezra
Nehemiah	Neh
Esther	Esth
Job	Job
Psalms	Ps
Proverbs	Prov
Ecclesiastes	Eccl
Song of Solomon	S of S
Isaiah	Isa
Jeremiah	Jer
Lamentations	Lam
Ezekiel	Ezek
Daniel	Dan
Hosea	Hos
Joel	Joel
Amos	Amos
Obadiah	Obad
Jonah	Jonah
Micah	Micah
Nahum	Nahum
Habakkuk	Hab
Zephaniah	Zeph
Haggai	Hag
Zechariah	Zech
Malachi	Mal

New Testament

Matthew	Matt
Mark	Mark
Luke	Luke
John	John
Acts	Acts
Romans	Rom
1 Corinthians	1 Cor
2 Corinthians	2 Cor
Galatians	Gal
Ephesians	Eph
Philippians	Phil
Colossians	Col
1 Thessalonians	1 Thess
2 Thessalonians	2 Thess
1 Timothy	1 Tim
2 Timothy	2 Tim
Titus	Titus
Philemon	Phlm
Hebrews	Heb
James	Jas
1 Peter	1 Peter
2 Peter	2 Peter
1 John	1 John
2 John	2 John
3 John	3 John
Jude	Jude
Revelation	Rev

About the Authors

Joe D. Batten

Mr. Batten is a world-renowned leadership consultant, author, and speaker on achieving goals, personal excellence, integrity, and motivation. His specialty is guiding and counseling corporate leaders and parents on how to build strong and cohesive corporate cultures and family structures.

He has written 13 books on management including the internationally best-selling *Tough-Minded Management*, called by Ross Perot

"the best management book ever written," and by Lee Iacocca, "legendary." He has appeared in 35 films on leadership, motivation, management, inspiration, and selling.

Batten has spoken to managers from over 80% of the Fortune 500 companies and has keynoted more international conferences than any other American. He has appeared on more than 300 television and radio programs. Emcees around the world often introduce him as the "Dean of Sales Trainers."

Gail Batten (deceased March 1996)

Gail was a motivational business-leadership consultant and speaker. She wrote television and film scripts and coauthored *The Confidence Chasm* with Joe Batten, her father. She was the creative script consultant for the classic film, "Keep Reaching," and for the

tape album recorded by Joe Batten entitled "How to Exceed Yourself."

Gail was a staff member of H.O.P.E. where she counseled with young children from families with alcohol and drug problems, grief and dysfunctional relationships. As the mother of two active young children, ages 6 and 12, she was able to apply many of the techniques outlined in her father's book, *Tough-Minded Parenting*.

Warren Howard

Mr. Howard is a native of Rhode Island and graduated from Brown University. After serving in the Army Air Force during World War II, he began his career with U.S. Rubber (UniRoyal) where he held an executive position. This was followed by similar responsibilities at Phillips Petroleum, Diamond-Shamrock Chemical Company, Tubbs Cordage Company, Certron Corporation, and Athena, Inc. He became widely known as a Project Management Specialist who consistently exercised successful leadership in the development of new processes and new products.

Howard has written five books and numerous technical manuals. He has conducted seminars on the techniques of leadership, statistical analysis, and the principles of quality control. In addition, he has been involved in church work for the past 45 years. At one time, he was Associate Editor of the *North American Christian Magazine*.

Howard's articles have appeared in a variety of Christian periodicals and he has been quoted in the *Harvard Business Review*. For many years, he has taught and lectured widely to both young and adult church groups.

Mr. Howard and his wife of 45 years now make their home in Tustin, California. They have two grown daughters and two granddaughters.

Although it has been fashionable the last few years to play arrogant "hardball" in many Congressional and corporate circles, based on deceit, greed, and contempt (there's even a TV program called that), these authors show that organizations seeking lasting growth, impact, and reward (including churches) are those with sound policies not only about finances and procedures, but about employees and those they reach out to serve, as well. In making their points—including the importance of small, mutually supportive groups—Batten and Howard stress biblical principles (such as those Jesus taught in His parables). Coupled with current business success stories, they then show practical ways to work these principles out in churches and other areas of life.

Bonnie Compton Hanson
Former editor, Scripture Press

The Leadership Principles of Jesus offers a comprehensive, thoroughly researched work on "Grass Roots Christianity"—why we need it, and how to make it work in our communities and the world. This book is chock-full of insights and information.

Laurie Beth Jones, author
Jesus, CEO* and *The Path

It seems Joe Batten and I have been friends forever (probably 25 to 30 years). He has always demonstrated the fundamental values and principles of Jesus Christ in his everyday behavior, so I'm not surprised by this excellent book, but I am impressed with how much practical data has been packed in these pages. The way these fundamental principles are illustrated, and the practical ways they can be applied will benefit tremendously any reader with an open mind.

Dr. DuPree Jordan Jr.
Jordan International Enterprises

The authors define, clearly and naturally, the practical application of *the leadership principles of Jesus* to management methods for all modern Christian churches. This book applies those principles to development of dynamic Christians and small groups. This is a new way to look at church leadership, and has been needed for a thousand years. Yet, it is applicable to *any* organization, and would benefit *any* reader. It should be read by everybody, of all religions. I wish that I could have read it many years ago, and I can hardly say enough for this book.

Paul Liston
US Army, retired, Legion of Merit

The Leadership Principles of Jesus is an excellent resource to equip Christians to become better leaders in their homes, in the workplace, and in their church work. What better example for the authors to use than Christ, Himself! This book provides tools to help readers know and accomplish God's will as well as dynamics for allowing God to work through them.

Susan Titus Osborn
Editor, *The Christian Communicator*
Adjunct Professor, Pacific Christian College

Joe Batten has masterfully connected issues of biblical faith with success in the marketplace. His book hits squarely at the need of the hour in America—to return to our moral and ethical roots as a basis for everyday life.

Merrill J. Oster, President
Oster Communications, Inc.
Chairman of the Pinnacle Forum

Joe Batten, known for his tender toughness, brings spirituality into the business world blessed by the vulnerability of one who has learned his lessons, on his knees, from the Master Teacher. What a gift!

Rosita Perez
President, Creative Living Programs, Inc.

This is an outstanding book for any person who wishes to grow in our changing world. Creative. Refreshing. Substantive.

Nido R. Qubein, CSP, CPAE
Chairman, Creative Services, Inc.

The Leadership Principles of Jesus cuts through the fog of tradition and detached religion to get to the basics of grass-roots Christianity. Batten, Batten, and Howard take seriously the methods of discipleship used by Jesus and they show how Jesus' methods have been adapted successfully by the business world. So why shouldn't the church also get back to these basics in order to reach God's real "customers," the lost world? My personal prayer is that this book will inspire the birthing of many dynamic cells of Christians who will interface effectively with the lost world, because they have adopted Jesus' own principles.

Robert Reese, missionary
Zimbabwe, Africa

This is a dynamite book! If it can change your life...it can change your world...and it will!! This book is an awesome example of applying Christ, the ultimate Servant Leader's Principles into our personal, professional, business, and church lives. It is written with the synergy of correct Biblical Principles consistently proven and applied. A deep and delightful challenge to individuals, small groups, and the entire Body of Christ.

Naomi Rhode CSP, CPAE
Past President National Speakers Association
Vice President, SmartPractice

This is an absolutely wonderful book, filled with ideas and insights that both inspire and uplift any manager of any enterprise.

Brian Tracy
Brian Tracy International

This magnificent book, *The Leadership Principles of Jesus* is the perfect marriage of the highest ideals with practical application to today's business. Just as Jesus did at the marriage at Cana, Joe Batten and Warren Howard have poured for us the best of the wines of life from the first page to the last. Every sentence is a delicious, delightful treasure of wisdom.

Dottie Walters, Publisher/Editor
Sharing Ideas Magazine for Professional Speakers
President, Walters International Speakers Bureau

If we but compare and contrast any measure of "success" or "effectiveness" in anyone who is truly *the very finest* in her role—at home, or in the world—we will find a person who opens herself to God, asking Him for guidance in motivating her towards the highest vision, mission and strength of leadership possible. It is with compelling courage and clarity that the authors write a book that should become a permanent source of reference for those who wish to go beyond "having and getting" and on to "being and becoming."

Bettie B. Youngs, Ph.D., Ed.D., Author
Gifts of the Heart: Stories That Celebrate Life's Defining Moments